English in Action
Band 4 R

English in Action

Band 4 R

Langenscheidt-Longman
ENGLISH LANGUAGE TEACHING

English in Action
Ein Lehrwerk für die Sekundarstufe I

Band 4 R
Für das 8. Schuljahr an Realschulen und
entsprechende Kurse an Gesamtschulen

Kursdesign: Malcolm Sexton

Autoren:
Shirley Söldenwagner und
Steve Elsworth, Viola Kessling, Malcolm Sexton,
Anne Wichmann, John Williams

unter Mitwirkung von
Schulamtsdirektor Waldemar Bindseil, Soltau

Mitarbeiter:
Prof. Dr. Wolf-Dietrich Bald, Aachen
Schulamtsdirektor Waldemar Bindseil, Soltau
Prof. Dr. Karlheinz Hecht, München
Konrektor Dr. Werner Kieweg, M.A., Schwabmünchen
Studiendirektor Adolf Schwarz, München
Fachbereichsleiterin Anne Wichmann, Bremen

in Zusammenarbeit mit der
Verlagsredaktion Langenscheidt-Longman
Shirley Söldenwagner
und Longman English Teaching Services

Beratung:
Realschullehrer Günter Diemer, Pforzheim
Studiendirektor Christoph Edelhoff, Grebenstein
Fachbereichsleiter Ulrich Grewer, Leverkusen
Realschullehrerin Barbara Lehmann, Rendsburg
Realschullehrer Gunnar Mößner, Pforzheim
Terry K. Moston, Fröndenberg
Oberstudienrat Ulrich Rösner, Heiligenhafen

Grammatik:
Prof. Dr. Wolf-Dietrich Bald, Aachen
Studiendirektor Adolf Schwarz, München

Zeichnungen:
Colin Shearing (Linden Artists), Jutta Bauer,
Jan Gulbransson, Sabine Kaske, Dietmar Noworzyn

Grafik: Sabine Kaske

English in Action 4 R besteht aus folgenden
Komponenten:

Schülerbuch	50047
Workbook	50067
Textcassette	57107
Folien	57095
Lehrerhandreichungen	50087

1. Auflage 1982

© 1982 Langenscheidt-Longman, München
Das Werk und seine Teile sind urheberrechtlich geschützt. Jede Verwertung in anderen als den gesetzlich zugelassenen Fällen bedarf deshalb der vorherigen schriftlichen Einwilligung des Verlages.

Druck: Kösel, Kempten
Printed in Germany · ISBN 3-526-50047-9

CONTENTS

UNIT 1 FIRE!

Here is the News

🎧 Listening	Three radio reports on the fire	2
Using the language	Telling someone about the news	3
Reading	Some extracts from the reports	4
Looking at the language	A note on the use of the Passive	5
Focus on grammar Can you do it?	***The Passive*** *Three firemen have been injured. /* *Can everybody be rescued? / They had to be taken to … /* *A press conference will be held*	6
Using the language	Writing about an accident	8
Extra: Some Facts about Chicago	Brief notes on Chicago	9
Focus on grammar Can you do it?	***More about questions with question words*** *Who did he see? / Who are you talking to?*	10
Focus on grammar Can you do it?	***More about relative clauses*** *I'm talking to a woman whose daughter …/* *The woman he spoke to…*	11
Looking at the language	A note on American English	12
Extra: Inferno Girl Plans Wedding	Popular newspaper article about the fire	13
Using the language	Writing a story	14

v

UNIT 2 BREAKING UP

Sally's Diary

Reading	Five diary entries	15
Looking at the language Can you do it?	**Asking for help** I don't know what to do. / Show me how to …/ A man told her where to … / when to …	18
Looking at the language Can you do it	**Talking about friends and relatives** A friend of mine / a cousin of his	19
Focus on grammar Can you do it?	**Present Perfect with "how long", "for", "since"** How long have you had that bike? She's known him for five months / since last year.	20
Using the language	Writing about oneself / Making up dialogues	21

Giving Advice

Looking at the language Can you do it?	**Some new expressions for giving advice** You ought to forget it. / You ought not to … It's no use worrying… It's not worth talking about it.	22
Using the language	Making up and acting dialogues	23

An Argument

Listening	An argument on the phone	24
Looking at the language	Finding the expressions which caused the argument	24
Listening	A friendly conversation on the phone	24
Focus on grammar Can you do it?	**Present Perfect Progressive with "how long", "for", "since"** How long has she been waiting? / They've been playing for two hours / since 4 o'clock.	25
Using the language	Writing about oneself / Completing dialogues	26

Avoiding Confrontations

Listening	Some extracts from arguments	27
Using the language	Making up and acting dialogues	27

How Will it End?

Using the language	Writing an ending for a picture story	29

UNIT 3 IT'S WORTH VISITING WALES!

The Holiday of a Lifetime

Reading	Brochure about a holiday camp	30
Using the language	Saying why you would/wouldn't like to go somewhere	32

What Are Your Interests?

Looking at the language	**More about the -ing form**	
Focus on grammar	*I'm keen on/fond of/interested in sightseeing.*	
Can you do it?	*She's looking forward to going.*	
	Aren't you tired of …ing?	33
Using the language	Talking about plans / Declining an invitation	35

Two Letters

Reading	Two formal letters	36

Extra: Welcome to Wales   Pages out of a brochure about Wales 37

Some Facts about Wales

Reading	Encyclopaedic texts on Wales	40
Using the language	Writing a formal letter	41

VII

UNIT 4   GETTING TO KNOW EACH OTHER

At Camp Cymraig

Listening	Four conversations	42
Using the language	Talking about what could happen	43
Looking at the language	Finding typical mistakes	43
Looking at the language Focus on grammar Can you do it?	**Comparison of adverbs** *The guide last week walked faster.* *I can understand them more easily.* *She played best.*	43
Using the language	Comparing how we do things	45

Rules Are Rules

Looking at the language Can you do it?	***Talking about what we must/mustn't do*** *We're supposed to be back by 10.30.* *We're not supposed to bring pets into the camp.*	46
	Asking permission	47
Can you do it?	Discussing which rules are silly/sensible	
Using the language	Writing your own rules	47

COOL   Pen Friends

Reading	Magazine ads for pen friends	48
Using the language	Talking about the people in the ads	
	Writing your own magazine ads	49

Extra: You Need a Friend   A science fiction story 49

UNIT 5 A TASTE OF AFRICA

Greetings from Mbour

Reading		Peter's first postcard	51
🔲 Listening / Reading		Peter's first conversation with Malick	52
Reading		Another postcard	53
🔲 Listening		Some more conversations	54
Reading		Peter's other postcards	55
Using the language		Talking about what's strange or new to you	56
Focus on grammar Can you do it?		***Reported speech*** *I told him I didn't speak French.* *He asked me if I was staying at the hotel.*	56
Focus on grammar Can you do it?		***More about reported speech*** *He asked me if I had been to Africa before.*	58
Extra: Something to Think about		Talking about some photos taken in Africa	59
Focus on grammar Can you do it?		***"Will" and "won't" in reported speech*** *I told them I would/wouldn't*	59
Focus on grammar Can you do it?		***Reporting commands*** *He told me to go in. / He asked me to*	61
Using the language		Talking about what we have to get done	63

Starting a Conversation

🔲 Listening		Extracts from conversations	63
Using the language		Making up and acting dialogues Reporting what others have said	64
Extra: Pidgin		A note on the English-speaking countries in Africa	65
Extra: Some Facts about The Gambia		Encyclopaedic texts on The Gambia	66
Extra: Project Africa		Making a wall chart about a country	67
Extra: Project Germany		Writing notes about your country	68
Extra: Chicken Yassa		An African recipe	69

UNIT 6   OVER THE SEA TO SKYE

Off the Beaten Track

Reading	A schoolgirl's account of a bike tour	70
Extra: Some Background Information	Brief notes on Skye and Bonnie Prince Charlie	73
Extra: The Skye Boat Song	Listening to a Scottish song	74

A Good Holiday?

Using the language	Talking about the bike tour	75
Looking at the language	**Saying that something applies to you, too** So do I. / Nor do I. / So did I. / Nor did I.	75
Using the language	Talking about being on your own	76

Useful Tips and Advice for Visitors

Reading	Short magazine article	76
Focus on grammar Can you do it?	**Talking about what's not necessary** You/He needn't take an umbrella.	77
Using the language	Tips for a visitor to Germany	77
Using the language	Talking about what's necessary for a holiday	78
Extra: North, East, South, West	Talking about the direction of places	79

"Can You Tell Us the Way?"

Looking at the language Focus on grammar Can you do it?	**Describing the way to others** Can you show it to me on the map please? A man explained to us how to get there.	80
Using the language	Asking the way and giving directions Giving directions to English-speaking visitors to your town/village	82
Extra: Rain, Rain ...	Talking about a weather forecast Three little riddles	83

UNIT 7   LOST IN THE CAVES

A Radio Play

Listening	Five scenes from the play	85
Using the language	Talking about the play and the characters	88

Talking it Over

Reading	Two conversations afterwards	89
Using the language	Talking about whose fault it was	89
Focus on grammar Can you do it?	***Reproaching others/Blaming yourself*** *If you had listened to me, this wouldn't have happened. / If I had been more careful, we wouldn't have been trapped.*	90
Using the language	Making up and acting dialogues	91

Don't Take Risks!

Looking at the language Focus on grammar Can you do it?	***Reporting warnings and instructions*** *He wanted them to put their helmets on.* *He told/warned them not to take risks.*	92
Using the language	Reporting your parents' instructions	94
Using the language	Making up and acting a dialogue	94

XI

UNIT 8   NELSON AND "VICTORY"

A British National Hero
Reading	Encyclopaedic texts on Nelson, Trafalgar Square, "Victory"	96

The Battle of Trafalgar
Reading	Beginning of a script for a school broadcast	98
Listening	Scenes from the battle	98

Talking about Heroes
Looking at the language	Finding out the meanings of new words	99
Using the language	Talking about heroes and well-known people Writing about somebody you admire	100

Do We Need Heroes?
Listening	A conversation about the necessity of heroes	100

Quiz: Famous People
Reading	Short descriptions of some famous people	101
Using the language	Writing a short description of a well-known person	101

On Board the "Victory"
Listening	A conversation on board the ship	102
Looking at the language Focus on grammar Can you do it?	**More about the Passive** *We were shown Nelson's cabin.* *They were given a lot of brochures.*	103
Using the language	Writing about a guided tour	104
Extra: Different Accents	A note on accents	105
Extra: What Were They Told?	Reporting what others said	105
Extra: Interpreting	Helping your English-speaking visitor to understand a German guide	106

UNIT 9 READING IS FUN

The Glove
Reading
Looking at the language

A "detective" story 108
Finding out the meanings of new words 110
Suggestions for further reading 111

Want to Read Some More?

Appendix
Irregular Verbs 112
Grammar 113
Vocabulary 140
Dictionary 154

Fire!

"Here is the News."

 Listening

You're going to hear three radio reports on the fire. While you listen, try to get the main facts. (Write your notes on a separate sheet of paper.)

Did you get it?

FIRST REPORT

1 *Listen carefully, and then say:*

- where the fire was.
- what was on fire (name, kind and size of building).
- if anybody was still in the building.

2 *What made the situation worse?*

Say why:
- the fire was spreading.
- helicopters couldn't be used.
- the firemen couldn't work properly.
- some of the fire engines couldn't get to the fire.

3 Do you know what caused the fire?

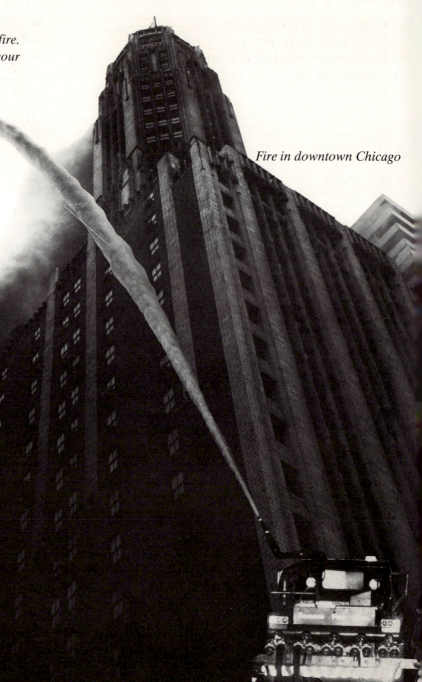

Fire in downtown Chicago

UNIT 1

SECOND REPORT

Now listen to the second report and try to get the new information. Again, write your notes on a separate sheet of paper.

○ Which floors did the fire spread to?
○ Who did the firemen rescue?
○ How many people were trapped in the building?
○ What did they plan to do to the neighbouring buildings?

THIRD REPORT

Listen to the news on the next day, and then try to complete this summary. (Use a separate sheet of paper.)

87 people were ... from the roof of .... Helicopters were ... to rescue the people. 30 people from the building and three ... were seriously .... They were ... to .... The number of dead is not .... According to the ... the fire has been brought under ....

Using the language

Now use your answers and the notes you've made to tell someone who didn't listen to the radio about the fire.

You can begin like this:

There was a big fire in ...
A very tall building │ was on ...
A skyscraper
The ... Building
Most people had already ..., but ...
The firemen had a lot of problems because ...
...

Skyscrapers in Chicago

UNIT 1

Reading

Extracts from the radio reports

1 The Victory Building in downtown Chicago is still on fire. According to reports the fire is out of control and is spreading fast. Most office workers left work at 5:30 p.m., but there are still some people in the building. News has just come in that Chicago's fire chief, Amos Dixon, has not been able to use helicopters because of bad weather, and help has been requested from neighboring cities. Reports say that the fire broke out on the 14th floor at about 5:45 p.m. Over 50 fire trucks have been sent to the burning skyscraper.

2 "We have a very bad situation down here. We're fighting the fire with sixty fire trucks at the moment, but we have high winds, and my men can't work because of the crowd. It's a very serious fire. My men will have a hard job stopping it. But we're doing our best. We hope everyone can be rescued. Our work has been made almost impossible by the crowd. Please tell your listeners to stay at home. This is a very urgent message. If you think you have relatives or friends in the building, please call 379 6066, our information number. Do not – repeat – do not enter Chicago's central district. Traffic has come to a stand-still and our fire trucks cannot get to the fire. Repeat. Stay in your homes and do not come near the fire."

3 The Victory Building is 120 stories high. It was built according to a new, fully computerized system which gives immediate fire warning and automatically closes the fire doors. People are already asking: "How did it happen? What went wrong?"

4 The fire which is now burning in downtown Chicago's Victory Building is the worst skyscraper fire in U.S. history. The 120 story building is now on fire between the 14th and 90th floors. Members of the cleaning staff and other workers who were trapped on the 17th and 18th floors have been rescued by firemen, but we have reports that about 80 people are still trapped in the building. The cause of the fire is not known and there has been a failure of the automatic alarm system. A huge crowd is watching the fire, and fire fighters from neighboring cities cannot get to the building because of sightseers who have driven into the city. High winds are making the situation worse, and have prevented the use of helicopters. According to reports all the neighboring buildings have to be evacuated. The question in everybody's mind is this: How can the 80 people be rescued?

5 87 people who had been trapped in the Victory Building last night were rescued from the roof of the 120 story skyscraper. Despite high winds Chicago's firemen were able to use helicopters to rescue the people from the flames. 30 people from the building and 3 firemen were seriously injured and had to be taken to the hospital. The number of dead is not known as fire fighters have not yet been able to enter the building, but it could be as high as 50. Police have pushed the crowd back half a mile from the scene and all the neighboring buildings have had to be evacuated. We can now report that the fire has been brought under control, but the building could still collapse. A press conference with the mayor of Chicago and Fire Chief Amos Dixon will be held this evening in the Maple Grand Hotel. The President of the United States has sent his congratulations and thanks to Chicago's fire department.

Looking at the language

The Passive

Try to find all the Passive forms in the extracts and write them down on a separate sheet of paper. Put them under the following headings.

You've already learnt these two Passive forms:

Here are four new Passive forms:

Simple Present	Simple Past	Present Perfect	Past Perfect	Will-future	Passive with auxiliaries

When is the Passive used?

Compare the following sentences on the left with those on the right.

In an interview, fire chief Dixon made the following statements to a newspaper reporter.

This is what appeared in the newspaper the following day.

"I immediately sent 50 fire trucks to the Victory Building."

Fifty fire trucks were sent to the Victory Building immediately.

"My men and I fight over 100 fires every week."

Over a hundred fires are fought every week by the Chicago Fire Dept.

"We have rescued all the office workers on the 18th floor from the smoke and fire."

All the workers on the 18th floor have been rescued from the smoke and fire.

○ Dixon tells the reporter what he and his men did. He uses the Active Voice.

○ The newspaper informs its readers about the events and the results. The Passive Voice is used.

The Passive is normally used in all kinds of official statements, reports and in the news.

UNIT 1

Focus on grammar — The Passive

As you have noticed, there are a lot of Passive forms in the reports.

Simple Present	Some people	**are** still	**trapped**	in the building.
Simple Past	Three firemen	**were**	**injured.**	
Present Perfect	Some workers	**have been**	**rescued**	**by** firemen.
Past Perfect	The people who	**had been**	**trapped**	were rescued.
Will-future	A conference	**will be**	**held**	this evening.

Subject + form of "be" + Past Participle + by-agent

Passive with auxiliaries:

	Three firemen	**had to**	**be**	**taken**	to hospital.
	Not everyone	**could**	**be**	**rescued.**	

Subject + Auxiliary + "be" + Past Participle

→ Grammatikanhang S. 116

Can you do it?

Talking about accidents

1 *What sometimes happens in accidents?*

People **are** sometimes seriously **injured**.

| The | people
driver
passengers
building(s)
aeroplane
car
bike | at the …
in the … | (be) | often
sometimes | (seriously)
(badly) | (injure).
(hurt).
(burn).
(kill).
(damage). |

6

UNIT 1

2 *Now imagine there has been an accident. You're at the scene now. Say what has happened.*

The car **has been** badly **damaged.**

Now you go on.

A	man	has	(be)	(seriously)	(injure).
	woman	have		(badly)	(hurt).
	child			(slightly)	(rescue).
Two	people				…
Three					
Nobody					
The	bicycle				
	train				
	gate (?)				
	house				

3 *A lot of things have to be done when there has been an accident. What are they?*

The people who are hurt		must	be	(take) …
The injured		should		(carry) …
The dead		(have) to		(bury).
The relatives	of the injured			(inform).
The family				
The police				(call).
The ambulance				
The fire brigade				

UNIT 1

4 *What had happened before?*

Example:
After the woman (take) to hospital, she died.
After the woman **had been taken** to hospital, she died.

1 After the fire (put out), the firemen had a rest.
2 As soon as the man's relatives (inform), they came to the scene.
3 After the boy (rescue) from the smoke, he was taken to hospital.
4 After the injured (take) out of the car, it exploded.
5 As soon as the police (call), they rushed to the scene of the accident.

Using the language

1 *Look at today's or yesterday's newspaper and write six sentences about the news, using the Passive where possible.*

Examples:

According to the ... an 82-year-old woman was killed in a fire.
According to a report in the ... Pele's ball was stolen.

2 *Write about an accident that you've seen or heard about.*

○ What happened? Where? When?

There was an accident in/at ...
Last week/Monday/... there was ...
A man/woman/... was riding/..., when ...

○ Was anybody injured/killed?
  Was anything damaged/broken?

Luckily/Unfortunately ...

○ Say what was done after the accident.
  police? ambulance? hospital? fire brigade?

The police and the ... came and ...

UNIT 1

By the way

Look at the first extract: **News has** just come in that …
On the tape you also heard the sentence: Here **is the news.**

"**News**" is always singular.

Look at the last extract: **Police have** pushed the crowd back.
Other examples: **Class 4B are** planning an outing.
The family want to go to Spain this year.
Manchester United have won the match.

These nouns are called "group nouns" as they refer to a group of people. They are **usually** plural.

⟶ Grammatikanhang S. 132

Some Facts about Chicago

1 Chicago

Chicago is the second largest city in the United States. It's an important industrial centre and an inland port on the west bank of Lake Michigan. Total population: about 3.5 million. A third of the population is black. The name Chicago is often associated with the underworld violence in the 1920's and 1930's. Chicago is famous for its skyscrapers. Some of the tallest skyscrapers in the world can be found in this city.

The Chicago Fire

In 1871 there was a huge fire in Chicago. About 300 people were killed and a great deal of the city was destroyed.

2

Perhaps you'd like to write a short text about a big city in Germany. Here's some help:
Berlin / Hamburg / Munich is the …
city – (not) badly destroy – in the war
a lot of – old / modern buildings – in the city
The … church / museum / theatre – build – in …

UNIT 1

Focus on grammar

More about questions with question words

1 *In the listening text a reporter asks Tom: "Who do you know?"*

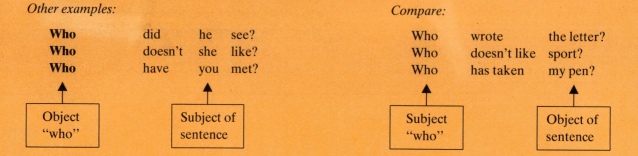

When we ask about a person we use "who" in the subject case and in the object case.

Note: In writing, it is also possible to use "whom" in the object case: "Whom have you met?"

2 *You also heard this question: "Who are you talking to now?"*

Look at these statements –   and questions:

A preposition following a verb stays with the verb when a question is asked. So we often use questions ending with a preposition.

→ Grammatikanhang S. 120

Can you do it?

What do you think they are saying?

Use the question words: what, who
the verbs: give, laugh, look, talk, write
and the prepositions: about, at, for, to

Focus on grammar

More about relative clauses

1 whose

A reporter said: "I'm talking to a woman **whose** daughter is still in the building."

Other examples: I'm talking to a man   **whose**   car was stolen.
                     I saw the woman   **whose**   son was injured in the accident.

> We use "whose" in relative clauses to show possession.

⟶ Grammatikanhang S. 123

2 The woman **that the reporter spoke to** saw her daughter afterwards.

Other examples:

There's the boy	who(m) / that	I was talking about.
There's the boy		I was talking about.
She found the book	that	she was looking for.
She found the book		she was looking for.

> A preposition following a verb stays with the verb in relative clauses.

⟶ Grammatikanhang S. 123

Can you do it?

1 Make sentences with relative clauses. Use: **"who"**, **"that"**, **"whose"**.

Example: building – on fire – built – ten years ago
The building that was on fire was built ten years ago.

1 crowd – watching – fire – made – situation worse
2 reporter – spoke to a woman – daughter – still in the building
3 Did – police – find – person – started – fire?
4 mayor – thanked – all the people – had helped – fight – fire
5 man – son – had been interviewed – reporter – rescued – by the firemen
6 last person – they rescued – woman's daughter
7 They – want – help – children – father – died – in the fire
8 Can – they – rescue – all the people – trapped – in the building?

 2 Rewrite the following sentences. The words in bold print should become the subject of your sentences.

Example: They're talking about an **accident** that happened in my street.
The accident they're talking about happened in my street.

1 The teacher told them about a **man** who used to live in this town.
2 I used to go to a **school** that was built 50 years ago.
3 The police were looking for a **man** who had already left the country.
4 They sent for the **doctor,** but he was ill.
5 The reporter spoke to the **fireman** who had rescued 10 people.
6 They went into the **building** that was badly damaged in the fire.
7 They took her to the **fireman** who had rescued her from the smoke.

Looking at the language

A note on American English

In this unit you've read and heard a lot of American English (AE) and have probably noticed that a few things are different to British English (BE).
Write down all the differences you've noticed on a separate sheet of paper. You can look at the texts again.

Any words or expressions that are different?	Any words that are spelt differently?	Any words that are pronounced differently?

Here are some words and phrases in BE that you already know. What are they in AE? How are they spelt or pronounced in AE? Look them up in a dictionary, or ask someone who knows.

different words or expressions	different spelling	different pronunciation
to hospital torch	colour	address [əˈdres]
underground holiday	theatre	adult [ˈædʌlt]
at the weekend go to the pictures	centre	either [ˈaɪðə]
football	favourite	

THE WORLD TRIBUNE, WEDNESDAY, JULY 10

Inferno Girl Plans Wedding

World Trib Exclusive

Sandra Casey, 19, who was rescued by fireman Peter O'Shaugnessy in the Victory Tower inferno, says she will marry her boss Gregory Jones, 42.

"He showed real courage in there. He was almost killed as he rescued our 'Bartholomew' here," she said, stroking the office cat which was also rescued from the terrible flames. "He's the kind of man I've always dreamed of."

She and Gregory were still in the office when the fire broke out. They did not notice the smoke at first. "The fire has changed our lives," said Sandra. "Now we are really serious about each other."

Millions

The fire could cost Victory and Mutual over two hundred million dollars. The fire started when cleaning woman Meryl Johnson, who had just come to work at 6 p.m., dropped a cigarette into a waste basket. "I was in my room on the 5th floor," she says, "and I dropped my cigarette into the waste basket and it set fire to the paper inside, and the next thing I knew everything was burning."

Fire Chief "Bootsy" Dixon said that over 500 fire trucks raced to the burning 160 story building. "It was a wall of flames," he said. "There were nearly 400 people trapped in that building and we knew we just had to get them out somehow. My men were very brave. I was real proud of them. 63 of them were badly burned and are now in the hospital."

Rescue

Not everyone was rescued. The number of dead has reached twenty already and firemen are still searching the building for more bodies. It was early this morning at about 4 a.m. when the last people in the building were brought out.

"Our boys have done a great job," says Chicago's mayor, "but this must never happen again."

As you know, some newspapers do not always get the facts right. Compare this account in the "World Tribune" with the extracts on page 4. What has the newspaper got wrong?

Here are some phrases you can use:

It is not true that …
The newspaper says that …, but …
According to the radio …
Nobody knows …
…

UNIT 1

Using the language

That evening...

 Can you tell the story?

 Imagine you're the boy or girl in the pictures. Write what happened.

Here are some adjectives and adverbs that you can use:

big	awful	quickly
huge	terrible	fast
large	afraid	hard
hot	frightened	suddenly
	nervous	

Breaking up

UNIT 2

Sally's Diary

Reading

March 10

A beautiful day today. Roger and I went for a walk along the river and talked about the future. We both want to work with animals — he'd like to work with cats and dogs and I'd love to work with horses. And we both want to work together in Yorkshire!

When we got to Tillot's farm, we saw a sheep with two little lambs. They were so beautiful — they could only just walk! They were so small and pretty. I wanted to take them home. I'm really looking forward to working with animals.

I love Roger very much, and he loves me, too. We've known each other for five months now. I'm sure we'll stay together for a long time. If I don't see him, I get moody — and he says, if he's unhappy, I always cheer him up!

I think we're perfectly suited to each other!

Why were they suited to each other?

April 15

Something was wrong with Roger today. I'm a <u>bit</u> worried about him. I had to help Dad in the garden this afternoon, so I left the house a little later than usual. When I got to the bus stop, I was ten minutes later – and Roger shouted at me! It's not like him. I've been late before and it didn't <u>matter</u>.

Anyway, we got to the Freaks concert on time, and they were very good, so Roger cheered up later on. Still, I've been thinking about our friendship the whole time. Roger and I met on a beautiful afternoon last autumn – October it was – and we've been together since that day. We've had such happy moments together. Of course, he sometimes gets moody, but I've never seen him so angry before. Maybe he wasn't feeling so well. If I see him tomorrow, I'll ask him.

Why was Sally worried?

April 16

Oh, yes, I saw him today all right, and he wasn't ill – he was with Liz Forman! I saw them walking down the High Street when I was going past on the bus. They went into the café. I don't understand – why Liz Forman? I'd go mad if he started going out with <u>her</u>! Anyway, I phoned Roger later and asked him about it. "Oh, it's nothing important," he said, "she's just a friend of mine. Lots of people go into that café after school."

I really don't know what to do. My mother says it's no use worrying..... But I've been thinking about Liz all evening – with her stupid smile and expensive clothes. Roger's coming to tea tomorrow because it's my birthday.....I feel a bit nervous about it......

APRIL 17

My birthday. Happy birthday to me. Just about the worst birthday I've ever had. First of all, Grandma fell down the stairs and broke her leg. Mum and Dad took her to hospital. Everybody's very worried - I hope she'll be OK ...
Well, I decided to have tea with Roger anyway because I wanted to talk to him. But he didn't come!!! I waited and waited, and then I rang him up. This is what happened:
"Roger?" - "Yes, ... oh, hello, Sally!"
- "I've been waiting for you for an hour - why haven't you come to tea?"
- "Tea? ... Oh, I'm sorry, I forgot ..."
- "You forgot! Look, Roger, I've been waiting for you since 5 o'clock!"
- "Sally, I've said I'm sorry."
- "Yes, Roger, but how long have we been together now? Six months and this has never happened before."
- "Well, it has happened now. Don't be so childish."
- "Childish? You've got a cheek!" - Click.
Roger put the phone down before I could finish speaking. Just wait until I see him tomorrow, I'll spit in his face!

APRIL 18

Well, I didn't spit in his face after all - but we were both rather miserable. He gave me a nice present, but it isn't the same the day after your birthday, is it? And now he can't come to Joan's party with me any more. He's got to study for his exam. We didn't really know what to say to each other, so we just said goodbye and went home. We've known each other for quite a long time now. Maybe he's getting a bit bored ... I don't know ... I could see he was very unhappy, though, and I was, too ... I'm still in love with him and I think he's still fond of me - we'll just have to wait and see. Mum's probably right - perhaps it's not worth worrying about.. and even Dad says I ought to forget it.

Why were Sally and Roger both "rather miserable"?

1 *How does the relationship between Sally and Roger develop? Look in the diary.*

In March Sally and Roger ...
A month later ...
The next day ...
Sally's birthday ...
They saw each other on 18th April, but ...

2 *What do you think of Sally's and Roger's behaviour?*

In my opinion ...	behaved	well.
I think ...		badly.
I don't think ...	was	childish.
	were	stupid.
		nice to ...

3 *What do you think will happen now?*
Perhaps …   I have no idea.
Maybe …   I don't really care.
… probably …

4 *What would you do if you were Sally / Roger?*
I'd / I would …
I wouldn't …

Did you get it?

Can you remember what happened?
This is a summary of what Sally wrote in her diary.
Can you complete it?

Roger was Sally's … . On 10th March they … walk by the river and talked about the … . They both wanted to work … . On that day Roger and Sally … and Sally thought they were perfectly suited to … .

Then things started going wrong in April. Sally was … and Roger … at her for the first time. The next day on 16th April she saw him with … . Sally felt really … , so she … Roger and asked him about it, but he said Liz was just a … . Sally didn't know what to … . The next day was her … . It was a … for her. First her grandmother … . She had to be taken to … . Then Roger, who had been invited to …, didn't come. After she … for over an hour, she … Roger. They … on the phone and Roger put … while Sally … still … . They saw each … day and Roger … a nice …, but they …

Looking at the language

Sally wrote:

I don't know   **what to   do.**
We didn't know   **what to   say** to each other.

Here are some more examples:

She told me   **what to   do.**
Did he know   **where to   go?**
I didn't know   **when to   get off** the bus.
Show me   **how to   open** this box, please.

⟶ Grammatikanhang S. 123

Can you do it?

1 *Sally didn't know what to do. What about you?*
What don't you know sometimes?

I	(sometimes)	don't know	what to …
We	(often)		where to …
			when to …
			how to …
			which (book) to …
			which way to …
			who to …

2 *Well, you can ask for help, using:*

Please	show	me	what to …
Can you	tell		where to … (?)
			…

3 *Complete the following.*

1 She didn't know the way, so a man told her where to …
2 Can you help me with this cake? Please tell me … the sugar in.
3 Both are beautiful. I don't know which one …
4 Can you help me, please? I don't know … mend this pullover.
5 Don't worry. I'll tell you …
6 I'm so worried. I don't know …
7 When they came to the traffic lights, they didn't know …
8 I didn't know the way, so a man told me which bus …
9 Then a woman told me … get off the bus.

UNIT 2

Looking at the language

Roger said:

It's nothing important – she's just a friend **of mine.**

The expression **"of mine"** *means* "one of my …".
So **"a friend of mine"** *means* "one of my friends".

Some more examples:

a friend	**of**	**yours**
an uncle		**his**
		hers
		ours
		theirs

> We normally use these structures when we're talking about **friends** and **some relatives** (cousins, aunts, uncles, nieces, nephews).

Can you do it?

1 *Now talk about some of your friends and relatives.*

A	friend	of mine	lives in …
	cousin		went to …
An	aunt		bought a …
	…		gave me …
			…

2 *Use the correct pronoun to complete the following.*

Focus on grammar — Present Perfect with "how long", "since", "for"

1 *On 10th March Sally wrote:* **We've known** each other **for** 5 months now.

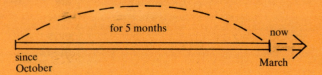

Sally and Roger met in October (= 5 months ago) and, of course, they still know each other.

How long have we **been** together? — We've **been** together	**for**	three months.
	since	September.

We first met in September, and we are still together.

> We use the Present Perfect when we talk about something that began in the past and has not ended yet.

Be careful! Which tense do we use in German?

They**'ve been**	friends	**since**	last Summer.
We**'ve known**	each other	**for**	two years.
How long have you **had**	this bike?		
I**'ve had**	it	**for**	six months.
Has he **known**	her	**for**	a long time?

> We always use the Present Perfect with **"be"**, **"have"** and **"know"** when we talk about something that began in the past and has not ended yet.

2 For / Since

I've been here	**since**	last week.
She's known him	**for**	two months.
I haven't written her	**for**	a year.
They haven't spoken to each other	**for**	4 days.

> ○ **for:** a period of time until now (for 5 months, for 2 hours, for a year etc.)
> ○ **since:** a certain point of time in the past (since April, since yesterday etc.)

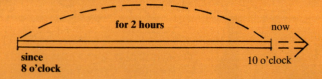

→ Grammatikanhang S. 126

Can you do it?

1 ***"For"*** *or* ***"since"***?
Use **"for"** or **"since"** with the following:

three hours – 3 o'clock – quite a long time –
last Christmas – a week – my last birthday –
last month – three years – yesterday – 1980 –
the day before yesterday – January –
last week – five days – a year – last autumn

2 *Now work with a partner.*

1 **A:** How long have you had | your | bike
 | ... | pen?
 | | ...

 B: For ... / Since ...
 How long have you ...?

 A: Oh, | for ...
 | since ...

2 **A:** How long (you – be) | here?
 | in this town?
 | at this school?
 | ...

 B: For ... / Since ...
 What about you?

 A: Oh, I ... | since ...
 | for ...

3 **A:** Have (you – know) | (Marion) for very long?
 | ...

 B: Yes, | for ...   *or:* **B:** No, only | for ...
 | since ... | since ...

Using the language

1 *Write 6 true sentences about yourself using the correct form of* **"be"**, **"have"** *and* **"know"** + **"for"** *or* **"since"**.

Example: I've known (Thomas) for over a year.

2 *Now make up a short dialogue with your partner for each of the following situations. Use* **"how long"**, **"for"** *and* **"since"** *where possible.*

1 Your partner has got a bike / etc. You don't know if it's new.
2 You're surprised that your partner knows a certain person.
3 You've heard that your partner is a member of a club. You want to know more.
4 You've heard that your partner used to live in another town/village.

Giving Advice

Looking at the language

Sally is talking to her parents.
Look at what they say:

By the way

You can give advice in a lot of different ways. Here are some new expressions you can use:

1 You **ought to** forget it.
  You **ought not to** speak to her again.

2 It's **no use** worry**ing** about it.
  It's **not worth** worry**ing** about it.

⟶ Grammatikanhang S. 128–129

Can you do it?

1 *What do you think Sally/Roger should do?*

Sally	ought to …
Roger	ought not to …
They	

2 *What else can you say to Sally or Roger?*

It's no use	(continue) like this.
It's not worth	(try) to be friends again.
	(go) out with …
	(argue) …
	…

Using the language

1 *Some friends are giving Roger and Sally advice. What are they saying?*

Be …
You shouldn't …
You mustn't …
You ought to …
Why don't you …?
If I were you, I'd …
You should …
You could …
Don't …
Well, I'd … if …
If you phone her now, she'll …
You ought not to …
It's no use …
If you gave her …, she'd …
It's not worth …

go out and meet other people
forget him/her
don't talk to him/her again
stop going out with him/her
find another boyfriend/girlfriend

say you are sorry
be nice to him/her
phone him/her
give him/her a present
write him/her a letter

2 *What advice would you give in the following situations? Act these situations out with a partner.*

1 A saw his/her boyfriend/girlfriend with someone else yesterday. A is worried, so he/she asks B for advice.

2 A's boyfriend/girlfriend forgot his/her birthday. A is now complaining to B.

3 A hears his/her best friend said something nasty about him/her. A doesn't know what to think and asks B for advice.

Here are some expressions you can use for asking for advice:

I don't know what to do.
I don't know what to think.
What shall I do?
What should I do?
Should I …?
Do you think I should …?
What would you do?

UNIT 2

An Argument

Listening

 Listen to Sally and Roger. They're having an argument on the phone.

How do they behave? Whose fault is it?

Looking at the language

Now look at the conversation you've just heard. Which expressions caused the argument? Find at least five and write them down on a separate sheet of paper.

Sally: Roger?
Roger: Yes … oh, hello, Sally!
Sally: I've been waiting for you for over an hour. Why haven't you come to tea?
Roger: Tea? … Oh, goodness! I'm sorry, Sally. I completely forgot.
Sally: Forgot? Roger, how could you? We've been going out for over six months now and you've never forgotten a date before. What have you been thinking about all day?
Roger: Now don't be silly, Sally. I'll come over later. I've been busy all afternoon.
Sally: Busy doing what?
Roger: Oh, stop it, Sally. You're being childish. I've been helping a friend of mine. That's all.
Sally: And I suppose this friend of yours is more important than my birthday?
Roger: Well, when someone is in trouble, you help them, don't you? You're being childish, and selfish, too.
Sally: Selfish? That's a joke, that is. You're the selfish one. You never think about other people at all.
Roger: Well, if that's the way you think. I'm not coming at all. I'll see you tomorrow. *(Click)*

How could the argument be avoided? What should they say instead?

 ## Listening

The conversation between Sally and Roger could have gone another way. Listen to the tape again.

How do the two young people behave this time? Can you remember any expressions which helped to avoid an argument?

Focus on grammar

Present Perfect Progressive (with "how long", "since", "for")

It's 6 o'clock. Sally is waiting for Roger.
How long **has** she **been waiting** now?

She's **been waiting** | for two hours.
| since 4 o'clock.

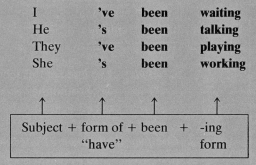

She started waiting at 4 o'clock, and she's still waiting now (at 6 o'clock).

So she **has been waiting** since 4 o'clock. OR
She **has been waiting** for two hours.

The Present Perfect Progressive:

I	've	been	waiting	since 4 o'clock.
He	's	been	talking	for two hours.
They	've	been	playing	for a long time.
She	's	been	working	all afternoon.
				the whole time.
				all the time.

↑ ↑ ↑ ↑

Subject + form of + been + -ing
"have" form

We use the Present Perfect Progressive when we talk about an action that began in the past, was going on all the time and is still going on now.

Compare: She's **playing** tennis *with* She's **been playing** tennis all afternoon.

⟶ Grammatikanhang S. 127

UNIT 2

Can you do it?

1 *What are they saying?*

Examples:

45 minutes

5 o'clock

Now you go on.

6 o'clock

two and a half hours

3 hours

nearly an hour

this morning

12.30

2 *Make sentences with the following words and phrases.*

e.g.: she – wait – the bus – 9 o'clock
   She's been waiting for the bus since 9 o'clock.
e.g.: I – have – book – a year
   I've had this book for a year.

1 they – play – football – 4 o'clock
2 he – not know – her – very long
3 we – learn – English – more than three years
4 we – sit – here – an hour and a half
5 she – have – that bike – last week
6 we – be – in this room – an hour
7 you – know – each other – very long?
8 she – stand – outside – forty minutes
9 I – work – all afternoon
10 she – think – him – the whole time

Using the language

1 *Write 6–8 true sentences about yourself or someone you know, using*

| (have) been -ing |
| (have) had/known/been |

+ for/since

Examples: I've been at this school for 4 years now.
My brother has been learning English for over 3 years.

2 *Complete the following dialogues. Use the correct tense of the verbs in brackets and other suitable words and phrases.*

1 A: I like your bike. Is it new?
  B: Oh, no. I (have) it … last summer / a year.

2 A: Your English (be) good. How long (you – learn) it?
  B: Oh, I (learn) it since / for …

3 A: Sorry I'm late. How long (you – wait)?
  B: That's all right. I (not wait) very long. I (come) at 5 o'clock.

4 A: Are you new here?
  B: Well, not quite. I (be) here ... last autumn / six months.
  A: I see. I'm new here. I (arrive) 2 days ago.

5 A: I (not – hear) from Jean ... such a long time.
  B: Oh, I have. As a matter of fact I (speak) to her on the phone yesterday.
  A: Oh, how is she?
  B: Fine. She has been on holiday and (just – come back).

6 A: I think I'm getting a bit bored with my boyfriend.
  B: Well, how long (you – go out) with ...
  A: Now let me see. We (know) ... 2 months now, but we (start) going out together 3 weeks ago.
  B: You're probably right. Maybe you (know) him too long.

Avoiding Confrontations

Listening

On the tape you'll hear some extracts from conversations. Each develops into an argument because the second person makes a provoking remark. Can you suggest a different reaction which would help to avoid an argument?

Here's some help, but you can think of other reactions of your own.

Do you think you could...?	I don't think that's ...
Oh – well – what about ... ing ...?	Well, I'm afraid I don't agree, but ...
Oh, really? I'm sorry, but ...	Couldn't you ...?
I'm sure that's not really ...	Well, I don't know ...

Using the language

A conversation can be polite and friendly, or it can develop into an argument. Work with a partner and act out one of the following situations. The chart and the expressions on the next page can help you.

1 A and B arranged to go to the pictures together last night. A waited for B outside the cinema but didn't see B. A asks B about it now.

2 Somebody has told A that her boyfriend (B) was at a party/the club with another girl. A asks B about it now.

3 A lent B his/her bike/dictionary/roller skates some time ago. When A gets it/them back, it's/they are damaged. A asks B about it now.

UNIT 2

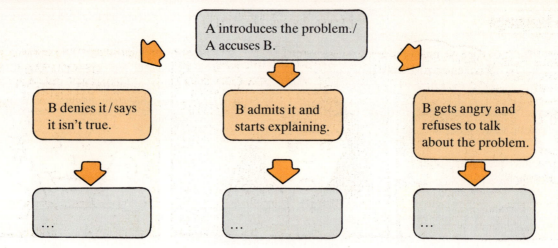

Why did/didn't you…?
Look, my … is broken/damaged.
Is it true that…?

Look, I haven't got time …
I'm not going to talk about it and that's that!
I don't know what you're talking about.

Why don't you want to talk about it?
Well, I think we should …
Don't you think we should …?

It's like this – I …
I really couldn't because …
This is what happened …

I'm really sorry.
I'm very sorry.
It's my fault.
I won't do it again.
Can you forgive me?

Well, I'm afraid you'll have to …
I'm sorry, but you'll just have to …
If you don't …, I'll …
I'm really sorry, but I …

Stop talking nonsense!
Don't be so stupid/silly/childish!

That's not fair/true.
It's not my fault.
Don't blame me.

All right. It really doesn't matter.
It's OK – it's not important.
Oh, never mind.
OK, I forgive you.

Using the language

How Will It End?

At the party   **Ten minutes later –**

 What do you think will happen? Write an ending for this story. You can begin like this:

 Sonya felt very unhappy at the party. Frank didn't ...

UNIT 3 — It's Worth Visiting Wales!

Meet Eva from Germany. She's thinking of spending her next holiday in Wales. She's reading a brochure about a holiday camp in South Wales.

Reading

The holiday of a lifetime at Camp Cymraig

For over 15 years we have been organizing adventure holidays for young people. And we get better at it each time.

- Every year we attract more guests to our camps;
- Every year we open at least one new holiday centre;
- And every year our adventure holidays get better and better.

This year we can offer you –

- modern, attractive camps with fully trained staff;
- a variety of sports and adventure activities;
- a full social programme with opportunities for meeting other young people from England, Ireland, Scotland, Wales and 15 other countries;
- the magnificent beaches and mountains of South Wales – one of the most beautiful parts of Britain.

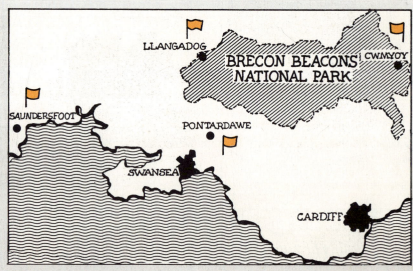

🚩 = Camp Cymraig holiday centre

All this, of course, with our unique money-back guarantee for guests who are not completely satisfied with our camps.

UNIT 3

And when you get tired of sightseeing and wind surfing, well – you can relax in our holiday centre or join in a variety of indoor activities. We're sure you won't be bored. We've got something for everyone for those lazy summer evenings.

- **Music Club** – musical evenings, folk music concerts, international music night, guitar classes, country dancing.
- **Games room** with electronic games, table tennis, jukebox.
- **Film Club**
- **Photography Club**
- **Disco**
- **Late-night snack bar**
- **Television room**
- **Arts and crafts corner**

CAMP CYMRAIG
1, Heol Waunvawr,
Cardiff CFI 2XN
Wales

So if you're between 14 and 20, and you are keen on adventure, sport and good company, write to our head office in Cardiff, and we'll send more information and an application form.

Did you get it?

What are the special attractions of the camp?

There is / are …
There are opportunities for …
If you want, you can …

Using the language

Would you like to go to this camp? Do you think you'd enjoy a holiday there? Give reasons.

Yes, I think …
I'd love to … because …
I wouldn't mind … because …
I don't think I'd …
Well, I'd get tired of …ing and …ing.
I wouldn't think of …ing …
I wouldn't dream of …ing …
Well, I'm not interested in …

What Are Your Interests?

Looking at the language

Eva plans to go to Camp Cymraig.

Look at what she says:

① I'm keen on caving and sightseeing, and all kinds of sport …

② … and I'm also very fond of meeting new people.

③ So I'm really looking forward to going to Camp Cymraig!

Focus on grammar

More about the -ing-form

| Why is Eva | thinking
looking forward
dreaming | of
to
of | go**ing** | to Camp Cymraig? |

| – Because she is | interested
fond
keen | in
of
on | sightsee**ing**
meet**ing** people
jogg**ing** |

and there are lots of **opportunities** for do**ing** these things.

> We can only use the -ing-form of the verb after verbs, adjectives and nouns with prepositions.

Other examples:

They're	**crazy**	**about**	jogg**ing**.
Aren't you	**tired**	**of**	look**ing** at historic buildings?
Thank you		**for**	com**ing**.

⟶ Grammatikanhang S. 114

Can you do it?

Before Eva goes to the camp, she's got to fill in a questionnaire about her interests. This is Eva's questionnaire:

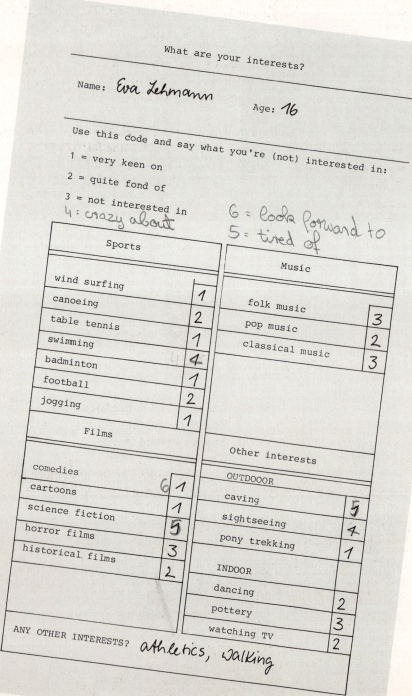

What can you say about Eva's likes and dislikes?

Eva		likes …
		enjoys…
	is	quite	interested in …
		rather	fond of …
		very	keen on …
isn't …		
doesn't …		

Using the language

1 *What about you? What are you fond of doing? Look at the questionnaire and talk about your likes and dislikes. You can use the phrases on page 34 and some of these, too.*

I prefer …
I love …
I don't mind …
I'm crazy about …
I hate …

2 *Work with a partner and ask each other about your plans for the weekend / the holidays / etc.*

You can begin like this:

What are your plans for the …?
What are you going to …?
Are you going to …?

Say what you are | **thinking of** | doing.
| **looking forward to** |

3 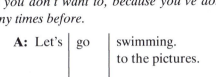 *Act out the following situations with your partner. He/She wants you to do something with him/her, but you don't want to, because you've done it so many times before.*

A: Let's | go | swimming.
| | to the pictures.
| | …
| have | a hot dog.
| | a pizza.
| | …
| play | …
| … |

B: Not again! | I'm tired of …
No thanks. |
Aren't you tired of …?
We always …
We … yesterday and the day before, too.
I'm really tired of …

Reading

Two Letters

1

Camp Cymraig
1, Heol Waunvawr
Cardiff CF1 2XN
Wales

Eva Lehmann
Königstr. 36
6110 Dieburg
15. April 198.

Dear Sir or Madam,
I have filled in the application form and the questionnaire. I hope that a place can be reserved for me at one of your camps in South Wales. I look forward to hearing from you soon.
Yours faithfully,
Eva Lehmann

2

CAMP CYMRAIG, Head Office,
1, Heol Waunvawr, CARDIFF CF1 2XN
Tel. 043-392481

23rd April, 198.

Dear Eva,
   Thank you for your letter of 15th April with the application form and questionnaire. We have reserved a place for you in our camp at Pontardawe from 17th June until 2nd July.
   When you come to London, you can catch a train from Paddington at 1.15 or 2.15 p.m. The trains arrive at Swansea Station at 4.54 and 6.01 p.m. We'll meet both trains at the station with our minibus.
   I enclose some brochures with information on Wales.
   I look forward to seeing you and I'm sure you will enjoy your stay at our camp.
                              Yours sincerely,
                              S. P. Trethowan
                              Director, Pontardawe Camp

 If you'd like to hear a traditional Welsh song, you could listen to the tape while you read the following texts.

Welcome to Wales

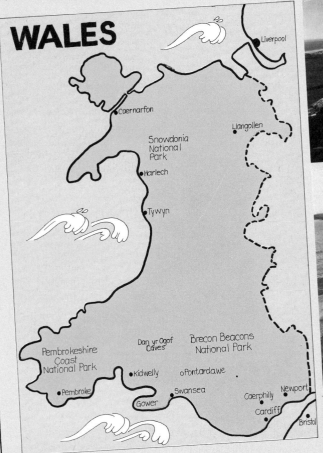

This brochure is an invitation to come to Wales, to see the historic and beautiful land which lies in the west of Britain.

○ You will be fascinated by the beauty and variety of the landscape. You will pass through mountains and hills, rivers and forests, deep valleys, rocky coastline and sandy beaches.

○ You will be impressed by the great medieval castles in Wales: Caernarfon, Caerphilly, Pembroke, Harlech and many more.

○ You won't have a dull moment in Wales. You can climb mountains and explore caves; go pony trekking, boating, fishing or sailing. You can visit museums and shows, go for rides on steam trains or visit local eisteddfodau where you'll hear the Welsh sing — and how they love to sing!

○ And you'll fall in love with the Welsh language, one of the oldest in the world. (But everyone you meet speaks English as well.)

So, come to the friendly land of Wales!

In this brochure we'll show you some of the attractions of the different areas in Wales.

**Wales Tourist Board,
Brunel House, 2 Fitzalan Road,
Cardiff CF2 1 UY, Wales**

EXTRA

Wales – a land of castles

Wales is famous for its medieval castles, and there are over 100 which you can visit. Each tells an exciting story – it is the story of Wales.

Here are a few of the many castles you just must visit.

Caernarfon Castle is in North Wales. It was built by Edward I, who, according to the story, presented his son "who can speak no English" to the Welsh people. In 1969, Prince Charles was made Prince of Wales in this castle.

Pembroke Castle in the south was the birthplace of Henry Tudor, one of the outstanding Welshmen in British history.

Caerphilly Castle, also in the south, is the largest medieval fortress in Wales. It is famous for its leaning tower.

So many attractions

Of course, we can't present all of Wales' tourist attractions. These are just a few.

Wales is full of some of the most unusual tourist attractions in Britain. You can, for example, ride on a narrow gauge railway and see some of Wales' most attractive countryside. There are nine lines in all, and they are called the "great little trains of Wales". These steam trains are a Welsh speciality – like the medieval castles or eisteddfodau.
For information on all the trains, contact:
**Talyllyn Railway, Wharf Station, Tywyn, Gwynedd.
Tel. Tywyn 710472.**

Narrow gauge railways, Wildlife parks, Caves

Arts Festivals and Eisteddfodau

Penscynor Wildlife Park
This beautiful park at Cilfrew in South Wales is protected from the north winds by the mountains and forests. You'll be fascinated by the variety of birds and animals.
Open 10 a.m. each day throughout the year.
Children's play area.

The Dan-yr-Ogof Caves, Britain's longest and largest showcaves, are situated between Brecon and Swansea in the Brecon Beacons National Park. Go on a guided tour of the caves and see some of the most fascinating stalagmites and stalactites.

Youth comes to Llangollen
Each July, hundreds of singers, musicians and dancers from many different countries come to the little town of Llangollen. They come to take part in the Llangollen International Eisteddfod.
Follow their example and come to Llangollen. You will be impressed by the beauty of the valley. It is also good country for walking, riding and fishing.

The Swansea Festival
This is one of the most important arts festivals in Wales. It offers concerts by famous orchestras, poetry, jazz, exhibitions, drama and ballet. Pembrokeshire, the Brecon Beacons National Park and the beaches of the Gower Coast are some of the places you can visit when you are in Swansea.

Some Facts about Wales

Reading

General information

Its Welsh name is Cymru, which means "land of comradeship". One of the three countries of Great Britain. Wales lies west of England.
Area: 8,016 square miles. Capital: Cardiff. Main ports: Cardiff, Swansea and New Port. Population: about three million.

Languages

English and Welsh. About 25% of the population can speak Welsh (as well as English).

Landscape

Many different kinds of landscape: there are mountains, plateaus and hills, valleys and the coastline. The two mountain areas are Snowdonia in the northwest and Brecon Beacons in the south. There are a lot of rivers and lakes in Wales.

Climate

It rains a lot. In winter there can be heavy snowfalls.

Economy

Agriculture, forestry, coal mining.

Culture

Wales has a traditional culture of its own, and the Welsh language is the medium of this culture. The National Eisteddfod is the most important cultural event in Wales. It is held each year either in North Wales or in South Wales for one week in August. There are competitions in music, literature, drama and art. During this week the National Eisteddfod is the meeting place for the whole nation. But smaller eisteddfodau are held in towns and villages throughout the year.

Did you get it?

True or false? If it's not in the text, say so.
Also correct the false statements.

1 Wales is in the west of England.
2 Cardiff is by the sea.
3 Most of the population can speak Welsh.
4 There is a great variety of scenery in Wales.
5 It can rain and snow heavily in Wales.
6 There are a lot of trees in Wales.
7 The National Eisteddfod is held in North Wales every year.
8 You can go to plays and listen to music at the National Eisteddfod.
9 Thousands of Welshmen go to the National Eisteddfod every year.
10 There are smaller eisteddfodau in many parts of Wales.

Using the language

 Perhaps you'd like to spend a holiday in Wales and would like some more information. Well, you can write to the Wales Tourist Board (address on page 37).

 Here's some help for your letter. You can also look at Eva's letter on page 36.

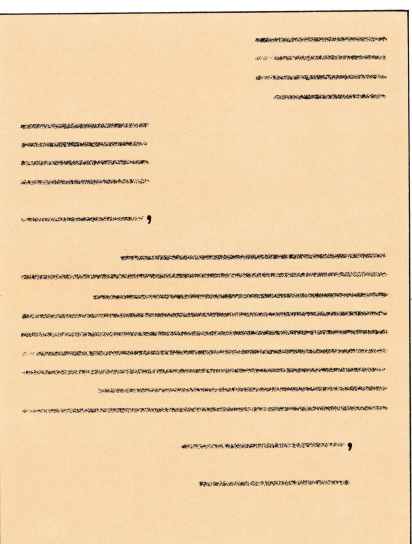

Your address

Date

Address of organization

Greeting

(1) Introduction / General reason for letter

(2) Say what kind of information you need and ask them to send you the material.

(3) Say you hope to hear from them soon / that they'll be able to help you.

Closing

Signature

You can use some of these phrases for (1), (2) and (3).

(1) We have read a lot about …
    We are pupils at …
    I'm interested in …

(2) Could you kindly …?
    Have you got any …?
    Can you send us …?

(3) I/We hope …
    I/We look forward to …

UNIT 4 Getting to Know Each Other

At Camp Cymraig

Listening

 Listen to each of the four conversations on the tape and try to find out:

who the people are (names, nationalities); where they are; where they are going; what they are doing; what they are talking about.

Did you get it?

Now listen to each conversation again and then try to answer the following questions.

1 In the refectory

1 *What's right? What's wrong? If it's not on the tape, say so.*

  a) Rieke has been at the camp for over two weeks.
  b) She's not interested in sport.
  c) She complains to Eva.
  d) Eva isn't too fond of music.
  e) Eva can play the piano.
  f) Rieke plays the guitar.

2 Do you think the two girls will get on well together? Why / Why not?

2 In the bus

1 a) Where have the girls been? Did they enjoy it?
  b) Whose English is better – Eva's or Rieke's?
  c) How are the two girls getting on now?

2 *What else have we learnt about the girls? Complete the following sentences.*

  a) Both girls are … films and they … the group, Monty Python.
  b) Eva likes … TV, but she isn't … watch it often at …
  c) She goes to a … because her mother …
  d) Rieke's mother is … and that explains why Rieke …

3 At the camp gate

1 *True or false?*

  a) Eva lives in Darmstadt.
  b) Rieke has been living in Utrecht for 3 years.
  c) The gate official is British.

2 What caused the argument?

4 On the walk

1 What started Rieke's interest in films?
2 How do we know that the girls really like each other?
3 How did the three people behave? What's your opinion?

Using the language

Do you think Eva and Rieke will remain friends? Give reasons.

They'll probably …
Perhaps they'll …
Maybe …
If they visit each other often, they'll …
I think …/ I don't think … because …

Looking at the language

Some common mistakes

As you might have already noticed, Eva's English is quite good. But sometimes she makes mistakes.

Here are some extracts from the conversations on the tape. Can you find the mistakes that Eva makes? Write them down on a separate sheet of paper, and then correct them.

1

Rieke: You look as if you're new here.
Eva: Yes, I've arrived an hour ago. And you? How long are you here?
Rieke: Oh, this is my second week. It's not bad. You'll like it – especially if you like sport.
Eva: Oh, yes, I like sport – that's why I've come here.
Rieke: Yes – just like everybody else. They're all crazy about sport.

wrong	right
I've arrived an hour ago.	I arrived an hour ago.

2

Rieke: Have you been enjoying yourself?
Eva: Oh, yes, very much. I went this afternoon to Kidwelly Castle. It was fun. And I've just went to the cinema … uuh, sorry … *(laughs)* I've just *been* to the cinema to see a film called …
Rieke: "The Life of Brian"?
Eva: Yes. How do you know?

3

Rieke: An actress? That's very interesting …
Eva: Yes – and she's travelling always, so I have to stay in the school.

Rieke: Mmm – My mother's English.
Eva: Oh, *that's* why you speak English so good. *well*
Rieke: Your English is very good, too. How long have you been learning it?
Eva: Oh, I learn it for 4 years now. … *I've been learning*

4

Rieke: Well – would you like to come and visit us next summer? You can stay at our house.
Eva: Thank you, Rieke. I'd love to. And then you can come to stay with us in Dieburg.
Rieke: Oh, great! I'll write to my parents this evening.
Eva: Good! And I write mine, too. – Oh, I'm looking forward to it already.

Looking at the language

Comparing how we do things

Now here are some more extracts from the conversations that you have listened to.

What adverbs can you find?

1

Rieke: Yes. Most of us play quite well, but there's a Portuguese girl who can play better than anyone else. Last night they had a little competition and she played best. She's really good. – Do you play anything? Piano? Guitar?
Eva: No, I'm afraid not.

2

Eva: Come on, Rieke, let's sit under that tree. That guide walks fast, doesn't he? I'm tired.
Rieke: Yes – there was one last week who walked even faster. Once we even had to ask him to stop. … I'm hungry. What is here in this picnic?
Eva: Mmmm – Er – Chicken sandwiches, boiled eggs, salad …

3

Eva: I've never seen an Australian film.
Rieke: I really liked those I saw. I can understand them more easily than American films – I think Australians speak more clearly than Americans. … Oh, look at those mountains! They're beautiful, aren't they?

Focus on grammar

Comparing how we do things: Comparison of adverbs

1 That guide walks fast.
The guide last week walked fast**er**.
In the competition Fred ran fast**est**.

> We compare adverbs that have the same form as adjectives by adding **– er** (comparative) and
> **– est** (superlative)

Other examples: hard   hard**er**   hard**est**
high   high**er**   high**est**

Note: lat**e**   lat**er**   lat**est**
far   **further**   **furthest** or
far   far**ther**   far**thest** (for distance only)

2 Rieke says:

Australians speak **more** clear**ly** than Americans.
I can understand them **most** easi**ly**.

> We compare adverbs that are formed by adding **-ly** with **– more** (comparative) and
> **– most** (superlative)

Other examples: careful**ly**   **more** carefully   **most** carefully
quick**ly**   **more** quickly   **most** quickly
quiet**ly**   **more** quietly   **most** quietly
slow**ly**   **more** slowly   **most** slowly

3 They all play quite **well**.
But the Portuguese girl plays **better** than anyone one else.
In the competition she played **best**.

Other special forms: **badly**   **worse**   **worst**
early   **earlier**   **earliest** (-ly is part of the word; it is not added as an ending)

⟶ Grammatikanhang S. 136

Can you do it?

1 *Compare how they do/did things.*

1 Eva speaks English ..., but Rieke speaks even ...
2 The two girls came back ..., but the others came even ...
3 The Portuguese girl played ... than all the others. She played ...
4 "Oh, that guide walks so ..." – "Yes. But there was one last week who walked even ..."
5 Rieke understands Australians ... than Americans because they speak ...

2 *Put in the correct forms of suitable adverbs.*

1 She won first prize in the competition because she sang ...
2 "Oh, I've broken your pen. I'm really very sorry." – "Oh, all right, but next time please be ..."
3 In the high jump, Ulrike jumped ... than all the other girls. She jumped ...
4 And in the long jump, Jack jumped farther than the other boys. He jumped ...
5 If you try ..., you'll do ... next time.
6 If you got up ..., you wouldn't come to school so late.
7 Joan did quite ... in German; she got a B. But Sylvia did even ...; she got an A.

high jump

long jump

Using the language

Now talk about yourself and some members of your family. Or talk about some friends. Compare how you/they do things. You can choose from the adverbs on page 44.

I/My sister/brother (Christian/Sabine)	get(s) up late every morning, but ... get(s) up even ...
	play(s) tennis quite ..., but ... play(s) even ...
	work(s) ...
	write(s) ...
	(can) speak(s) English ...
	...
...	

UNIT 4

Looking at the language

Rules Are Rules

Some of the campers are reading the rules at Camp Cymraig. *Look at what they say.*

By the way	**Talking about rules (What we must/mustn't do)**

The campers	should must	be back in camp by 10.30 p.m.
They	shouldn't are not allowed to mustn't	bring pets into the camp.

We can also use these expressions to say what we must/mustn't do:

I	'm		
He/She	's	supposed to	be back in camp by 10.30 p.m.
We	're	not supposed to	bring pets into the camp.
You	're		
They	're		

⟶ Grammatikanhang S. 130

Can you do it?

1 Talking about rules

Here are some of the rules at Camp Cymraig.

> 3. Don't drop litter on the camp site, please. Report any broken glass to the camp office.
> 4. Alcohol is not allowed in the camp area.
> 5. Smoking in the rooms or tents is prohibited.
> 6. You are not allowed to bring electrical equipment into the camp.
> 7. You are not allowed to play radios after 11.00 p.m.
> 8. You should park your cars, motorbikes and mopeds in the car park only.
> 9. The camp gates close at 10.30 p.m. All guests must be back in camp by this time.

Now say what the guests at Camp Cymraig | *are supposed to do.*
| *are not supposed to do.*

Then discuss which rules are sensible and which aren't. Give reasons.

2 Asking permission

Eva and Rieke would like to go and see a film which ends at 10.30 p.m., so they have to ask permission to come back later.
What can they say?

May we stay out later, please?

Could we ...?

We know we're not supposed to ..., but ...

We'd like to ...

Using the language

1 *Imagine you are at Camp Cymraig and you'd like to ask permission to do certain things that are not allowed. What can you say?*

2 *What rules have you got at your school? Work with the others in your group and discuss which ones are sensible or silly. Then write a set of sensible rules for your school.*

UNIT 4

Reading

Cool Pen Friends Cool Pen Friends

Do you want to make friends with young people from other countries? Well then, this is the place for you! Every month you'll find the addresses of other young people who are looking for pen friends. So choose a friend now and write today. He or she is waiting for your letter!!!

PEN FRIENDS   PEN FRIENDS   PEN FRIENDS

Karmele Gomez (16)

28 Fernando Calle, Barcelona 856, Spain.

Speaks Spanish and English. Keen on reading, history, music. Can't stand going to discos.

Gaston Snyder (15)

29 Rue de la Culture, St. Rhode 341, Belgium.

Speaks French, German and English. Loves music, films, photography. Also likes going to discos and parties.

Mary Boyle (16)

14 St John's Rd., Limerick, Ireland.

Speaks English and Spanish. Friendly, quiet. Good at painting, music, football. Likes dancing. Loves animals.

Fabio Severini (14)

63 Via Cantonale, 6501 Bellinzona, Switzerland.

Speaks Italian and French, and a little English. Shy. Keen on football, skiing. Doesn't like pop music.

Francoise Bertrand (15)

4, Rue d'Orleans, Bordeaux, France.

Speaks French and English. Fond of all kinds of music. Enjoys skiing. Hates discos.

Volker Richter (16)

Meggendorfer Str. 12, 8110 Murnau, W.-Germany.

Speaks German. Has been learning English for 5 years. Crazy about football, table tennis. Also loves going to discos.

Want a pen friend of your own? Send your name, age, address and other information (likes, dislikes etc.) to Cool Magazine, 14 Grosvenor Place, London WC 2 3

UNIT 4

Using the language

1 *If you wanted a pen friend, would you write to any of these six people? Say why/why not.*

I would write to ... because ...
I certainly wouldn't choose ... because ...
Well, I'm | interested in ..., too, | so I would ...
 | fond of ..., too, |
 | keen on ..., too, |
... sounds | boring, so I wouldn't ...
 | interesting, so I would ...

2 *If these six young people met, who do you think would get on with whom? Give reasons.*

Perhaps ... b ... like the same things.
Maybe ... e ... fond of ... and ...
... would probably ... c ... interested in ...
I | think ... a
 | don't think ... u ... don't like the same
 s things.
 e

3 *Now write a short description of yourself (similar to those on page 48).*

You Need a Friend

Eric Wilmslow opened his eyes and yawned. Then he got up and went to the bathroom. He washed his face and brushed his teeth. Then he opened a <u>drawer</u>, took out a pair of scissors and started cutting his toenails. He could hear them outside – they were asking questions, looking at their <u>guide</u> books and talking quietly to each other. Eric smiled to himself – they were always <u>puzzled</u> when he brushed his teeth, or cut his nails. Of course, the <u>guides</u> knew what he was doing, but the five hundred tourists out there had never seen anyone from Earth before. They didn't understand what he was doing. Then one of the <u>guides</u> started speaking over the loudspeaker. "What are you doing now, Mr Wilmslow?" he asked. So Eric explained that Earth people had to wash, and cut their nails and hair, or they would feel very uncomfortable. The <u>explanation</u> was <u>translated</u> into <u>Ballantarian</u> for the tourists who were watching Eric with great interest.

Why were the Ballantarians watching Eric "with great interest"?

UNIT 4

The Ballantarians were very happy with Eric – he was the latest attraction in their interplanetary zoo. Every day three to four thousand visitors came to see the strange creature which had only one head. The busiest time was when he went to sleep or got up. As the Ballantarians didn't ever go to bed, they found this behaviour most interesting.

The Ballantarians, in fact, found a lot of things very interesting. They had visited 384 planets and had brought back something from 180 of them. They were fascinated by Earth because they found people there who were intelligent, although not very developed. After they had studied Earth for several years, they decided to take two people back with them to start a small colony in Ballantaria. They had chosen carefully, and Eric was actually very happy in his new home, although it was more than three billion light years away from his old one.

The experiment was now at a critical stage – it was time to find Eric a friend. So the Ballantarians studied some more Earth creatures and then made their choice. Again, they were very careful. They were sure the person would be right for Eric.

When they told him about their plans, however, he was furious. "You want to find me a mate – just like an animal?" he said. "That's just not possible. I don't know the lady, and she doesn't know me. You can't arrange these things – they have to happen naturally." But the Ballantarians didn't listen. They kidnapped the young woman they had chosen for Eric and brought her to Ballantaria.

At first everything was strange to Jane, but she soon got used to her new home. And after a while she even started liking it. She wasn't as lonely as she had been in her old home, and because the Ballantarians had chosen carefully, she and Eric found that they had a lot in common. So they soon became good friends. At first she missed the sea, but the Ballantarians found a solution to this problem: they projected a film of the ocean on to a wall.

Eric was glad that Jane was with him, but he still couldn't believe that things had gone so well. He decided to talk to the Ballantarians about this. "How did you know that Jane and I would get on well with each other?" he asked. The Ballantarians smiled and answered: "There's an Earth saying, 'To know someone, is to love him'. Earth people are naturally friendly. In most cases, if they get to know one another, they'll become friends. Earth is full of people, who could have been your friends. The only reason they weren't, is that you didn't get to know them properly."

Eric thought about it, but he wasn't sure if he agreed or not.

What do you think an interplanetary zoo is? What would you expect to find in such a zoo?

Why did so many visitors come to the zoo every day?

Why did the Ballantarians find Earth so interesting?

Did they plan to take back more Earth people with them? How do you know?

Why did Eric get so angry?

How did Jane feel in her new home? Why did she feel this way?

What about you? Do you agree with the Ballantarians?

A Taste of Africa

UNIT 5

Greetings from Mbour

Peter Robinson, 16, is an English boy. He lives with his aunt and uncle in Liss in Hampshire. Peter's parents are in The Gambia, a small country in West Africa, because Mr Robinson has got a job there for two years. Last Easter Peter visited his mother and father in The Gambia. They all went to the seaside in Senegal, the neighbouring country, for a few days. They stayed in a little town called Mbour. From there, Peter wrote to his friend Alan in England.

Reading

oresque de Mbour
sque view of Mbour
sche Ansicht von Mbour

Dear Alan,
Greetings from Africa! The weather is marvellous, but I'm <u>bored stiff</u>. We are staying in a beautiful hotel by the sea. But everybody is so <u>old</u>. I'm the only young person here! I go swimming every day. I haven't been in the town much. Frankly it scares me a bit. It's all so strange.
I'll write again soon.
Peter

Mr Alan Ross,
8, Oak Tree Drive
Liss, Hants
GU 33 7 HW
England

51

UNIT 5

Listening

  Now listen to the tape.

1 Who has Peter met?
2 Where are they?
3 What do they plan to do?

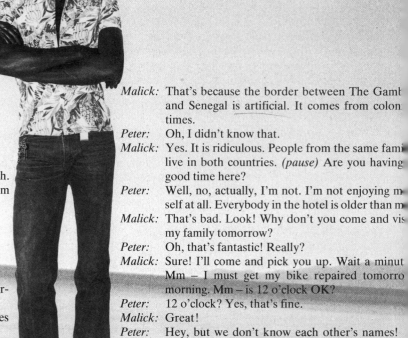

Reading

Here's the conversation that you have listened to.

Malick: Bonjour! Ça va?
Peter: Oh! Er – mm – I'm afraid I don't speak French.
Malick: Oh, that's OK. Er – I speak English. You see, I'm Gambian. Are you English?
Peter: Yes.
Malick: I say, I like your jeans.
Peter: They're GEE!
Malick: Uh, uh – Are you staying at the hotel?
Peter: Yes. And you?
Malick: I'm staying with my family. My uncle's a fisherman here.
Peter: Here in Mbour? But you're Gambian. Why does your family live here?
Malick: It's only my uncle and aunt. You see, they're Wolof. That's the name of a tribe. Some of them live in Senegal and some of them live in The Gambia.
Peter: But why is that so?
Malick: That's because the border between The Gambia and Senegal is artificial. It comes from colonial times.
Peter: Oh, I didn't know that.
Malick: Yes. It is ridiculous. People from the same family live in both countries. *(pause)* Are you having a good time here?
Peter: Well, no, actually, I'm not. I'm not enjoying myself at all. Everybody in the hotel is older than me.
Malick: That's bad. Look! Why don't you come and visit my family tomorrow?
Peter: Oh, that's fantastic! Really?
Malick: Sure! I'll come and pick you up. Wait a minute. Mm – I must get my bike repaired tomorrow morning. Mm – is 12 o'clock OK?
Peter: 12 o'clock? Yes, that's fine.
Malick: Great!
Peter: Hey, but we don't know each other's names!
Malick: Yes, you're right. I'm Malick.
Peter: Malick – And I'm Peter, or Pete.
Malick: OK, Pete, 12 o'clock, then. In front of the hotel. See you!
Peter: 'Bye, Malick!

UNIT 5

Reading

Peter wrote this postcard after he had met Malick.

Scène typique d'un marché au Sénégal
Typical market scene in Senegal
Typische Marktszene in Senegal

Dear Alan,
 Everything has changed. Yesterday I was walking along the beach when an African boy spoke to me. I told him I didn't speak French, but he said he spoke English. Then he asked me if I was staying at the hotel. I told him I wasn't enjoying myself because everyone in the hotel was older than me. He invited me to visit his family today. Wow, it's 12 o'clock, and he said he'd come at 12. I must go and meet him now. Peter

UNIT 5

Listening

 Now let's see how Peter is getting on in Africa. Listen to the three conversations and try to find out:

○ who the people are
○ where they are
○ what they are doing
○ what they are talking about

Did you get it?

With the help of the following catchwords, summarize the main points of the story.

Peter – family – stay – hotel – Senegal

he – bored – only old people

meet – Malick – Gambian – invite – meet – family

Peter – meet – family – talk – life in Africa

eat – chicken – hands

the next day – go – boat – little village

talk – dangers – tourism

last evening – disco – Peter – Aissouta – dance

A typical market scene

Fishing boats

Wolof women

Reading

Here are Peter's other postcards to Alan.

①

Dear Alan,

Malick, that's my Gambian friend, arrived late yesterday. I told him I had been waiting half an hour. He was surprised I was angry. People have more time here. He took me home and I met his uncle, aunt, his cousin Aissouta, and Lamine, a friend. His uncle asked me if I had been to Africa before. I said it was the first time. So he told me a bit about his life. He said that he's a fisherman, and it's very dangerous work – fishermen often drown.

For lunch we ate chicken with our hands! And Malick suggested we had an hour's sleep afterwards. It was all very interesting.

See you soon!
Peter

②

Dear Alan,

Yesterday we went to two little places near here – Joal and Fadiouth. We went from Joal to Fadiouth in a boat. It was fantastic! I mentioned that a lot of tourists had been waiting for boats, and asked about tourism. I thought it was good for the people here in Senegal. But no! They told me everything had been cheaper before the tourists came. People had eaten every kind of fish, too. Now the best fish goes to the hotels. It's very sad. So now I've changed my mind about tourism.

Peter

③

Dear Alan,

This will be my last card. I'm leaving here in an hour. My last evening was great! We all went to a disco together. Incredible! The noise! All the people! I was almost scared. But Malick just told me to go in. They were sad I was leaving – and I was sad, too. They gave me their address and I promised to write often. I told them I would come back again and they said they wouldn't forget me. Aissouta, that's Malick's cousin, asked me to dance with her. And that's the last thing I remember!

Peter

Did you get it?

What do the conversations and the postcards tell us about:

○ Senegal
○ The Gambia
○ Muslims
○ Tourism

Here's some help:

two countries in Africa	believe in Allah
neighbouring countries	pray five times a day
used to be colonies	give money to the poor
Wolof – a tribe in Senegal and The Gambia	don't drink alcohol
eat with their hands	everything has got expensive
sometimes can't get jobs	the best fish now goes to the hotels
live off fish	

Using the language

1 You now know a little about Senegal and The Gambia. Talk about the things that are strange or new to you.

I didn't know that ...

That's new to me, too.

That's not so strange. | We do that, too.
That happens here, too.

That isn't new to me. I knew that before.

2 You've probably been on a holiday in another country or another part of Germany. Did anything seem strange to you? Make notes first, and then tell the class about it.

Focus on grammar

Reported speech (Reporting what people said)

Look at the conversation between Malick and Peter, or listen to the tape:

Peter said: "I **don't** speak French."
Malick asked Peter: "**Are** you **staying** at the hotel?"

Look at what Peter reported in his postcard:

I told him I **didn't** speak French.
He asked me if I **was staying** at the hotel.

> When we report something that was said in the past, we change the tense of the verb.

Some more examples:

DIRECT SPEECH

The boy said: "I**'m** tired."
"I **can't** see anything."
"I **have** a toothache."

She asked me: "**Are** you keen on films?"
"**Do** you **want** a coke?"

Tim asked me: "What **are** they **doing**?"
"Why **don't** you **like** sport?"
"Where **do** you **live**?"
"How **are** you?"

REPORTED SPEECH

The boy said (that) | he **was** tired.
He told me (that) | he **couldn't** see anything.
| he **had** a toothache.

She asked me | **if** I **was** keen on films.
She wanted to know | **if** I **wanted** a coke.

He asked me | what they **were doing**.
He wanted to know | why I **didn't like** sport.
| where I **lived**.
| how I **was**.

> In reported speech, Simple Present becomes Simple Past; Present Progressive becomes Past Progressive.

⟶ Grammatikanhang S. 124

UNIT 5

Can you do it?

Here are three little scenes. Report what the people said in each scene.

1

The girl wanted to know if …

2

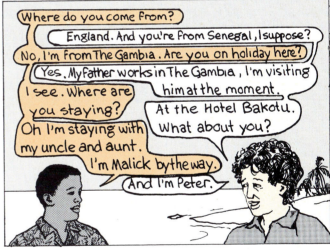

Malick asked Peter …

3

Malick asked Peter …

Focus on grammar

More about reported speech

Malick's uncle said:

"**Have** you **been** to Africa before?"
"People **ate** every kind of fish."

Peter reported what he said like this:

He asked me if I **had been** to Africa before.
He told me people **had eaten** every kind of fish.

Some more examples:

DIRECT SPEECH

Janet asked Alan:

"**Have** you **seen** Peter, Alan?"
"**Did** he **have** a good time?"

Alan said:

"I **have** just **spoken** to him on the phone."
"He **met** a very nice family in Senegal."

Some friends asked Peter about his holiday:

"What **have** you **brought** back from Gambia?"
"Who **did** you **meet**?"

REPORTED SPEECH

Janet asked Alan if he **had seen** Peter.
She wanted to know if he **had had** a good time.

Alan said (that) he **had** just **spoken** to …
Alan told her (that) Peter **had met** a nice …

They asked him what he **had brought** back.
They wanted to know whom he **had met.**

In reported speech Present Perfect and Simple Past become Past Perfect

⟶ Grammatikanhang S. 124

Can you do it?

When Peter came back from Gambia, Janet asked him about his holiday there.

Janet: Hello, Peter. When did you come back?
Peter: Hello. I've just arrived. How are you?
Janet: Fine, fine. But how are *you*? Did you have a good holiday?
Peter: Yes, it was great.
Janet: Tell me all about it. What did you do?
Peter: Now where should I start …? Well, I went swimming every day … Oh, and I met a nice family. They showed me round Senegal.
Janet: Senegal? Weren't you in Gambia?
Peter: Of course, I was. But we went to Senegal for a few days. It's not far. It was great.
Janet: Oh, you're lucky. Have you brought back any souvenirs?
Peter: Just one or two. I didn't have any time to go shopping.

Now take Janet's part and tell another friend what Peter said. Report the parts that are underlined.

Peter said his holiday had been …

Something to Think about

Here are some photos that Peter took while he was in Gambia and Senegal.

Look at these two scenes. What's African about them?

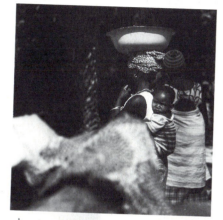

Can you see anything African or European in this photo?

How do these two young men look? What kind of clothes have they got on?

Focus on grammar

"Will" and "won't" in reported speech

Listen to the tape.

Peter said: "I'**ll** come back again."
And his friends answered: "We **won't** forget you."

Look at the postcard. Peter wrote to Alan:

I told them I **would** come back again and they said they **wouldn't** forget me.

In reported speech **"will"** in Future forms becomes **"would"**.
The negative form **"won't"** becomes **"wouldn't"**.

⟶ Grammatikanhang S. 124

UNIT 5

Can you do it?

Look at the three little scenes and report what the people in each scene said.

Alan said he hoped Peter …

Malick said …

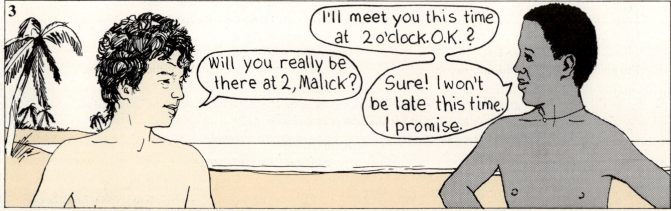

Malick said …

Focus on grammar

Reporting commands

When they went to the disco, Malick said:
"Go right in, Peter."

Peter reported what Malick said like this:
Malick told me to go in.

Other examples of commands in direct speech:

Alan said: "Write soon, Peter."
Peter said: "Don't be late again, Malick."

In reported speech they become:

Alan told Peter to write soon.
Peter asked Malick not to be late again.

> When we report commands we use "tell" + indirect object + "to" + infinitive
> "ask" "not to"

⟶ Grammatikanhang S. 124

Can you do it?

Report the following commands.

Janet said: "Tell us about your trip, Peter."
"Show me the photos you took."

Malick said: "Don't forget us, Pete."
"Come and meet my family."
"Write us when you're in England."

By the way

1 *In reported speech we often change the adverbial phrases of time or place.*

DIRECT SPEECH	REPORTED SPEECH
"I'll visit you **tomorrow**."	He said he would visit me **the next day.**
"I saw him **yesterday**."	He said he had seen him **the day before.**
"I live **here**."	He said he lived **there.**
"I haven't seen Malick **today**."	He said he hadn't seen Malick **that day.**
"I'm going to meet him **this afternoon**."	He said he was going to meet him **that afternoon.**

2 *We don't have to change the tense of the verb when we are reporting something that's still true at the time of reporting. There is an example of this in the first postcard on page 55.*

Malick's uncle said:
"I**'m** a fisherman."

Peter wrote:
He said that he**'s** a fisherman.

⟶ Grammatikanhang S. 124

Can you do it?

1 *Look at the first postcard (page 53) that Peter wrote to his friend, Alan. Now take Alan's part and tell Janet what Peter said. You can start like this:*

Janet: Heard from Peter, Alan?
Alan: Yes. As a matter of fact I got a postcard from him yesterday.
Janet: What did he say?
Alan: He said …

2 When Peter came back to England, his friends asked him a lot of questions about his holiday. Here are some of their questions and some of Peter's answers.

1 "When did you come back?"
2 "Have you brought back any souvenirs?"
3 "How are your parents?"
4 "Is it very hot in Gambia?"
5 "Did you like the food there?"
6 "Were you sorry to leave?"
7 "Do you think you'll see Malick again?"
8 "Show us the photos you took."
9 "Can you tell us about Chicken Yassa?"
10 "When are you going to visit your parents again?"

1 "One day we went out in a boat."
2 "Malick took me to a disco the night before I left."
3 "At first it was boring."
4 "Now I can eat with my hands."
5 "The people were very nice to me."
6 "I want to go back soon."
7 "I won't forget this holiday."
8 "I'll show you how to cook Chicken Yassa."

Can you report what they said?

They	asked him …	Peter	said …
	wanted to know …		told them …
	said …		
	told him …		

By the way

In the first conversation between Malick and Peter, Malick said:

"I must get my bike repaired tomorrow." *This means:* He will take his bike to someone who will repair it.

There are lots of things that we do ourselves, but there are also lots that others normally do for us.

We normally **get** our hair **cut.**
get a car **repaired**

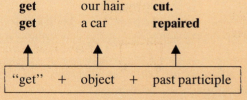

"get" + object + past participle

⟶ Grammatikanhang S. 115

Using the language

1 Talk to your partner. Ask each other what you can do yourself and what you have to get done.

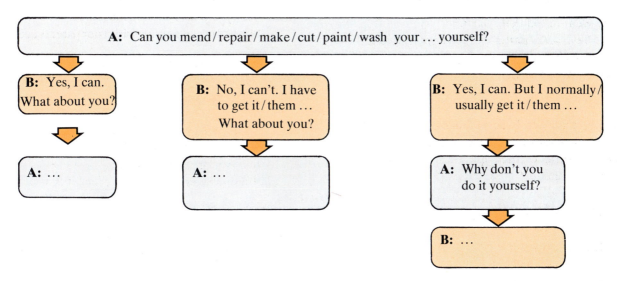

2 Now make a list of all the things | you're going to get done | tomorrow.
you're going to do | next week etc.

Starting a Conversation

You can start a conversation in many different ways. In our story Malick just went up to Peter and said "Hello" (in French "Bonjour"). Here are some other ways of starting a conversation.

You can | ask for help.
talk about the weather.
apologize.
ask someone if he/she has been here before.
comment on the behaviour of others.
introduce yourself.
ask the way.

Listening

 Listen to the extracts on the tape and say how the conversations started.

Example: In the first extract a woman introduced herself.

Now you go on. In the 2nd extract ...

Using the language

Form groups of four. Each pair in a group should use one of the following charts as a guide and make up a dialogue. First write out the dialogue, (or make notes), then act it out. While one pair is acting, the other should listen and take notes, and then report what was said. The pair that acted out the dialogue should say whether the other pair got it right or not.

(Barbara) said that the weather was …
and (Gerd) agreed. Then he asked her if …

(Barbara): Yes, that's right.
(Gerd):   No, I didn't. I asked …

1

A	comments on the weather.
B	agrees with A and asks if A is at the hotel.
A	says he/she is and asks what B has done today.
B	tells A what he/she has done.
A	finds it interesting and asks about B's plans for tomorrow.
B	tells A his/her plans.

2

A	introduces him/herself.
B	introduces him/herself and asks if A is enjoying his/her holiday.
A	says he/she's not enjoying his/her holiday.
B	asks why not.
A	gives reasons.
B	suggests doing something together.
A	accepts/agrees.
A	refuses and explains.

3

A	asks B the way to a place.
B	tells A the way.
A	asks if B is enjoying his/her holiday.
B	says he/she is, and tells A about something interesting that he/she did yesterday.
A	finds it interesting and suggests doing something together.
B	accepts/agrees.

Pidgin

You now know that in The Gambia people speak English as a second language. There are a lot of other countries in Africa where this is so.
You can see them on this map:

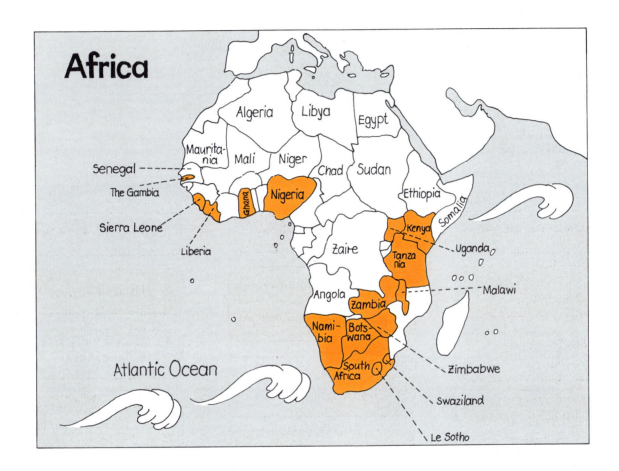

In some of these countries people speak a special kind of English, often called Pidgin. Here is a short example. Can you work out what it means? Have a try, then check your version against the Standard English version on page 68.

'Dis ole woman, sah, she be mammy for dat picken woman. Dat picken woman be wife for dat man. Dat man 'e done go for bush all day, an' when 'e done come back 'e find 'e wife never make him food. 'E belly de cry out, an' de man angry too much, so 'e like beat 'e wife. De wife 'e run, de man 'e run for beat 'e wife, an de ole woman, 'e run for beat dis man.'

picken = young, small. From Portuguese "pequeno" = small

UNIT 5

Some Facts about The Gambia

Here's some more information on The Gambia.
Perhaps it will interest you.

General information
The Gambia is a West African republic. It is one of the poorest and smallest countries in Africa. Size: about 10,500 square kilometres. Capital: Banjul.

Geography
The Gambia is a narrow strip of land on both sides of the Gambia River. It is about 300 kilometres long and 25–45 kilometres wide. It is an enclave in Senegal. The country is generally flat.

Climate
Tropical. Summer is the only season. Short and intense rainy season between June and October.

Population
About 500,000 inhabitants in 1979. 85% of the population lives in rural areas. Population in Banjul in 1977: about 51,700. About 40% of the population is Mandingo. Other important groups: the Wolof, Fulani, Dyola and Soninke. All these different groups also live in Senegal. A lot of Senegalese live and work in The Gambia. There are also a few Europeans, Syrians and Lebanese.

Religions
The majority of the population is Muslim. There are some Christians, especially in the capital.

Languages
Besides the local languages, English is spoken and is the official language. (French is the official language in Senegal.)

History
British colony from 1821. The Gambia became an independent country on 18th February, 1965.

Economy
The Gambia is dependent on peanuts (groundnuts).

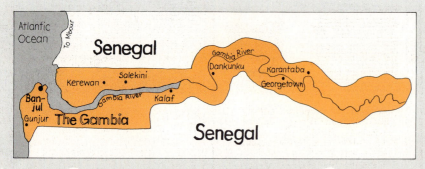

Did you understand the texts?

True or false? If it's not in the text, say so. Also correct the false statements.

1. The Gambia is the smallest and poorest country in Africa.
2. Banjul is a town in The Gambia.
3. The country is quite mountainous.
4. It's very warm throughout the year.
5. It can rain heavily between June and October.
6. In 1979 there were about half a million people in The Gambia.
7. Most Gambians live in the country.
8. The Mandingo, Wolof and Fulani live in Senegal, too.
9. A lot of foreigners live in The Gambia.
10. You can meet Christians in Banjul.
11. The people in The Gambia speak only English.
12. The Gambia used to be a British colony.
13. Peanuts grow in The Gambia.

Project Africa

Perhaps you would like to find out about one of the other countries in Africa where English is spoken.

Collect information from

○ your library
○ an encyclopaedia
○ brochures from your travel agent's

You can ask your teacher, too, if you want to know more about the country. Also try to find pictures. Then prepare a wall chart about the country you have chosen and put it up in your classroom. You can use some of the headings on page 66, but you can, of course, think of others of your own. Also find a title for your wall chart. Here's an example:

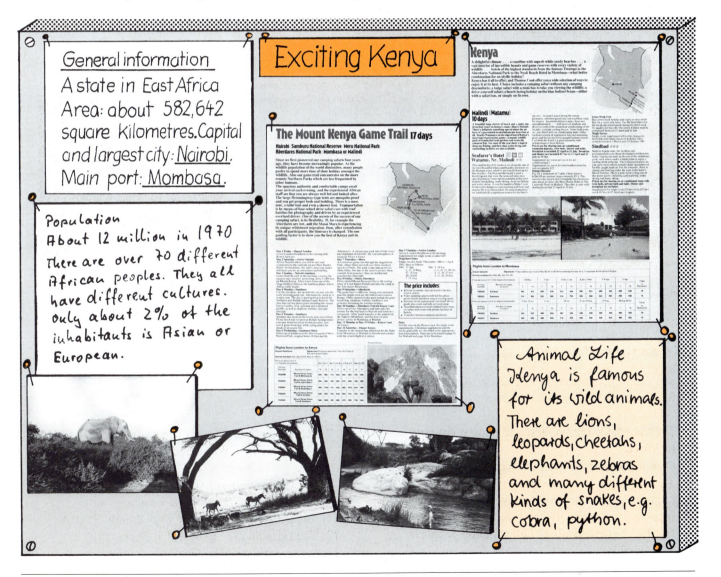

Project Germany

Perhaps you'll meet someone from abroad who'll ask you about your country. What can you say about Germany, or your area? Write notes about:

- the landscape
- the climate
- the language (dialects)
- the population
- ...

Standard English version of the Pidgin text on p. 65:

This old woman, sir, was the mother of this young woman. And this young woman was the wife of this man. The man went off into the bush all day, and when he came back, he found his wife hadn't prepared him any food. He was very hungry and very angry. So he wanted to beat his wife. The wife ran away and the man ran after her to beat her, and the old woman ran after the man to beat him.

Chicken Yassa

Perhaps some of you would like to know what Chicken Yassa is like. It's easy to cook and it tastes good, too. Here's the recipe:

Chicken Yassa
for 6–8 people

Ingredients

2 chickens (3 kilograms)
juice of 6 lemons
6 big onions (finely chopped)
1 hot pepper (finely chopped)
Salt, black or white pepper
9–10 tablespoons peanut oil

The day before …

Cut the chickens into small pieces and put them in a bowl. Make a sauce with the lemon juice, salt, pepper, the finely chopped pepper, the onions and 2 tablespoons of oil. Mix well. Pour the sauce over the chicken and mix well. Cover the bowl and leave in the refrigerator overnight.

Today …

Fry the pieces of chicken in a big frying pan until brown. Take the pieces out of the frying pan, then fry the onions in the rest of the oil. Add sauce from the day before. Add chicken and a cup of water. Cover frying pan and cook gently for $1/2$ hour. Serve with rice.

UNIT 6

Over the Sea to Skye

Reading

Travel

Jill Southwell, a 17-year-old schoolgirl from Manchester, sent us this account of a cycling holiday spent with three friends on the Isle of Skye.

Off the Beaten Track

The road followed the coast for the first three miles. It was a sunny day and we could see the grey green coast of Scotland across the water. The fresh air felt good. "This is nice after sitting in that train all the way from Manchester," said Chris. After a short while we got off our bikes and looked around. There were not many trees. The countryside was hilly, and a few sheep were grazing on the short grass. In the distance we could see the Cuillin Hills. The atmosphere was calm and peaceful – very different from the noise of Manchester. The road left the coast and turned northwest towards Broadford. It was quite steep in places, and we had to push the bikes uphill.

It was late afternoon when we reached the youth hostel in Broadford. We were tired and hungry, and we were very disappointed when they told us we had to cook for ourselves. Peter and Chris offered to ride down into the village to buy some food. They came back with some bread and a huge haggis. "What on earth do you do with that?" asked Sally. Neither she nor I had seen a haggis before. Chris explained it to us. "It's easy – you just boil it. It's a Scottish speciality."

The next day was sunny but windy. We set off again early in the morning. The road leading to Portree ran along the coast again. It was flat here, so cycling was easier. Suddenly, as we came round the corner, we saw that the road was blocked by a large number of sheep. We were fascinated by the sheep dog. He kept the sheep together and guided them into a neighbouring field. Five

Portree

hours later we reached Portree, the biggest town on the island. There was no youth hostel in Portree, so we found a bed and breakfast place. It was a bit expensive, so Chris sent a telegram to his parents, asking them to send more money. Then we went to the Tourist Information Centre and collected some brochures about the island and its history. While we were sitting on a wall by the harbour, we read our brochures and talked about where to go.

"Hey, listen to this!" That was Chris. He had found something about Bonnie Prince Charlie, and he read it aloud. We heard about the many battles that the prince and his men had fought – and about Flora Macdonald and how she had helped Bonnie Prince Charlie to escape. It was all very interesting. That night in the bed and breakfast place we discussed where to go the next day. The choice was between Kilmuir where you can visit Flora Macdonald's grave, and Glen Brittle. In the end we decided to go to Kilmuir.

It was raining the next day, so we took the bus for a change. Some of the people in the bus were talking a different language. "Excuse me, is that Gaelic?" Sally was interested. "That's right," said the woman. "Most of us speak Gaelic here, but we all speak English, too." In Kilmuir we visited Flora Macdonald's grave and then looked round the Skye Museum. On our way back to Portree, Peter noticed a sign saying "Kingsburgh". "This is where Bonnie Prince Charlie landed," he said. "Shall we get out and have a look? We can take the next bus to Portree."

Kingsburgh was very romantic. Just a small bay, but a man who thought he should be king had landed there more than two hundred years before. The rain had stopped, and we sat for a while watching the water, then went back to the bus stop. There was no timetable, so we went up to an old man who was leaning on his garden gate and asked him when the next bus went. "There are no more buses today," was the answer. We looked at each other. It was too far to walk. The old man seemed to understand and after a moment's pause he told us not to worry. "The baker will soon pass by," he said. "Maybe he'll take you back to Portree." He did, and we really enjoyed the ride, sitting among the cakes and bread in the back of the van. That night we were really exhausted, so we went to bed quite early because we wanted to see some more places the next day. It was going to be our last day on Skye.

"I'm glad we've taken the bikes today," said Sally. "It's easier."

We were in Trumpan, looking at the ruins of an old church. Here a terrible thing happened many years ago. The people from the village were in the church, when suddenly the church was surrounded by enemies from another island. They locked the door and then set fire to the building with all the people inside. Then they attacked the village, but the villagers there were saved by other members of their clan who came to their rescue. It was an awful story, and hard to imagine in that peaceful valley. But then ... that is what makes Skye such a fascinating place.

Next week: Jim Barnes writes about sailing in Denmark.

Did you get it?

1 *With the help of the following catchwords, say where the young people went on their holiday.*

go – bike tour – Isle of Skye
first day – ride – Broadford – stay – youth hostel
second day – ride – Portree – no youth hostel – stay – bed and breakfast place
next day – rain – bus – Kilmuir
visit – Flora Macdonald's grave – Skye Museum
afterwards – Kingsburgh – then – back to Portree
last day – go – Trumpan – look at – ruins – church

2 *Did you get the details?*
Here are some of the letters which the young people wrote while they were on holiday. Can you complete them? (Use a separate sheet of paper.)

1 Dear Mum and Dad,

Here we are on…. It was lovely to start our bike … after that long train … from…. We rode along the … at first. Then we went through some … countryside. Sometimes the road was so … that we had to … our bikes uphill. We were really … and … when we reached the … here in …, so you can imagine how … we were when we heard we had to … for ourselves. The boys … a haggis. Pat and I had never seen one before but it tasted quite nice. Tomorrow we are going to …. The weather was … today. Hope it will stay that way.

        Love,
        Sally

2 Dear Mum,

Today we … very early and set off for Portree. Luckily the weather was…. When we got to Portree, they told us that there was no…. So we had to … some extra money for a … and … place. Later we went to the … and got some … about the island. We read about a Scottish … called…. It was all very…. We're going to … tomorrow.

        Love,
        Pat

3 Dear Michael,

For the first time we've had bad weather, so we took the bus and went to Kilmuir. Did you know that a lot of people here still … Gaelic? In Kilmuir we … the Skye Museum and Flora Macdonald's grave. From there we went to Kingsburgh to see where Bonnie Prince Charlie … two hundred years ago. But then – guess what – we found out that there were no more … back to Portree. Luckily the baker … and took us back to Portree. We really enjoyed … among the … and … in the back of the …, but I think we should take the bikes again tomorrow – it's easier!

        Chris

4 Dear Mum and Dad,

Our last day on Skye. Today we rode to…. It's a lovely village – so…! It's difficult to imagine what happened here in the past. Some people from another … attacked the … when it was full of people from Trumpan. Then they … to the church. Afterwards they … the village, too. I think we read about it in our history lessons, but it didn't seem so exciting.

        See you soon.
        Love,
        Peter

Some Background Information

Isle of Skye

The largest island of the Inner Hebrides, off the west coast of Scotland. Population: about 7,500. People live mainly from fishing, sheep farming, some agriculture and tourism. Main town: Portree. Beautiful countryside, good roads. Quiet sandy bays in the south; rough hilly countryside in the north. Highest mountains: the Cuillin Hills (over 1,000 metres). Home of the Macdonald and Macleod clans for centuries. Of historical interest: Kilmuir – grave of Flora Macdonald (1721–90), who helped Bonnie Prince Charlie to escape after the Battle of Culloden.

Bonnie Prince Charlie (1720–88)

Prince Charles Edward Stuart, a national hero of Scotland. He was the grandson of James II who was the last catholic king of England. He was born in Rome. He returned to England in 1745 to claim the throne, but was defeated in 1746. He spent months hiding in the islands west of Scotland before he escaped to France. He went to Italy in 1766 and later died in Rome.

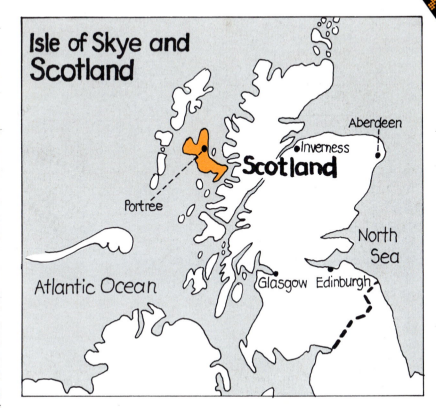

Did you understand the texts?
Try to answer the following questions.

Isle of Skye

1. What group of islands does Skye belong to?
2. How many people live on the island?
3. What kind of work do they do?
4. What's the landscape like on Skye?
5. Why is Skye of historical interest?

Bonnie Prince Charlie

1. Where and when was Bonnie Prince Charlie born?
2. What was his real name?
3. Who was his grandfather?
4. What did Bonnie Prince Charlie want to become? Did he succeed?
5. Where and when did he die?

UNIT 6

The Skye Boat Song

1 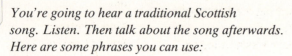 You're going to hear a traditional Scottish song. Listen. Then talk about the song afterwards. Here are some phrases you can use:

I didn't understand some of the words.
I didn't get it. What was it about?
The English sounded | a bit strange.
                    | old-fashioned.
                    | ...

2 Here's part of the song you've listened to. The glossary below will help you to understand the text.

Speed bonnie boat like a bird on the wing,
'Onward' the sailors cry,
Carry the lad that's born to be king,
Over the sea to Skye.

Loud the winds howl, loud the waves roar,
Thunderclaps fill the air.
Baffled, our foes stand by the shore,
Follow they will not dare.

Glossary

speed	= go fast
bonnie	= beautiful, nice
onward	= go on, go forward
lad	= boy, young man
thunderclaps	= noise of thunder
baffled	= confused and angry
foes	= enemies

A Good Holiday?

Using the language

1 *Tell the class what you think of the young people's holiday. Give a reason.*

| I | think it was
thought it was | rather
quite
very

too | interesting
dull
boring
nice
tiring

awful
terrible
great
fantastic | because
as | … enough money.
nothing really happened.
the weather was …
there was nothing to …
… |

2 *If you don't like this kind of holiday, say what you would rather do.*

| I would rather
I would prefer to | go …
travel …
… |

I don't think …
I didn't think …

Looking at the language

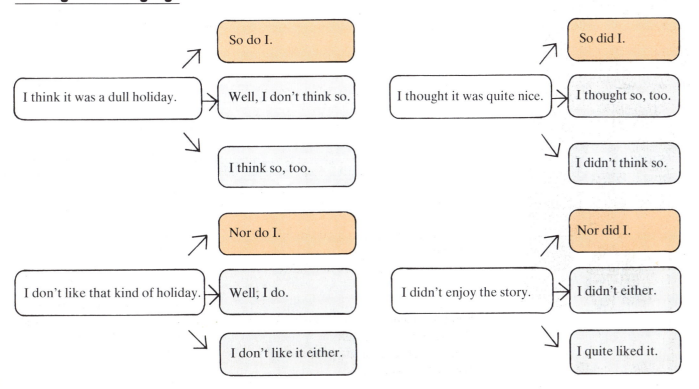

By the way

If someone makes a statement and you want to say that you think the same way, or that it applies to you, too, you can use expressions like these:

So do I. *(for positive statements)* **Nor do I.** *or* **I don't either.** *(for negative statements)*

Positive statements

I **like** travelling.	– **So do** I.
We **went** abroad last year.	– **So did** I.
I **can** speak English.	– **So can** I.
I **would** like to go to Skye.	– **So would** I.
They**'re** hungry.	– **So am** I.
He **has** a lot of photos of the island.	– **So have** I.

Negative statements

I **don't** like travelling.	– **Nor do** I.	*(or* I don't either.*)*
I **didn't** know that.	– **Nor did** I.	*(or* I didn't either.*)*
I **can't** speak Gaelic.	– **Nor can** I.	*(or* I can't either.*)*
I **wouldn't** live there.	– **Nor would** I.	*(or* I wouldn't either.*)*
I**'m** not keen on sport.	– **Nor am** I.	*(or* I'm not either.*)*
We **haven't** any money.	– **Nor have** I.	*(or* I haven't any either.*)*

⟶ Grammatikanhang S. 119

Using the language

The young people in the story spent their holiday together because they probably like doing things in a group.
What about you? Work with a partner and tell each other what you like / don't like doing. You should agree or disagree with your partner.

like	go to concerts	alone
enjoy	go into town	on my own
prefer	go out	with my friends
fond of	do things	in a group
don't like		

Reading

Useful Tips and Advice for Visitors

You needn't have a lot of money to enjoy a holiday on the Isle of Skye!

Where to stay

There are <u>reasonable</u> hotels, guest houses and holiday flats. We <u>recommend</u> youth hostels or bed and breakfast in private houses.

What to wear

The weather is not <u>reliable</u>! So you need <u>waterproof</u> clothes. Take jeans, strong <u>waterproof shoes</u> and either an anorak or a raincoat. You needn't take a warm <u>coat</u> between June and August.

Where to eat

There are plenty of <u>cheap</u> restaurants and snack bars, so you needn't spend a lot of money on food.

How to get around Skye

It's easy to travel around Skye. There are <u>coach</u> tours round the island and good <u>local</u> bus services. So you needn't spend a lot of money on transport.

Look at the tips again. What's necessary for a holiday on Skye? What's not necessary? Say why.

You need ... because ...
You don't need ... because ...
You needn't | have ... | because ...
             | take ... |
             | ... |

Focus on grammar — Talking about what's necessary / not necessary

They		need	waterproof clothes.
She	doesn't	need	an anorak.
He	needn't	take	a warm coat.
They	needn't	take	a lot of money.

auxiliary + verb + object

→ Grammatikanhang S. 129

Can you do it?

What's not necessary?
Use "**needn't**" + suitable phrases.

1 It has stopped raining, so you needn't ... (take)
2 It's very warm today, so the girl ... (put on)
3 Everything's cheap in this country, so we ... (spend)
4 His cold has got better, so he ... (go)
5 Your teeth are all fine, so you ... (go)

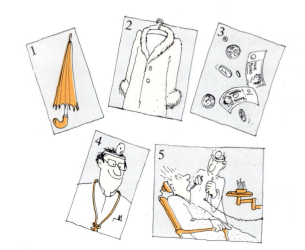

Using the language

What tips would you give a foreigner who wants to visit Germany in spring / summer / autumn / winter? Give reasons.

You need	a ...	in	spring	because ...
You don't need	a lot of ...		summer	
			autumn	
			winter	

You	should	take	a lot of money with you	because	everything's expensive here.
You	shouldn't	bring	...	as	...
	ought to	...			
	needn't				

UNIT 6

By the way

Do you like **those jeans**? – Yes, **they're** quite nice.

Some other examples:

My **trousers**   **are** dirty.
These **shorts**   **are** lovely.
The **scissors**   **are** on the table.

> These nouns are always plural in English.
> What are they in German?

Be careful: When you are counting these things, you have to say:

a (or one)	**pair of** jeans
two	**pairs of** scissors
three	**pairs of** …

Example:
A: I've only got one pair of shorts. How many have you got?
B: I've got three pairs.

⟶ Grammatikanhang S. 132

Using the language

Imagine you were going …

skiing in the Alps

on a bike tour through Germany with friends

to Camp Cymraig in Wales

on holiday in The Gambia

What would you take with you? The following illustration will help you.   I would take three pullovers and a pair of … / … pairs of …

toothbrush, bra, pants, briefs, boots, anorak, vest, cap, gloves, scissors, toothpaste, comb, scarf, soap

78

North, East, South, West

Do you know how to express direction?

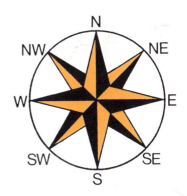

N = north
E = east
S = south
W = west
NE = northeast

What do SE, SW and NW stand for?

1 Look at the map of Great Britain on the right.

Can you say where | Wales | is?
 | Scotland | lies?
 | the Isle of Skye |
 | London |
 | Edinburgh |
 | Liverpool |
 | Cardiff |
 | Birmingham |

Wales is in the west of Britain.
Wales is ☐ west of England.

2 Now look at a map of your country. Find the main towns and say where they are. Also find your town / village and say where it is.

Hamburg is in the north of Germany.
Bonn is …

My town is | in the … of Germany.
 | northeast of | Stuttgart.
 | east of | …
 | … |

UNIT 6

Looking at the language   "Can You Tell Us the Way?"

Youth hostels are not always easy to find. When these two people were touring Scotland last summer, they often had to ask the way.

Look at what they said and the answers they got.

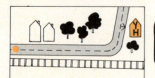

Excuse me. Can you tell us the way to the youth hostel, please?

Yes, of course. Go down here. The road follows the railway track, then it turns left. The youth hostel is the big white building on the right.

Excuse me. We can't find the way to the youth hostel. Could you show it to us on the map, please?

Yes, look. Here we are. Walk along this road until you come to the square. Walk right across the square. Then take the first street on your left. The youth hostel is at the end of that street.

Excuse me. We're looking for the youth hostel. Could you explain to us how to get there?

Er – let me see. Yes. Now, go back down this road until you come to the bridge. Walk across it, then turn right. Walk along that street until you come to the post office. The youth hostel is opposite the post office.

Excuse me, please. We're looking for the youth hostel. Can you describe the way to us, please?

Certainly. Go straight down this road. Then turn left at the next traffic lights. The youth hostel is the third building on the right.

UNIT 6

Focus on grammar — Verbs with 2 Objects

1 Could you show it to us?

I showed **John** the photos.   I showed the photos **to John.**

indirect object + direct object   direct object + indirect object

If we want to emphasize the indirect object (= the person), we put it after the direct object, together with **"to"**.

Other examples:

He	gave	**me**	that book.	He	gave	that book	**to me.**
Did he	write	**you**	a letter?	Did he	write	a letter	**to you?**
	Bring	**me**	that chair, please.		Bring	that chair	**to me,** please.

If the direct object is **"it"** or **"them"**, we must use **"to"** + indirect object.

| He | gave | **it** | to | her. |
| We | showed | **them** | to | the boy. |

2 describe, explain, say

The man	**described**	the way	**to** the group.
She	**explained**	the meaning of the word	**to** the class.
What did he	**say**		**to** you?

When we mention the indirect object with **"describe"**, **"explain"**, **"say"**, we must always use **"to"**.

Note: Sometimes we do not mention the indirect object with these three verbs.
○ The man described the way. ○ She explained the meaning of the word. ○ What did he say?

3 say and tell

The boy said: "I don't know the way."

What did he **say** ☐ ?   – He **said** ☐ he didn't know the way.
What did he **tell** ☐you☐ ?   – He **told** ☐me☐ he didn't know the way.

"Tell" always takes an indirect object. We don't normally use an indirect object with **"say"**.

⟶ Grammatikanhang S. 113, 114

UNIT 6

Can you do it?

1 *You need help in the following situations. What do you say? Use the expressions below to ask for help.*

1 You're in a strange town. You don't know the way to the station.
2 You don't know the meaning of a word.
3 You can't find a town on the map.
4 You're at the airport in London. You want to go to Oxford Street.
5 You want to use the phone, but you don't understand the instructions in the phone box.

Could you Can you	tell me	how to …? which … train to …?
	explain … to me, please? describe … to me, please? show it to me, please?	

2 **A very helpful person**
What did he do? Complete the text. Use the correct forms of:
"tell", "show", "explain", "describe"
and suitable phrases.

Bruce met a lot of tourists last week, and they all needed help. Two girls from Germany didn't know the way to the Skye Museum, so he …. A group from France wanted to find the youth hostel, so Bruce …. One of them didn't know how to use the phone box, so Bruce …. Later he met a boy who was looking for Flora Macdonald's grave. Bruce ….

Using the language

Could you give directions to some English-speaking visitors to your town/village? Work in groups and act out the situation. The visitors ask the way to the **church/police station/ museum/etc.** *(Before you begin, decide where the people should be.)*

Here are some phrases you can choose from:

Asking the way

Excuse me. I'm looking for …
Could you	show it to me, please?
Can you	tell me	how to …? the quickest way to …?
	describe the way to me, please? explain to me how to get to the …?

Giving directions

Walk right across the …
Turn left/right (at the …)
When you come to the …, …
Walk past the …
Go straight down this street, then turn …
| The … is | next to the …
opposite the …
the 2nd / 3rd building on the … |

Rain, Rain …

 Listen to the weather forecast on the tape.

Will there be rain?
Will it be sunny/warm?
Will it be windy?
What would you do in this kind of weather?
Would you go to the Isle of Skye?
Would you go on a picnic?

cloudy
rain
sunny
wind/storm
temperature

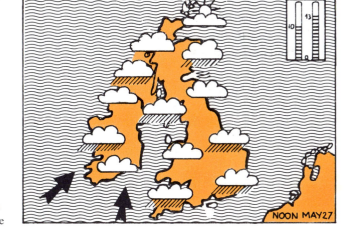

 What goes up when the rain comes down?

An umbrella.

 What did the ground say when it began to rain?

If this goes on, my name will be mud.

 What is the difference between a big black cloud and a lion with a toothache?

One pours with rain, and the other roars with pain.

UNIT 6

UNIT 7 Lost in the Caves

Dos and Don'ts

Use your head.
Take a watch.
Tell someone where you're going.
Take warm clothes.
Take enough food.
Take spare batteries for torches.
Don't take risks.
Turn back if you run into difficulties.
Study the map before you set out.
Keep together – never go alone.
If you run into trouble, don't panic.
Don't take your helmet off at any time.

Next Expedition to Green Grotto Cave
Date: Sept. 8

Rucksack
in very good condition
Price: £10.—

Price per photo 50p

A Radio Play

In this unit you're going to hear a radio play "Lost in the Caves". This is the beginning of the script:

```
Title:         Lost in the Caves
Written by:    Angus Miller
Recording:     4th October, 1 p.m. - 6 p.m.
Broadcast:     12th December, 8 p.m.
Directed by:   Elizabeth Cook

Cast:          Nick (Leader), 19    Sam Jones
               David, 14            Peter Franklin
               Ian, 16              Simon Fletcher
               Melanie, 16          Jennifer Johnson


Scene 1

(At the entrance of the cave - sound of rain, boots on stones)

Nick:   Well, this is it. It's going to be a long day. Let's check
        the equipment before we go in. Have you all got extra clothes
```

Listening

 Now listen to the play, and find out what it's all about.

UNIT 7

Did you get it?

Listen to each scene, and then answer the questions.

Scene 1

1 The young people talked about the equipment they had to take.
  Who had what?

The leader	rucksack
David	helmet
Ian	food
Melanie	map
All of them	torch
	spare batteries
	first aid equipment
	extra clothes

2 Now say what last warnings the leader gave.

They	must	keep …
	mustn't	walk …
		check …
		put on (wear) …
		leave …
		take off …

Why did he give the warnings?

Scene 2

True or false?

1 Nick said that stalagmites grow slowly.
2 David was more interested in food than in the caves.
3 David and Melanie didn't get on well together.
4 They were going to have lunch.
5 There were no animals in the cave.
6 They had never used a rope-ladder before.
7 Nick went first.
8 Ian didn't dare to go down the rope-ladder.

UNIT 7

Scene 3

1 *Can you remember who said what?*

1 "Are we really supposed to wear the helmets all the time?"   M
2 "Perhaps we ought to change our plans and go to a different part of the caves."
3 "You said we're not supposed to take risks."
4 "I don't really dare to try the other way. I don't know it very well."
5 "Oh, come on, Nick. The roof won't fall."
6 "Please, Nick. Let's go on."
7 "Let's just go and look at the stalagtites and come straight back."

2 The young people couldn't agree on what to do next.
Say what their opinions were.

Nick	thought they should …
David	said …
Melanie	wanted to …
Ian	

3 *What do you think they should do?*

They	ought to …	because …	might …
Nick	ought not to …		could …
…	should …		
	shouldn't …		

Scene 4

Here is a map of the cave. Look at it while you listen to the 4th scene.

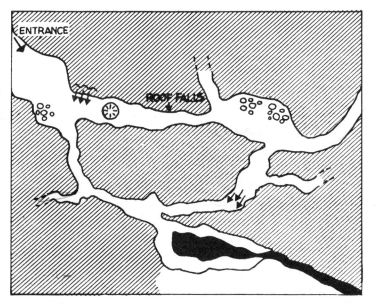

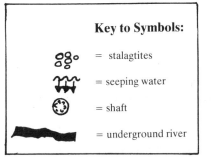

Key to Symbols:

- ⊙⊙⊙ = stalagtites
- 〰〰 = seeping water
- ⊕ = shaft
- ▬ = underground river

UNIT 7

Now here are two short summaries of the fourth scene. Which fits the scene better? Give reasons.

1

When the roof fell in, the young people were very worried. They were glad that they had food, light and warm clothes, but they didn't know how to get out of the cave. Nick, the leader, said they shouldn't worry. He was confident because he knew that a search party would look for them. Then they studied the map and found a different route. This led them back to the entrance. They arrived just as a search party was coming.

2

When the young people were trapped, they were very frightened, and Melanie asked what they should do. Nick said they shouldn't worry, they would soon think of something. They were glad that they had extra pullovers because it was very cold. They were also glad that they had food with them, and torches so that they could see. They tried to find a way out because they didn't want to stay in the cave. Then Nick remembered another route. There were arrows on the map and that meant it was quite steep. But Nick thought they could make it. The route went near a place called the Black Pool. Then the tunnel branched. The group went to the right and the Black Pool was to the left. Soon they found the way out, so they were safe again.

Scene 5

True or false?
Correct the false statements.

1 The leader said they had not reached the steep part yet.
2 Ian said he was very tired.
3 Melanie thought she could hear the sound of water.
4 Melanie said the way out was to the left.
5 David said he could hear voices.
6 David hoped the search party would have some warm clothes for them.

Using the language

1 Talking about the play

Did you enjoy the play?

Yes, I did. It was …
Yes. It was …

No, I didn't. It was …
No. I thought it was …

It was all right.
It wasn't bad.

2 Talking about the characters

What did you think of the young people in the play?

Nick	seemed	quite	sensible.
Melanie	sounded	a bit	childish.
Ian	was	rather	silly.
David		very	confident.
			…

I rather liked (Nick) because …
I didn't like …

Talking It Over

Reading

The following two conversations were part of the radio play "Lost in the Caves".

1

Father: I can imagine how frightened you all were when you saw the roof fall in.
Nick: We didn't actually see it happen. We only heard the crash.
Father: Didn't you notice anything unusual before it happened?
Nick: Well, the roof was a bit lower than I remembered.
Father: Why didn't you turn back, then? You were supposed to turn back in case of difficulties.
Nick: Well, I don't know the other way very well, and Melanie wanted to see the stalagmites.
Father: You mean if Melanie hadn't wanted to see them, you wouldn't have gone on?
Nick: It wasn't Melanie's fault. It was David who insisted on going on.
Father: You shouldn't have listened to him. I'm sure the warden warned you not to take risks.
Nick: I'm sorry. If I had been firmer with the others, it wouldn't have happened.
Father: Well, never mind. You're all safe. That's the main thing.

2

Ian: I'm sorry, Nick. If I had supported you, it wouldn't have happened.
Nick: Don't worry. It wasn't your fault. I was responsible. If I had been more sensible, we would have gone straight back to the entrance.
Ian: It wasn't really your fault, Nick. David insisted on going on.
Nick: If I hadn't listened to him ...
Ian: ... and Melanie – she wanted to see the stalagmites.
Nick: That was no reason to take such a risk. If I hadn't agreed to go on, we wouldn't have been trapped.
Ian: Don't blame yourself, Nick. We should have listened to you. It wasn't your fault at all.
Nick: Thanks, Ian. Oh, well. It turned out all right in the end.

Using the language

Whose fault was it? What do you think?

It was	Nick's ...	fault.
It wasn't	anybody's Nick's ...	

| They Nick ... | should have shouldn't have | turned back immediately. been firmer with the others. listened to ... gone on. ... |

UNIT 7

Focus on grammar

What would have happened if ...?

| If | I | **had** | **been** | firmer with the others, | it | | **wouldn't have** | **happened.** |
| If | she | **hadn't** | **wanted** | to see the stalagmites, | they | | **would have** | **turned** back. |

| if-clause: | Past Perfect |

| main clause: | would have + Past Participle |
| | wouldn't have |

You can use this structure:

○ **if you want to reproach someone for something he did or didn't do**
   If you had listened to me, this wouldn't have happened.

○ **if you want to blame yourself for something you did or didn't do**
   If I had been more careful, this wouldn't have happened.

Note: You can also start with the main clause:
This wouldn't have happened if they had turned back immediately.

→ Grammatikanhang S. 122

Can you do it?

1 The four young people are talking about their adventure in the caves.
What are they saying?

If they had stayed at home, they wouldn't have got into trouble.

1 If we ... (turn back) immediately, we wouldn't have been trapped.

2 If I had not wanted to see the stalagmites, it ... (not happen).

3 We ... (not be trapped) if we ... (listen) to you, Nick.

4 If we ... (be) more sensible, we ... (not get) into trouble.

5 If I ... (not insist) on going on, ...

6 We (not run) into difficulties, if ...

2 Now look at these pictures. Can you say what **would (not) have happened if...?**

come – earlier
catch – train

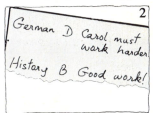

work – harder
do – better in German

be – more careful
burn – finger

drive – more carefully

run – ...

...

Using the language

1 Now think of some things that happened in the past which you now regret.
What can you say? Use the structure:

> If ... had (not) ..., ... would (not) have ...
> ... would (not) have ... if ... had (not) ...

Here are some things that probably happened, but you can, of course, think of others yourselves.

1 You didn't work very hard – you did badly in the test.
2 You rode your bike too fast and hurt a little child.
3 You left your anorak/raincoat at home. It rained, you got wet and caught a cold.
4 You watched TV until 11.30. You couldn't wake up next morning – you were late for school.
5 You ate too much ice cream – you had stomach-ache afterwards.
6 You weren't very careful – you broke your friend's record or you lost his/her pen, dictionary etc.

2 Work with a partner and act out one of the following situations.

1 A rode his/her bike too fast and had an accident. The bike was broken. A is now talking to his/her mother or father (B).
2 A played badly in a ... match. The team lost the game. A is now talking to B, one of the girls/boys in the team.

Here are some more phrases you can use:

| I | should have ... |
| You | shouldn't have ... |

I'm so sorry. It won't happen again.
I'll be more ... next time.
I'll try harder next time.

UNIT 7

By the way

When they were in the cave,

Melanie **remembered** another route.   You **remember something**.

Nick **reminded** the others of the rules.   You **remind another person of something**.

"Remember" or "remind"?

Complete the following.

1 Please … him to mend his rucksack.
2 Can you … what happened in the play?
3 … me to get a new torch, please.
4 He … the others in the group of the rules.
5 Did you … to bring spare batteries?
6 The leader … them to keep their helmets on.
7 You should always … to take warm clothes.
8 Thanks for …ing me to take the map.

Don't Take Risks!

Looking at the language

Before the group set out, they had a talk with the warden.

Later, Nick reminded the others of the instructions.

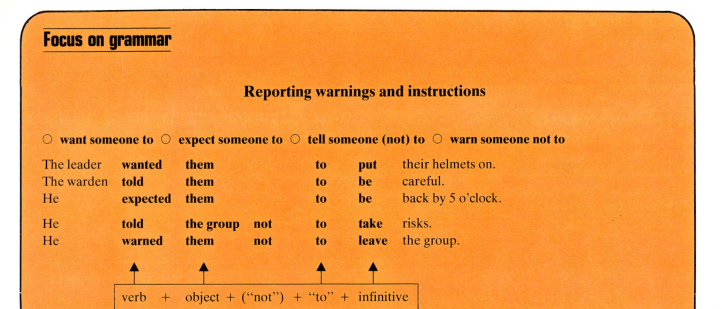

Can you do it?

The warden gave the young people a lot of instructions.
What do you think he said to them? Look at the dos and don'ts at the beginning of the unit, but you can, of course, think of other things yourselves.

| He | wanted / told | them to | keep together. … |

| He expected them to | come … … |

| He | told / warned | them not to | take their helmets off. … |

UNIT 7

Using the language

Have you ever been on an outing or a trip with a group of other young people? What instructions did your mother (father, teacher) give you?

My	mother	wanted me to …
	father	told me to …
	parents	expected me to …
Our teacher		told us not to …
		warned us not to …

Wir erwarten Dich um 6 Uhr zurück.

Ruf sofort zu Hause an.

Geh nicht so spät ins Bett.

Using the language

Some dos and don'ts of mountaineering

- Never go alone.
- Find out the weather forecast before you go.
- Tell someone where you're going.
- Wear suitable shoes.
- Wear suitable clothes.
- Don't push stones down the mountain.
- Never leave the marked track.
- Turn back if you run into difficulties.

 Work with a partner and make up a dialogue for the following situation. Write out the dialogue first, or make notes, then act out the situation.

 Two young people went mountaineering and ran into difficulties because one of them (or both of them) ignored some of the dos and don'ts. They now talk about whose fault it was.

The following language chart and the expressions and structures below will help you.

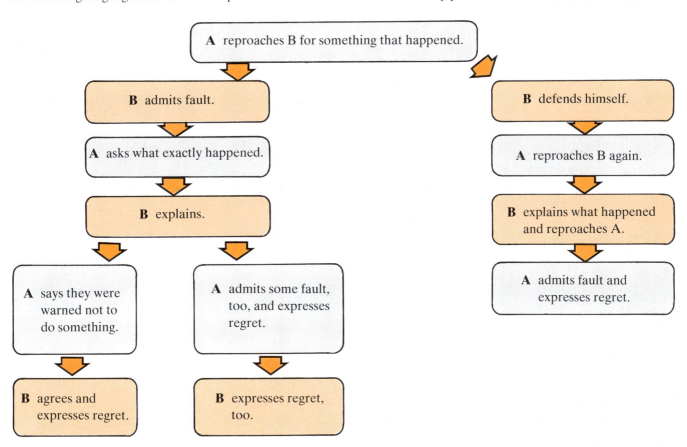

Reproaching or blaming someone

Why did you …?
Why didn't you …?
You | should have …
    | shouldn't have …
You | were supposed to …
    | were not supposed to …
I told you to …
I told you not to …
I warned you not to …
If you had …, this wouldn't have …
If you hadn't done that, we …

Defending yourself / Denying fault

Don't blame me. It's not my fault.
You should have …
It's *your* fault really.

Admitting fault / Expressing regret

You're right. If I | had …
                   | hadn't …
Yes, it's my fault. I | should have …
                      | shouldn't have …

95

UNIT 8 Nelson and "Victory"

If you go on a sightseeing tour of London, you'll be shown a number of famous buildings, monuments and squares of historic interest. Here's one of the squares you'll definitely be taken to:

Nelson's column at Trafalgar Square

Scene at Trafalgar Square

Do you know anything about Nelson?

Why is he famous?
Why was a monument put up in his honour?
Why was the square given the name "Trafalgar Square"?
If you don't know the answers, read the following texts and find out.

Reading

A British National Hero

Nelson, Lord
Horatio Nelson, British national hero, the most successful and popular British admiral in the wars against France under Napoleon. His two most important victories were the Battle of the Nile (1798) and the Battle of Trafalgar (1805). In the Battle of the Nile, he destroyed the French fleet, and in the Battle of Trafalgar, both the French and the Spanish fleets. The victory at Trafalgar saved England from Napoleonic invasion.
Nelson was born in Burnham Thorpe, England, on 29th September 1758. He married Frances Nisbet in 1787. After the Battle of the Nile he fell in love with Emma Hamilton. He shocked English society when he brought her to live in the same house as his wife. He and Emma Hamilton had a daughter, Horatia.
Nelson was killed by a French bullet on board his ship the "Victory" during the famous Battle of Trafalgar. He was buried at St Paul's Cathedral in 1806. In 1842 a monument with Nelson's statue was put up in Trafalgar Square.

Trafalgar Square

The most famous of all squares in London. Here stands the statue of Nelson, the hero of the Battle of Trafalgar (1805).
In 1832 the square was named after the great victory of Trafalgar, and in 1842 Nelson's column was put up. Many meetings are held in this square every year. It is also a favourite resting place for tired tourists.

"Victory"

Lord Nelson's flagship in the famous Battle of Trafalgar (1805). The ship is preserved today at Portsmouth, England. In this battle, the "Victory's" flags gave the famous signal: "England expects that every man will do his duty." Nelson died on board the "Victory" during the battle, after he had been hit by a French bullet.

Did you get it?

Lord Nelson

True or false?

1 Nelson was well liked by a lot of people.
2 He only won two very important battles.
3 The French were beaten by the British in the Battle of the Nile and the Battle of Trafalgar.
4 Napoleon invaded England.
5 Emma Hamilton was Nelson's wife.
6 They had one child.
7 Nelson was shot by the French during the battle.
8 He died in 1806.

Trafalgar Square

Can you remember?

1 It is the ... square in London.
2 It was named after the ...
3 Here you can see the ... of Nelson.
4 A lot of meetings ... there every year.
5 ... often go there to rest.

"Victory"

Can you remember?

1 This was Nelson's ...
2 Today the "Victory" can be seen at ...
3 Lord Nelson died ... the "Victory".
4 The famous signal: "England expects that every man will do his duty" was given by the "Victory's" ...

The Battle of Trafalgar

Reading

Here's the beginning of the script of a radio programme you're going to hear on the tape. Read this extract first.

> Announcer: In this programme we are bringing you scenes from one of the most important battles in the last century - the Battle of Trafalgar. It was important because, after this battle, the British were masters of the sea for more than a century.
>
> In 1805 France was at war with Britain. Napoleon Bonaparte, Emperor of France, had plans to invade England. The French fleet under Villeneuve was lying in the port of Cadiz. The British fleet waited and watched outside Cadiz to make sure that the French could not get out. On board the "Victory", Nelson was discussing his battle plan with Captain Keats.
>
> Nelson: What we shall have to do

Listening

Now listen to the tape. You'll learn more about Nelson and the famous Battle of Trafalgar. While you listen, try to find out:

○ who is talking;
○ where and when the conversation takes place;
○ what they're talking about.

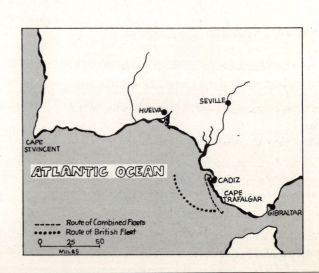

Did you get it?

Put the following sentences in a logical order, so that you get a summary of what you have heard and read about the Battle of Trafalgar.

a) Although he was in great pain, he was carried to the doctor's cabin.
b) The British ships were ordered to attack as soon as they saw the French fleet.
c) It was fought because Napoleon had planned to invade England.
d) Just before the battle started, Nelson gave his famous signal: "England expects that every man will do his duty."
e) Before Nelson died, he was happy to hear of his great victory although he destroyed fewer ships than he had expected.
f) Then the battle started, and after hours of fighting Nelson was hit by a French bullet.
g) Nelson's plan was to show only his small ships so that the French would think it was safe to come out of port.
h) The Battle of Trafalgar was one of the most important battles which were fought in the last century.

Looking at the language

*Here are some adjectives you can use when you are talking about people:**

stupid	egoistic	loyal	confident
weak	thoughtless	intelligent	independent
unkind	mean	generous	strong
selfish	cruel	brave	kind

If you don't know the meanings of some of these words, you can look them up in your dictionary.

How to use a dictionary

Here are two questions you should always ask and answer when you look up a word in a dictionary:

1 In what **context** *(Zusammenhang)* is the word used?
2 What **part of speech** *(Wortart)* is it?

e.g.: Let's take the word "confident" in this sentence:
Nelson was very **confident** when he discussed his new battle plan with Captain Keats.

Context? Describing Nelson
Part of speech? Adjective

Talking about Heroes

You'll find this in your dictionary:

> **con·fi·dent** ['kɔnfidənt] *adj.* □ →
> **confidently**; **1.** (*of, that*) über'zeugt
> (von, daß), gewiß, sicher (*gen.,* daß);
> **2.** vertrauensvoll; **3.** selbstsicher,
> zuversichtlich; **4.** eingebildet, kühn;
> **con·fi·den·tial** [kɔnfi'denʃəl] *adj.* □
> **1.** vertraulich, geheim; **2.** in'tim,
> vertraut, Vertrauens...: ~ *agent* Ge-
> heimagent; ~ *clerk* † Prokurist;
> **con·fi·den·tial·ly** [kɔnfi'denʃəli]
> *adv.* im Vertrauen: ~ *speaking* un-
> ter uns gesagt; '**con·fi·dent·ly** [-li]
> *adv.* getrost; **con·fid·ing** [kən-
> 'faidiŋ] *adj.* □ vertrauensvoll, zu-
> traulich.

In this case **"zuversichtlich"** *or* **"selbstsicher"** *seems to be the best meaning.*

Here are two more sentences with some of the adjectives from above:

1 He was a great leader – strong and intelligent, but in private life he was mean and egoistic.
2 Everybody hated her because she was so cruel and selfish.

Now look up the new adjectives in your dictionary.

---

* Um die Arbeit mit dem Wörterbuch zu ermöglichen, werden die neuen Adjektive nicht im Anhang erscheinen.

UNIT 8

Using the language

1 Talk about Lord Nelson.

1 What do you think of him? What do you like/
don't like about him?

I think he was a …
He also seemed … and …
In my opinion he …

2 Would you call him a hero? Give a reason.

Yes, I would. He …
No, I wouldn't. He …

2 Think of some well-known German men or women and talk about them. Say why you like/don't like them. Do you think they are heroes?

You can choose well-known people from the fields of:

| sport | music | politics |
| art | science | etc. |

3 Everybody has someone that he or she looks up to. You must have someone, too. It may be a famous person, or someone in your family, or a friend, or your neighbour.

Write a short text about this person. You should say something about his/her life and character. Also say why you like or admire this person. (Make notes first.)

In the first part of your text, you could mention:

- where and when the person was born, how old he/she is, relationship to you;
- where the person lives, what job he/she does.

In the second part, write about:

- the person's character – what he/she is like;
- some of the things he/she did which you like or admire.

Do We Need Heroes?

Listening

 Listen to Jack and Sally. They're having an argument. Take notes of the main points.
(Write on a separate sheet of paper.)

Did you get it?

1 What did Jack think? What was Sally's opinion?

Here's some help:

Jack	thought …
Sally	said …
He/She	also said …

| Jack's | opinion was … |
| Sally's | |

1 always something wrong with – people – you admire
2 everybody – need – hero
3 not right – look up to people
4 we need people – can admire – learn from them
5 dangerous – have – heroes – countries – get – dictators

2 Who do you agree with: Jack or Sally?
Say why you think we need/don't need heroes.

Reading

Quiz: Famous People

Here are short descriptions of some famous people.
Do you know who they are? Which picture goes with which description?

He lived in the 16th century and wrote marvellous plays. One of them is about two young people in Verona who loved each other very much.

She had a German husband who was known as Prince Albert. She had many children and gave her name to a whole period of English history.

They were famous for their haircuts, but not only for that. They were very musical people and wrote beautiful songs.

One was fat and one was thin. One was American and one was English. They did a lot of silly things to make people laugh.

Have you ever seen this man eat his own shoes? He had a funny walk, a bowler hat, and a tiny moustache.

He designed St Paul's Cathedral and many other famous buildings. He was England's greatest architect.

Did you get it?

After you've matched the pictures with the descriptions, talk to your partner about these famous people.

A:	Who	was were	Shakespeare? the … …		
B:	He was That was They were She was	the man …	who	wrote …	…

Using the language

Now write a short description of a well-known person. Don't tell the others in the class who it is. They should guess who the person is that you've described.

101

UNIT 8

On Board the "Victory"

You know what happens when you go on a guided tour of a place where a famous person was born, or where he lived and worked, don't you? You're told all about the person – when he was born, which schools he went to, who he married, how many children he had, how he lived and how he died. Then you're shown the rooms in which he ate, slept, worked and played.

Well, it's no different on board the "Victory". If you visit this famous ship in Portsmouth one day, you'll be told a lot of things about Nelson and the Battle of Trafalgar.

Listening

 Listen to what some visitors were told during a guided tour of the "Victory".

Did you get it?

True or false?

Find out which of the sentences below are wrong and which are right. Can you correct the wrong ones?

1. The guide was showing people around Trafalgar.
2. A woman was surprised to hear that the sailors used to wash.
3. The tourists were shown the battle-plan for Trafalgar.
4. One visitor thought that there were not enough electric lights in the dining cabin.
5. The guide showed the tourists the furniture in the museum.
6. The guide dropped a musical box.
7. One of the visitors thought that Nelson had been a brave man.
8. Another visitor said he would like to take part in a sea-battle.
9. The guide explained what the rigging of a ship was.

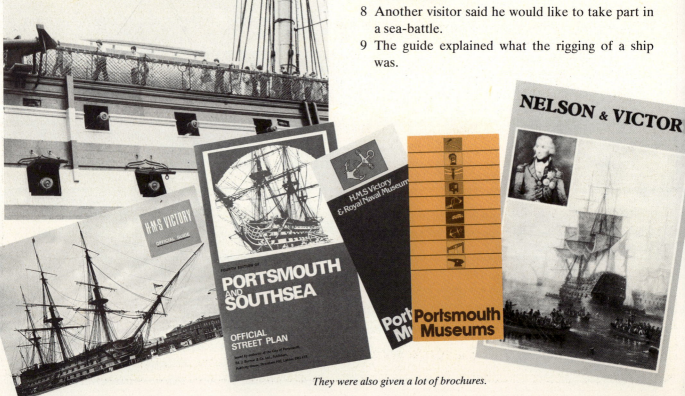

They were also given a lot of brochures.

Looking at the language

The woman you heard on the tape talked about the tour afterwards.
Look at what she said:

> … Then we were shown Lord Nelson's sleeping cabin with a washing and toilet cabinet. I was surprised because I thought sailors just stayed dirty.

Focus on grammar — More about the Passive

1 *Remember?*

The fireman		rescued	**the woman.**
The woman	was	rescued	by the fireman.

- The direct object in the active sentence becomes the subject in the passive sentence.
- We use the Passive when we are mainly interested in the action or the object of the action (the woman).

2

The guide	showed	**the tourists**	Nelson's cabin.
The tourists	were shown	Nelson's cabin.	

He	gave	**them**	brochures.
They	were given	brochures.	

He	told	**them**	about the battle.
They	were told	about the battle.	

> The indirect object often becomes the subject in passive sentences.
> This happens when the "agent" (= the person who performs the action) is of no interest to us.

Other examples:

She has promised **me** a pen for my birthday.	**I**'ve been promised a pen for my birthday.
They paid **me** two pounds.	**I** was paid two pounds.
Did they offer **you** a drink?	Were **you** offered a drink?
He'll pay **her** three pounds.	**She**'ll be paid three pounds.
They are going to ask **you** your name and address.	**You** are going to be asked your name and address.

Be careful: How would you translate these passive sentences into German?

⟶ Grammatikanhang S. 116

UNIT 8

Can you do it?

Look at what somebody said about a guided tour that he / she had been on.

1 "The guide gave us a map of the castle."
2 "He told us a lot of interesting things about the castle."
3 "Then he gave us our tickets."
4 "First he showed us the room where the prince was born."
5 "He told us not to touch the bed."
6 "Then he showed us the room where the jewels were kept."
7 "He asked us not to take any photos of the jewels."
8 "He told us to meet at the main entrance."
9 "He said he expected us to be there at 4 o'clock."
10 "He warned us not to be late."

Later he/she wrote a report on the tour. *What did he/she write? (Use a separate sheet of paper.)*

Example: "He took us to the castle and showed us the rooms."

We were taken to the castle and shown the rooms.

Using the language

Describe a guided tour that you've been on.

1 **Introduction**

Where did you go? When? Why?
Who did you go with?

Last year/summer my cousin came to ...
She had never seen ..., so ...

2 **Beginning of the tour**

Where did you go? What were you given/told?

After we had been ...
Then ..., but ...
Afterwards we ..., so ...

3 **Main part of the tour**

Where did you go? Where were you taken to?
What were you shown/told? What were you warned not to do?

When ...
While ...
Suddenly ...

4 **End of the tour**

What did you do? How did you feel?

I was glad/sorry ...
My cousin ...

Different Accents

As you have already noticed, the people on the "Victory" spoke English with different accents. This chart shows some of the features of their speech.

Woman	American	Cockney guide	German	Irishman
Speaks Standard British English. You can't tell exactly where she comes from.	Pronounces [r] differently. Listen to it in the word *dark*.	Says: *sleepin'* and *washin'* instead of *sleeping* and *washing*.	Says: *vot* and *ziss* instead of *what* and *this*.	Says: *dose* instead of *those*.

Now listen to the people again. Try to find some other features of their speech, and write them down in a chart similar to the one above.

What Were They Told?

1 Here are parts of the conversation on board the "Victory". Can you match them?

1 "Did the sailors wash, then?"
2 "Vot is ziss?"
3 "The ceiling's kinda low."
4 "What did they do with the furniture during a battle?"
5 "Vot is a rigging?"

a "When there was a battle, the furniture was all stowed away."
b "Those are the ropes that hold up the sails."
c "That's a musical box, sir. Please don't touch it."
d "Sailors have always washed."
e "Well, sir, they was a bit shorter in dem days than you Texans."

2 Now say what the tourists asked or mentioned and what the guide told them.

When the	woman American German Irishman	asked mentioned said	if/what … that …	she he	was told that … was told to … was told not to … was warned not to …

105

Interpreting

Imagine you are showing a visitor from an English-speaking country around your town. You have taken him/her on a guided tour, but your visitor doesn't understand what the guide says. Can you explain? Don't translate word for word.

Example:

Here are some more scenes. Be an interpreter for your visitor.

UNIT 9 Reading is Fun

Reading

Now let's see how much English you understand. Read the following story and try to get the main points. Don't look up any new words yet.

The glove

R. U. Joyce

James Dunne hung from the window and, after a moment, dropped to the ground. He had made no noise. He looked about him. The house was on the edge of the town and it was not too near the road. It was almost two o'clock and the night was dark. "Nobody will see me at this time of night," he thought. He ran quickly across the garden. He felt fairly safe now.

Can you describe the scene?

He felt clever, too. He had been a thief once. But that was before he had come to live in the little town of Brampton. Now he was a jeweller. He had had a jeweller's shop in Brampton for ten years. And nobody in the town knew that he had once been a thief. He had not stolen anything in all this time. Tonight was the first time in ten years. But he was not nervous. He climbed easily over the garden wall. He could even think coolly of the dead man he had left in the house. He had not wanted to kill Richard Strong, but it had been necessary. He had not wanted to steal from Strong either. But he needed money.

What had Dunne been before he became a jeweller?

What had he just done in the house?

Dunne needed money because someone had found out about him. A man he had once met in prison recognised him. The man demanded money. He knew that Dunne had been a thief. He said that he would tell people in Brampton about this. Dunne was afraid so he gave him the money. Then the man wanted more money. Dunne's jewellery business was good, but the man demanded so much that Dunne could not pay him. He tried to win some money, but he lost instead. Now he was in real trouble. He had to get money so he became a thief again.

Why did he need money so badly?

Richard Strong had a lot of valuable old things in his house. Dunne knew this. He often bought old gold and melted it down. He had decided to melt the gold from Strong's house and then sell it. He was a jeweller so he knew that he could sell it easily.

Say what he planned to do.

It was easy to get into the house. The valuable things were all in one room. Dunne knew this so he just climbed up to the window. In Brampton no one thought it was necessary to worry about thieves. In the room Dunne filled his pockets with gold pieces. He soon had more than enough.

Why was Dunne able to get into the house so easily?

He was about to leave when he heard a sound behind him. He turned quickly. The door had opened and Strong was standing in front of him. "Dunne!" It was the only word Strong said. Dunne picked up an old knife which he had admired a few seconds before. He hardly thought before he used it. In a few seconds Strong was dead. Dunne pulled the body into the room and closed

108

the door. Then he turned off the light, drew back the curtains and climbed out through the window.

He did not blame himself for killing Strong. "I could do nothing else," he told himself. "He recognised me. If I hadn't killed him I would have gone to prison." He remembered the look of surprise on Strong's face. It even made him smile. "I had to kill him," he thought. "Besides, he was an old man. He had only a few more years to live."

Why didn't he feel sorry?

He felt safe. Nobody had any reason to think that he had been to Strong's house. "I left nothing there," he thought. "Nobody saw me going or returning." The little street was empty and dark when he went into his own house by the side door.

Why did he feel so safe?

He lived alone in the house. A woman came in every day to cook and clean for him but she did not live there. His bedroom was at the back of the house, but he drew the heavy curtains across the window before he turned on the light. Then he felt in his pocket und pulled out a glove. A look of surprise came onto his face. He felt in his pocket again. His hand moved among the gold pieces there but he did not take them out. He was afraid to look at them. He was white with fear. The other glove was not there!

Why was he "white with fear" now?

He remembered finding the gloves in his pocket when he was at Strong's house. He had put them on a table while he filled his pockets with gold. He was certain that he had picked them both up before he left. But now one of the gloves had gone. And it had his name and address inside!

He thought of the room where the dead man lay. The thought of returning filled him with fear. He gave a little cry. "I can't do it," he said to himself. "I can't!"

Then he thought of prison. The rest of his life in prison. This thought made him go out into the street again. The return journey to Strong's house was like a terrible dream. He thought he saw strange shapes at every corner. Once he nearly screamed at a piece of paper on the ground. For a moment it had looked like a dead body.

What made him decide to go back to Strong's house in the end?

Describe in your own words how Dunne felt on his way back to the house.

He reached the house and climbed slowly up to the window. The room was dark as he had left it. But he thought he could see a darker thing on the floor near the door. He needed to turn the light on to find his glove. He had to go towards the body. His feet touched something soft. He almost screamed. Then his nervous fingers turned on the light.

Richard Strong lay on the floor at his feet. Dunne tried not to look at the body. But something made him look. He put out his hand and touched the knife. "Put up your hands! Put up your hands, you –!"

Dunne looked up with a cry. The door had opened and Strong's son stood there. He was pointing a gun at him. Slowly, Dunne raised his arms above his head.

UNIT 9

A detective and two policemen took him to the police station. On the way, the detective said to Dunne, "Well, this is a surprise. You know, if Strong's son hadn't found you in the room, you would have been safe. We would never have thought of you if he hadn't found you with the body – and with your pockets full of gold. You just didn't get away in time."

Dunne said nothing.

His house was on the way to the police station. He asked if he could go in and fetch his overcoat. He was cold.

"Certainly," said the detective. "But we'll go with you."

He opened the side door and went in. Dunne came next and then the two policemen. Dunne's foot touched something on the floor.

He picked it up and at that moment the detective turned on the light. Dunne looked at the thing in his hand.

It was his glove.

How did the glove get there?

Looking at the language

If you'd like to find out the meanings of some of the new words in the story, you can look them up in your dictionary.*

Remember to ask and answer these two questions:
1. In what context is the word used?
2. What part of speech is it?

Did you get it?

1 *Can you tell the story in your own words?*

2 *Write a summary of the story. Here's the beginning of each section.*

1 James Dunne was a jeweller. He had had the shop for ten years and business was good. Nobody knew that he had been a thief before he became a jeweller. Then one day a man …

2 One dark night he climbed into Strong's house and filled his pocket with gold. Suddenly the door …

3 But when he went home he couldn't find one of his gloves. He was frightened, and thought he …

4 On the way to the police station, they had to go past …

* *Um die Arbeit mit dem Wörterbuch zu ermöglichen, werden die neuen Wörter der Geschichte nicht im Anhang angegeben.*

Want to Read Some More?

If you enjoyed reading "The Glove", and would like to read some more stories, here's the book this story was taken from. It contains five other stories which you might also like to read.

And perhaps you'd enjoy reading these books, too.

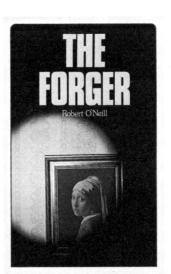

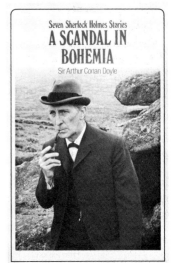

Contains seven Science Fiction stories by seven different authors.

Five of Daphne du Maurier's best-known and most popular stories.

Who is the forger? David tries to answer this question and discovers that the forger is not only a great artist, but also has a beautiful daughter.

Seven Sherlock Holmes Stories.

IRREGULAR VERBS

Present	Past	Past Participle [1]	Present	Past	Past Participle [1]
be	was/were	been	lend	lent	lent
beat	beat	beat(en)	let	let	let
become	became	become	lie	lay	lain
begin	began	begun	lose	lost	lost
bite	bit	bitten	make	made	made
break	broke	broken	mean	meant	meant
bring	brought	brought	meet	met	met
broadcast	broadcast	broadcast	pay	paid	paid
build	built	built	put	put	put
burn	burnt, burned	burnt, burned	read	read [red]	read [red]
buy	bought	bought	ride	rode	ridden
catch	caught	caught	ring	rang	rung
choose	chose	chosen	run	ran	run
come	came	come	say	said	said
cost	cost	cost	see	saw	seen
cut	cut	cut	sell	sold	sold
do	did	done	send	sent	sent
draw	drew	drawn	set	set	set
dream	dreamt, dreamed	dreamt, dreamed	shake	shook	shaken
drink	drank	drunk	shine	shone	shone
drive	drove	driven	shoot	shot	shot
eat	ate	eaten	show	showed	shown
fall	fell	fallen	sing	sang	sung
feed	fed	fed	sink	sank	sunk
feel	felt	felt	sit	sat	sat
fight	fought	fought	sleep	slept	slept
find	found	found	smell	smelt	smelt
flee	fled	fled	speak	spoke	spoken
fly	flew	flown	spell	spelt	spelt
forget	forgot	forgotten	spend	spent	spent
forgive	forgave	forgiven	spill	spilt	spilt
get	got	got	spit	spat	spat
give	gave	given	spread	spread	spread
go	went	gone	stand	stood	stood
grow	grew	grown	steal	stole	stolen
hang	hung	hung	stick	stuck	stuck
have	had	had	swim	swam	swum
hear	heard	heard	take	took	taken
hide	hid	hid(den)	teach	taught	taught
hit	hit	hit	tell	told	told
hold	held	held	think	thought	thought
hurt	hurt	hurt	throw	threw	thrown
keep	kept	kept	understand	understood	understood
know	knew	known	wake	woke	woken
lead	led	led	wear	wore	worn
learn	learnt, learned	learnt, learned	win	won	won
leave	left	left	write	wrote	written

[1]) Mit dieser Form werden das Passiv, Perfekt und Plusquamperfekt gebildet.

GRAMMAR

Diese Grammatik hilft dir beim Erkennen von Satzformen und beim Bilden englischer Sätze.

Diese Pfeile (———→) hinter verschiedenen Abschnitten verweisen auf die Units des Bandes IV, in denen die besprochene grammatische Erscheinung eingeführt oder geübt wird; z. B.: IV 1 = Band 4, Unit 1.

Der Satz

I. Der einfache englische Satz (The Simple English Sentence)

I.1 Die Wortstellung in der Aussage (Word Order in Statements)

Subject S	Auxiliary Verb av	Verb V	Object O
We	will	send	more information.
I		enclose	some brochures.
Sally		smiled.	

Die Reihenfolge der Satzglieder im Aussagesatz ist festgelegt:
S (– av) – V (– O)

Subject S	Auxiliary Verb av	Verb V	Indirect Object Oi	Direct Object Od
We	will	send	you	more information.
I	didn't	show	Mary	the way.

Wenn zwei Objekte vorhanden sind, ist die Reihenfolge: Oi – Od. ———→ IV 6

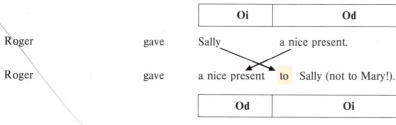

	Oi	Od
Roger gave	Sally	a nice present.

	Od		Oi
Roger gave	a nice present	to	Sally (not to Mary!).

Wenn das indirekte Objekt besonders hervorgehoben werden soll, wird es mit **to** an das direkte angeschlossen:

Od – to – Oi ———→ IV 6

Could you send **it to me** ?
Could you show **them to us** ?

Wenn das direkte Objekt **it** oder **them** ist, wird das indirekte Objekt immer mit **to** nachgestellt.

Reihenfolge: Od – to – Oi ———→ IV 6

Beachte:

a) Bei Verben wie **bring, give, send** und **show** kann die Reihenfolge von indirektem und direktem Objekt vertauscht werden; das am Schluß stehende Objekt ist hervorgehoben. Bildet das indirekte Objekt den Schluß, steht **to** davor.

Bei einigen Verben gibt es nur die Reihenfolge: Od – to – Oi (describe, explain):

	Od		Oi
The policeman	**described**	the way	to	the campers.
He	**explained**	the route	to	them.

———→ IV 6

b) **Say** und **tell**:

She	said	that she had lost the way.
Alison	told us	that she had lost the way.

Bei **say** erscheint normalerweise kein indirektes Objekt. Bei **tell** hingegen erscheint das **Oi** immer.

Say wird bei direkter und indirekter Rede verwendet.
Tell wird nur bei indirekter Rede verwendet (siehe Unit 5).

I.2   Verschiedene Verbergänzungen (Objects and Complements)

2.1 | O |

I	like	jogg**ing**.
Mary	enjoys	meet**ing** people.
She	hates	danc**ing**.

Die **ing**-Form des Verbs kann als Objekt verwendet werden (= Gerund). (Siehe I.2.2.)

S		Complement C
Mary	is	a teacher.
Her hobby	is	sightsee**ing** .
Watch**ing** TV	is	his hobby.

		O	
Watch**ing** the football match	made	me	tired.

Das Gerund kann ebenfalls als Komplement nach **to be** oder als Subjekt erscheinen.

I am	fond **of**	camp**ing**.
Eva is	dreaming **of**	go**ing** to Camp Cymraig.
There are lots of	opportunities **for**	do**ing** things.
He is	good **at**	tell**ing** jokes.

Das Gerund steht immer nach Adjektiven, Verben und Substantiven + Präposition.   ⟶ **IV 3**

2.2 | V | O |

Peter **wanted**	to meet	his friend.
They'**d like**	to go	by hovercraft.
I'**d love**	to live	there.
Alison **preferred**	to leave.	

Der Infinitiv mit **to** kann bei Verben wie **want, like, love, prefer** wie ein Objekt folgen.

Beachte:

a) Tim **likes** `watching` TV.
   He'**d like** `to watch` TV now.
   I **hate** `doing` housework.
   I'**d hate** `to do` the housework now.

b) **Stop** talk**ing**!
   Let's **go** shopp**ing**.
   John **enjoys** writ**ing** letters.
   Have you **finished** eat**ing**?

Auf Verben wie **like, love, prefer, hate**, die Wünsche, Vorlieben oder Abneigung ausdrücken, kann das Gerund oder der Infinitiv folgen, die aber verschiedene Bedeutungen haben: Gerund signalisiert eine Gewohnheit, der Infinitiv dagegen eine Aussage zu einer bestimmten zeitlich begrenzten Gelegenheit. Das Verb, das dem Infinitiv vorausgeht, steht oft mit **would ('d)**.

Nach **stop** (= *aufhören, etwas zu tun*), **go, enjoy, finish** (= *beenden, fertig sein*) folgt nur das Gerund, nie der Infinitiv.

fragen + bitten

2.3 | V | O + Infinitive |

Mother **wanted** `the children to do` the shopping.
She **told** `them to stop` playing.
The children **asked** `her to give` them money.
She **expected** `them to come` home by 10.

Mother told them `not` to take their bikes.
They asked her `not` to leave the house.

Ausdrücke wie „*wollen, daß jemand etwas tut, sagen, daß jemand etwas tun soll, fragen, ob jemand etwas tun kann, jemanden bitten, etwas zu tun, erwarten, daß jemand etwas tut*" werden im Englischen mit **V - O + Infinitiv** gebildet.

Auch beim Berichten von Verboten, Warnungen oder Aufforderungen, etwas zu unterlassen, wird die Struktur **O + Infinitiv** verwendet, wobei **not** zwischen **O** und **to** steht.

Beachte:
Tell und **ask** können mit **not** oder ohne **not** in solchen Berichten verwendet werden.
Warn (= *ermahnen*) wird nur mit **not** konstruiert, **want** und **expect** jedoch nie.

He **warned** them `not to be` late. ⟶ IV 7

Aber:
He **didn't expect** us to come so early.
She **doesn't want** us to go out together.

2.4 | V | O + past participle |

I must `get` `my hair cut.`
The baker had to `get` `his car repaired.`

Get - O + past participle ist im Deutschen mit *lassen* (= Haare schneiden, Auto reparieren lassen) wiederzugeben; die Konstruktion signalisiert, daß andere eine Arbeit ausführen als der im Subjekt des Satzes Genannte. ⟶ IV 5

I.3 Passivsätze (Passive Sentences)

3.1

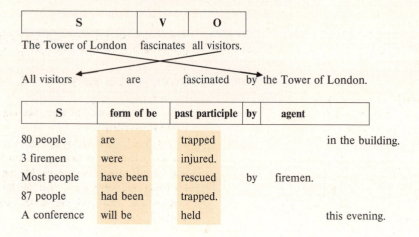

Wenn ein aktiver Satz in einen passiven umgeformt wird, erhalten Subjekt und Objekt neue Positionen: das Objekt übernimmt die Rolle des Subjekts, während das Subjekt mit **by** an das Ende des Satzes gestellt wird (als *by-agent*). Das Verb wird ersetzt durch sein *past participle* und eine Form von **to be,** die in der entsprechenden Zeit steht.

Häufig fehlt **by** + **agent** (in Nachrichten, Berichten usw.), weil man die Ursache oder den „Täter" nicht kennt oder weil die von der Handlung Betroffenen oder das Geschehen selbst in den Vordergrund gerückt werden sollen. ⟶ **IV 1**

3.2

	av	form of be	past participle	
Three firemen	had to	be	taken	to hospital.
Not everyone	could	be	rescued.	

Passivsätze können wie Aktivsätze modale Hilfsverben enthalten (siehe III.2.3).
⟶ **IV 1**

3.3

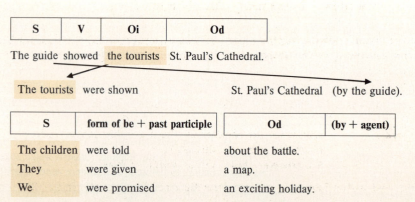

Wenn indirektes und direktes Objekt vorhanden sind, kann auch das indirekte im Passivsatz Subjekt werden. Es dient dazu, Personen (**Oi**) in den Mittelpunkt zu stellen (*persönliches Passiv*). ⟶ **IV 8**

I.4 Die Stellung der Adverbien (Position of Adverbs)

4.1

S	V	Adverb Adv	
The new star	sang	beautifully.	
The man	ran	quickly	to his house.

S	Adv	V	O
The girl	quickly	put on	her jeans.

Besteht der Satz aus **S – V**, folgt das Adverb der Art und Weise *(Adverb of Manner)* dem Verb.
Besteht der Satz aus **S – V – O**, steht es vor **V**.
(**Adv** kann aber auch **O** folgen: **She put on her jeans quickly.**)
Ist bei **S – V** eine Richtungsangabe oder ähnlich vorhanden (**to the house**), kann **Adv** vor **V** erscheinen: **The man quickly ran to his house** oder aber auch nach der Richtungsangabe: **The man ran to his house quickly.**

4.2

S	av	Adv	V	O/Adv
Lord Nelson		often	thought	about his new plan.
Peter	had	never	eaten	with his hands before.

Adverbien, die aus einem Wort bestehen (und oft eine Häufigkeit angeben, *Adverbs of Frequency*), stehen *vor* dem Verb. Sind Hilfsverben vorhanden, folgen diese Adverbien unmittelbar dem ersten Hilfsverb.

4.3

Adv (Time/Place)	S	V	O	Adv (Place)	Adv (Time)
In the evening	the boys	prepared	the meal.		
	The boys	prepared	dinner		in the evening.
	They	had bought	everything	in the village	two days before.
At home	they	would have eaten			at seven.
	They	met	the others	in the kitchen	after 12 o'clock.

Adverbien des Ortes und der Zeit, vor allem solche, die aus mehreren Wörtern bestehen, stehen am Anfang oder am Ende des Satzes. Treffen verschiedene Adverbien am Ende des Satzes zusammen, ist die Reihenfolge festgelegt: Adverb des Ortes + Adverb der Zeit.

4.4

| Unfortunately, | I can't find your book. |
| Frankly, | I'm a bit scared. |

Hier drückt der Sprecher des Satzes mit dem Adverb seine Einstellung zum folgenden Satz aus:
It is unfortunate that . . . oder **I want to be frank.**

Trotz ihres Namens *Ad-verb* können Adverbien auch andere Satzglieder wie auch ganze Sätze modifizieren (siehe III.3, IV.4).

I.5 Die Wortstellung in Fragesätzen (Word Order in Questions)

5.1 Entscheidungsfragen in Sätzen mit Hilfsverb (Yes/No-Questions in Sentences with Auxiliary)

Aussage ⇒ Frage ⇒ Kurzantwort

S	av	V

av	S	V

Sally	is		at home.	Is	Sally		at home?	Yes, she	is.
Nelson	was	born	at Burnham Thorpe.	Was	Nelson	born	at Burnham Thorpe?	Yes, he	was.
She	would	like	to go to Africa.	Would	she	like	to go to Africa?	No, she	wouldn't.

5.2 Entscheidungsfragen mit do-Umschreibung (Yes/No-Questions with do)

Aussage ⇒ Frage ⇒ Kurzantwort

S	V

av	S	V

Malick	lives	in The Gambia.	Does	Malick	live	in The Gambia?	Yes, he	does.
The people	speak	French there.	Do	they	speak	French there?	No, they	don't.
Peter	wrote	several postcards.	Did	Peter	write	several postcards?	Yes, he	did.

Die Bildung der Frage mit **do** kommt nur in Sätzen ohne Hilfsverben vor und nur im *simple present* und *simple past* (weil alle anderen Zeiten mit Hilfsverben gebildet werden). Die Form von **do** signalisiert die Zeit (**do – did**) und die Person (**do – does**); sie wird wie ein Hilfsverb vorangestellt, so daß die Wortstellung **S – V** erhalten bleibt.

5.3 Fragen mit Frageanhängsel (Tag-Questions)

Paul is German, isn't he?
Sally has talked to Roger, hasn't she?
Your parents could go by train, couldn't they?
Nelson won the Battle of Trafalgar, didn't he?
You can't speak French, can you?
The bus hasn't left yet, has it?
He didn't write any letters, did he?

Mit *Tag-questions* signalisiert der Sprecher, daß er eine Antwort oder Reaktion erwartet (eine positive bei positivem Aussagesatz, eine entsprechend negative bei negativem Aussagesatz).

5.4 Kurzantworten auf Entscheidungsfragen

Is	Sally at home?	– No, she	**isn't.**	(No, she's not.)
Would	you like a cup of tea?	– Yes, I	**would.**	
Has	she been to England?	– Yes, she	**has.**	
Did	she like it there?	– No, she	**didn't.**	(No, she did not.)

Eine höfliche Kurzantwort besteht im Englischen aus Pronomen und dem Hilfsverb, mit dem die Frage gebildet wurde (und nicht nur aus **yes** oder **no**).

5.5 Kurzsätze mit so/nor/not either

I	**have**	Irish stamps.	– So	**have**	I.
Mary	**is**	very fond of dancing.	– So	**am**	I.
Peter	**would**	like to go to America.	– So	**would**	we.
I	like	going to the theatre.	– So	**do**	I.
We	went	to Africa last year.	– So	**did**	she.
I	**can't**	stand operas.	– Nor	**can**	I.
			(I	**can't either**	.)
We	**didn't**	like the weather much.	– Nor	**did**	he.
			(He	**didn't either**	.)

Um auszudrücken, daß eine positive Aussage für sich oder andere auch zutrifft, verwendet man Kurzsätze mit **so + do/did** oder vorhandenem Hilfsverb (*ich auch, sie auch, wir auch usw.*).

Bei negativen Aussagen verwendet man **nor + do/did** oder vorhandenes Hilfsverb. Eine weitere Möglichkeit auf negative Aussagen zu reagieren, sind Kurzsätze mit verneintem Hilfsverb + **either** (*ich auch nicht, er auch nicht, du auch nicht usw.*). → **IV 6**

5.6 Fragen mit Fragewörtern (Ergänzungsfragen; Wh-Questions)

Frage

S	av+V	
Who	lives	in Scotland?
Who	is	his sister?
Who	can speak	French and German?
What	went wrong	that day?
Which boy	lost	his torch?

Wenn mit **who, what** oder **which** + *noun* nach dem Subjekt des Satzes gefragt wird, nimmt das Fragewort die Stellung des Subjekts ein. Die Wortstellung bleibt erhalten: **S - (av) - V - (O)**.

wh-word	av	S	V
What	can	Mike	see?
Where	is	Anne	waiting?
Where	was	Peter	going?
When	had	he	left?
Why	was	Malick	late?
How	did	he	get home?
How long	does	the journey	take?

Wenn das Fragewort (*wh-word*) sich nicht auf das Subjekt des Satzes bezieht, wird es auch dem Satz vorangestellt; die Wortstellung des nachfolgenden Satzes wird jedoch wie bei einer Entscheidungsfrage geändert (siehe I.5.1): **av - S - V**.

| Aussage | ⟶ | Frage | ⟶ | Kurzantwort |

S	av	V		Wh-word (+ noun)	av	S	V
I'	ve	got	Anne's dictionary.	Whose (dictionary)	have	you	got? — Anne's.
I		wanted	the French dictionary.	Which (dictionary)	did	you	want? — The French one.

Das Substantiv kann nur wegfallen, wenn der Zusammenhang und der Bezug von **whose** oder **which** eindeutig ist.

Beachte:

a) Who / Whom did you meet at the station?

Wen? heißt im Englischen **who** oder **whom**. Gesprochenes, umgangssprachliches Englisch bevorzugt **who**, schriftliches, formelleres Englisch **whom**.

b) I talked to Jane yesterday. – Who did you talk to yesterday?
I was thinking of our holiday. – What were you thinking of?

Verben mit Präposition stehen am Schluß einer Frage, wobei die Präposition hinter dem Verb bleibt. ⟶ IV 1

I.6 Die Wortstellung im Befehlssatz (Word Order in Imperatives)

V	
Be	quiet!
Stop!	
Open	the door.
Now close	it slowly.

Beachte:

a) Durch Hinzufügen von **please** wird der Befehlscharakter gemildert:
Please, be quiet. – Be quiet, please.

b) Let's go. *Laß/Laßt uns gehen!*

Let's drückt eine Aufforderung aus, die den Sprecher einschließt.

I.7 Verneinung (Negation)

7.1 Verneinung von Aussagen (Negated Statements)

Peter	was	late.		Peter	wasn't	(was not) late.
He	should	say that.		He	shouldn't	(should not) say that.
The boy	has	been injured.		The boy	hasn't	(has not) been injured.
They	laughed	at him.		They	didn't	(did not) laugh at him.
Mary	likes	cats.		Mary	doesn't	(does not) like cats.
Her parents	like	her boyfriend.		Her parents	don't	(do not) like her boyfriend.

Werden Sätze ohne Hilfsverb verneint, wird wie bei der Frage (I.5.2) die entsprechende Form von **do** verwendet.

7.2 Verneinung von Fragen (Negated Questions)

Is	Sally at home?	–	Isn't	Sally at home?
Can	we meet tomorrow?	–	Can't	we meet tomorrow?
Did	you see her?	–	Didn't	you see her?

Verneinte Fragen drücken Überraschung aus, z. B.: "Is it really true that Sally isn't at home (I thought she was)."

7.3 Verneinter Befehlssatz (Negated Imperative)

Don't | stop!
      | open the door!

Verbote werden formuliert, indem **don't** vor den Befehlssatz gestellt wird. Auch hier sind Abschwächungen mit Hilfe von **please** möglich (siehe I. 6).

II. Das englische Satzgefüge (The Complex English Sentence)

II.1 Adverbialsätze (Adverbial Clauses)

Hauptsatz	Konjunktion	Nebensatz
(Main Clause)	(Conjunction)	(Subordinate Clause)

S	V	O/Adv etc.		S	V	O/Adv etc.
They	were watching	TV	when	the lights	went out.	
The telephone	rang		while	they	were having	dinner.
Judy	wrote	a report	after	she	had returned	to England.
I	went	home	because	it	was	late.

Beachte:

Im Englischen ist die Wortstellung in Haupt- und Nebensatz identisch: **S – V – O** etc.

II.2 Bedingungssätze mit if (Conditional Clauses with If)

2.1 If-Sätze im Präsens (Open or Neutral Condition)

If-Clause		Main Clause	
If you	go	to the disco, you	'll meet a lot of people.
If we	use	light paint, the room	will be nicer.

Die Bedingung im **if**-Satz ist eine reale Möglichkeit und erfüllbar; das Verb des **if**-Satzes steht im *simple present,* das des Hauptsatzes im Futur mit **will.**

2.2 If-Sätze im Präteritum (Unreal Condition)

If people	drove	more carefully,	many accidents	wouldn't	happen.
If he	didn't get up	so early,	he	wouldn't	wake up all the others.
If I	were	you,	I	would	spend my holidays in Britain.

Das Eintreffen der Bedingung im **if**-Satz ist äußerst unwahrscheinlich oder ganz irreal; das Verb des **if**-Satzes steht im *simple past,* im Hauptsatz steht **would** (oder **wouldn't**) + Infinitiv.

2.3 If-Sätze im Plusquamperfekt (Unreal Condition in the Past)

If I	had been	firmer with the others,	it	wouldn't have	happened.
If Melanie	hadn't wanted	to see the stalagmites,	they	would have	gone back.

Wie in II.2.2 wird das Eintreffen der Bedingung als irreal angesehen; zusätzlich wird durch das *past perfect* im **if**-Satz und **would** (**wouldn't**) + *present perfect* der ganze Satz in die Vergangenheit verlegt. ⟶ **IV 7**

Beachte:

a) Die Reihenfolge von **if**-Satz und Hauptsatz kann vertauscht werden:
   You'll meet a lot of people if you go to the disco.

b) **If**-Sätze, die eine *unreal condition* ausdrücken, werden oft verwendet, um jemanden zurechtzuweisen **(If you had worked harder . . .)**, zu warnen **(If you listened, you would notice . . .)** oder auch um Vorschläge zu machen **(If I were you, I would . . .)**.

c) Das Verb **to be** hat für **if**-Sätze mit *unreal condition* bei allen Personen die Form **were (If I were, you were, he were,** usw.**).** Bei **he/she/it** ist auch **was** möglich: **If she was interested, . . .**
   Unreal condition in the past wird durch das normale *past perfect* ausgedrückt.

II.3 Relativsätze (Relative Clauses)

3.1

	Relative Clause		
The fireman	who	rescued the cat	was injured.
The ship	which / that	Nelson commanded	is preserved in Portsmouth.
The boys	who / that	came late	missed the bus.
The tree	which / that	was too close to the road	had to be cut down.

Das Relativpronomen **who** bezieht sich nur auf Personen, **which** auf Sachen. **That** kann sich auf Personen oder Sachen beziehen.

I talked to the children	whose	parents couldn't come.
This is the building	whose	roof fell in.

Das Relativpronomen **whose** bezieht sich auf Personen und auf Sachen.

3.2

The boys	who / whom / that / –	she met were also club members.
The letter	which / that / –	Mary wrote never reached London.

Wenn das Relativpronomen Objekt im Relativsatz ist, kann man **who** oder **whom** gebrauchen. **Whom** ist formell oder schriftsprachlich.

In Objektfunktion kann das Relativpronomen auch ganz wegfallen (das gilt für **who/whom, which** und **that**), was sehr häufig im Englischen vorkommt. (= *contact clause*).

Beachte:

(They talked about stamps.) The stamps | which they talked about / they talked about / about which they talked | were Swedish.

(The warden listened to the girls.) The girls | who the warden listened to / whom the warden listened to / the warden listened to / to whom the warden listened | were members of the youth club.

Wie bei der Frage mit Fragewörtern (siehe I.5.6) bleiben im Relativsatz Präpositionen hinter dem Verb. Nur in formeller Sprache steht die Präposition vor dem Relativpronomen (**about which, to whom**). ⟶ IV 1

II.4 Infinitivsätze (Infinitive Clauses)

Main Clause	Infinitive Clause
We didn't know	what to do.
	(= what we should do.)
Show me	how to open this box.
	(= how I should/open this box.)

Infinitive können als Objekt erscheinen (I.2.2), doch auch als Verkürzung eines Nebensatzes. ⟶ IV 2

II.5 Indirekte Rede (Reported Speech)

5.1 Die Zeiten

	Direkte Rede			Indirekte Rede
Malick to Peter:	"I **like** your jeans."	*Peter*	⇨	Malick said he **liked** my jeans.
	"**Do** you **speak** English?"	*reported*	⇨	He asked me if I **spoke** English.
	"**Are** you **staying** at the hotel?"	*like*	⇨	He asked me if I **was staying** at the hotel.
	"**Have** you **been** to Africa before?"	*this:*	⇨	He asked me if I **had been** to Africa before.
Peter to Alan:	"I **met** a very nice family in Senegal."	*You*	⇨	Peter told Alan he **had met** a nice family in Senegal.
	"**Did** you **get** my postcards?"	*can*	⇨	Peter asked Alan if he **had got** his postcard.
A friend to Peter:	"When **did** you **come** back?"	*report*	⇨	Alan asked Peter when he **had come** back.
Peter to Malick:	"I'**ll write** soon."	*like*	⇨	Peter said he **would write** soon.
Malick to Peter:	"I **won't be** late again."	*this:*	⇨	Malick told Peter he **wouldn't be** late again.

Wenn über ein Gespräch, eine Aussage, eine Frage usw. berichtet wird, entsteht ein Satzgefüge: im Hauptsatz steht ein Verb des Sagens (say, tell, ask usw.) meistens im Past und im Nebensatz indirekte Rede. Wenn das Verb des Hauptsatzes im Past steht, ändert sich die Zeit in indirekter Rede wie folgt:

Direkte Rede		Indirekte Rede
Simple Present	⇨	Simple Past
Present Progressive	⇨	Past Progressive
Present Perfect	⇨	Past Perfect
Simple Past	⇨	Past Perfect
will + infinitive	⇨	would + infinitive

Beachte: Die Zeit im Nebensatz ändert sich nicht in folgenden 2 Fällen:

1) wenn der Inhalt, über den berichtet wird, noch allgemeine Gültigkeit hat.
   Malick's uncle: "I'm a fisherman." – He said he **is** a fisherman. *(Malick's Onkel ist noch Fischer, daher* **is**.*)*

2) wenn das Verb des Sagens im Present Tense steht.
   Mary: "I'**m coming** next week." – She **says** she '**s coming** next week.

5.2 Aufforderungen in indirekter Rede werden mit **tell/ask** + O + **Infinitiv** wiedergegeben (vgl. I.2.3).

Janet:	"**Tell** me about your holiday, Peter."	⇨	Janet **asked Peter to tell** her about his holiday.
Malick:	"**Don't forget** us, Peter."	⇨	Malick **told Peter not to forget** them.

5.3 Pronomen und Adverbien werden auch in indirekter Rede geändert.

Bill to me:	"I'll visit **you** soon."	⇨	Bill said **he** would visit **me** soon.
Mary to John:	"I'll phone **you** tomorrow."	⇨	She said that **she** would phone **him** **the next day**.
	"**We** saw **you** yesterday."	⇨	Mary told John **they** had seen **him** **the day before**.

⟶ **IV 5**

Die Satzglieder

III. Der Verbteil

III.1 Hauptverben (Main Verbs)

1.1 Die Zeiten (The Tenses)

Präsens (Simple Present)

She **is** happy.
I **have** a bike.
She **looks** at her cat.
We **hate** skating.

Im *simple present* ändert sich die Verbform (= Infinitivform) nur in der 3. Person Singular (**she looks**). Zu beachten sind die Formen von **be** und **have**: **I am, he/she/it is, you/we/they are; he/she/it has, I/you/we/they have.**
Das *simple present* kennzeichnet Zustände oder Ereignisse als gegenwärtig. Oft drückt es Gewohnheiten oder die Zeit überdauernde Gegebenheiten aus (**He works in a garage. Paris is the capital of France.**)

Beachte:

She kiss**es** her daughter.
School finish**es** at four.
John hurr**ies** to school.
Peter go**es** home for lunch.
He look**s** sad.
He live**s** far away.

	Schreibung	und	*Aussprache*
	Nach Buchstaben, die für Zischlaute stehen (**sh, s, dg** usw.), ist die Endung der 3. Person Singular **-es**; ebenso nach Buchstaben, die Vokale wiedergeben (**goes**). Dabei wird **y** zu **i** (**hurries, carries**). In allen anderen Fällen wird nur **s** angehängt.	[ɪz],	wenn der letzte Laut des Infinitivs ein Zischlaut ist (= [s, z, ʃ, ʒ, tʃ, dʒ]; [kɪsɪz, fɪnɪʃɪz]).
		[s],	wenn der letzte Laut des Infinitivs stimmlos, aber kein Zischlaut ist ([lʊks]).
		[z],	wenn der letzte Laut des Infinitivs stimmhaft (aber kein Zischlaut) oder ein Vokal ist ([lɪvz, pleɪz]).

Präteritum (Past)

He **was** a teacher.
The boys **were** late yesterday.
They **had** four children.

Anne **visited** her aunt last week.
I **spoke** to the policeman.

Im *past* ändert sich nur die Form von *be*: **I/he/she/it was, you/we/they were**. Alle anderen Verben haben nur noch eine Form für alle Personen.

Das *past* kennzeichnet Zustände oder Ereignisse, die in der Vergangenheit liegen und als abgeschlossen betrachtet werden. Zeitadverbien wie **yesterday, last week, some time ago** usw. signalisieren oft das Präteritum.

Beachte:

They want**ed** to leave.
We need**ed** a holiday.
John phon**ed** again yesterday.
He hurri**ed** home.
I travel**led** all over England.

	Schreibung	und	*Aussprache*
	Das *past* der regelmäßigen Verben wird gebildet, indem **-d** an den Infinitiv auf **-e** und **-ed** an alle anderen Infinitive gehängt wird. Dabei wechselt **y** zu **i** (**hurried**). Nach kurzem Vokal werden einfache Konsonanten in der Regel verdoppelt. *Unregelmäßige Verben:* siehe Anhang, S. 112.	[ɪd],	wenn der letzte Laut des Infinitivs **t** oder **d** ist (wan**t**ed, nee**d**ed).
		[d],	wenn der letzte Laut des Infinitivs stimmhaft (außer **d**) oder ein Vokal ist (pho**n**ed, mar**r**ied).
		[t],	wenn der letzte Laut des Infinitivs stimmlos (außer **t**) ist (sto**pp**ed).

Perfekt (Present Perfect)

I have lived in London all my life.
They haven't met for years.
Have you seen your friends?
I haven't talked to them since Easter.
We 've been to London twice.
She 's had a marvellous time there.
Her postcard has just arrived.
I haven't done my homework yet.
I 've never been here before.

Das *present perfect* wird mit einer Präsensform von **have** + *past participle* gebildet (Bei regelmäßigen Verben endet das *past participle* auf **-ed**. Aussprache und Schreibung siehe vorigen Abschnitt über *past*. Das *past participle* der unregelmäßigen Verben siehe Anhang, S. 112).

Das *present perfect* drückt aus, daß zwischen einem Ereignis in der Vergangenheit und dem Zeitpunkt der Äußerung eine Verbindung besteht: das Ergebnis ist noch wichtig, die Handlung verläuft bis zum Sprechzeitpunkt; das Ereignis selbst kann zeitlich festgelegt sein **(since Easter)** oder einen unbestimmten Zeitraum lang andauern **(for years)**

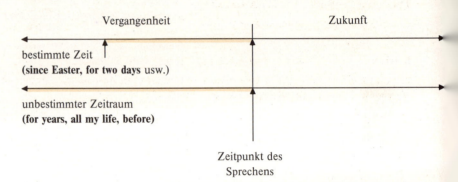

Beachte:

Das Deutsche unterscheidet nicht streng zwischen *past* und *present perfect* (Ich lebte in London. - Ich habe in London gelebt.) Im Englischen dürfen die beiden Zeiten nicht verwechselt werden. Eine in der Vergangenheit abgeschlossene Handlung oder ein Ereignis (oft durch Signale wie **yesterday, last week, two months ago** usw. angezeigt) erfordert das *past*. Will der Sprecher eine Verbindung mit der Gegenwart, mit dem Sprechzeitpunkt signalisieren, muß er das *present perfect* verwenden; Signalwörter sind oft **just, often, already, for** (**weeks, 3 months** usw.), **since** (**last Christmas** usw.); in Fragen **ever**. Zum Beispiel: **Have** you ever been to London? - Yes, I **was** there two weeks ago .

⟶ IV 2

Plusquamperfekt (Past Perfect)

Nelson died after he had heard the good news.
I knew that I had done badly in the test.
She told us that she had had fish for lunch.

Das *past perfect* wird gebildet mit **had** + *past participle*. Es wird verwendet, um eine zeitliche Reihenfolge in der Vergangenheit auszudrücken (früher = *past perfect*, später = *simple past*). In indirekter Rede erscheint es, wenn bei direkter Rede *past* oder *present perfect* vorlag (siehe II.5.1).

Futur (Future)

I `'ll go` to London as soon as possible.
`Will` Sally `meet` Roger again?
He `will be` happy in France.

She `is going to` see her aunt tomorrow.
We `'re going to` stay for three weeks.
I `'m not going to` learn Russian.

They `are coming` to lunch next Sunday.
I `'m leaving` for Italy next week.

Will + *infinitive* drückt im Englischen am neutralsten das Futur aus: das Ereignis oder der Zustand werden nach dem Zeitpunkt der Äußerung eintreten.

Be going to + *infinitive* wird verwendet, wenn der Sprecher eine Absicht für die Zukunft signalisieren möchte.

Das *present progressive* (siehe III.1.2) wird verwendet, wenn ein festgelegter Plan oder eine konkret geplante Absicht ausgeführt werden soll.

Beachte:

Im realen **if**-Satz steht das *simple present* mit futurischer Bedeutung, während im Hauptsatz **will** + *infinitive* stehen: **If** I `see` the warden, I `'ll ask` him about the canoes (siehe II.2.1).

1.2 Verlaufsform (Progressive Aspect)

Look, the baby `is jumping` up and down.
Hurry! Peter `is waiting` for you.
He `was reading` when Anne came in.
We `have been listening` since 8 o'clock now.

Der *progressive aspect* wird ausgedrückt durch die verschiedenen Zeiten von **be** + **ing**-Form des Verbs *(present participle)*; er kann mit jeder Zeit verbunden werden.
Durch den *progressive aspect* betont der Sprecher, daß eine Handlung oder ein Ereignis andauert oder sich wiederholt, aber zeitlich begrenzt ist. ⟶ **IV 2**

Beachte:

a) Im Deutschen existiert keine Form, die den *progressive aspect* ausdrückt, sondern man muß die einfache Form + Adverbien wie *gerade, schon* usw. für eine Übersetzung zu Hilfe nehmen.

b) Handlungen oder Ereignisse (Gewohnheiten), die man als zeitlich unbegrenzt ansieht, stehen in der *simple tense* (oft verknüpft mit Adverben wie **always, usually, every day** usw.), während Dauer *und* zeitliche Begrenzung durch die Verlaufsform gekennzeichnet wird:

He `drinks` a glass of milk `every day`. He `is eating` right now, so he can't answer the telephone.
John `always` `watched` TV in the evening. He `was watching` TV, `when` the fire broke out.

Wenn ein Adverb wie **always** mit dem *progressive aspect* verknüpft wird, signalisiert der Sprecher Verärgerung: He **is always watching** TV! One can never really talk to him!

c) Schreibung der **ing**-Formen:

stop – sto**pp**ing
begin – begi**nn**ing
sit – si**tt**ing

Wenn der Infinitiv einen kurzen, betonten Vokal und einen Schlußkonsonanten enthält, wird dieser verdoppelt, wenn **-ing** angehängt wird.

III.2 Hilfsverben (Auxiliary Verbs)

2.1 Be

The taxi	is	waiting outside.
The thief	was	seen by all the neighbours.
You	weren't	looking at her.

Als Hilfsverb findet **be** Verwendung beim *progressive aspect* (siehe III.1.2) und beim Passiv (siehe I.3): **av + V-ing** oder **av + past participle**. **Be** wird auch als Hauptverb verwendet (**I am German. Mary is a teacher**).

Beachte:

a) Hilfs- und Hauptverb haben die gleichen Formen. **Be** kann alle Zeiten bilden (siehe III.1.1).

b) Hilfs- und Hauptverb haben die gleichen Verkürzungen in positiven und verneinten Sätzen (siehe III.1.1): **I'm, he's, she's, it's, we're, you're, they're. He/she/it isn't, we/you/they aren't** (aber: **I'm not**); **I/he/she/it wasn't, we/you/they weren't**.

There als Subjekt von **be**:

There's	a book on the table.	*Es liegt (da liegt) ein Buch auf dem Tisch.*
There was	an abstract picture on the wall.	*Es hing (da hing) ein abstraktes Bild an der Wand.*
I think there was	a reason for his behaviour.	*Ich glaube, es gab einen Grund für sein Verhalten.*
There are	many people who collect stamps.	*Es gibt viele Leute, die Briefmarken sammeln.*

There + be, verknüpft mit Ortsangaben (**on the table**), ist meistens zu übersetzen mit *liegen, stehen, hängen* usw. Wenn es sich nicht um Positionsangaben handelt, heißt **there + be** = *es gibt/gab* usw.

2.2 Have

Have you been	to London?	
She has seen	most countries in Europe.	
He said he had had	a cat and a dog some years before.	
They hadn't visited	their aunt for weeks.	

Als Hilfsverb wird **have** für die Bildung des *present perfect* und *past perfect* aller Hauptverben gebraucht (siehe III.1.1). **Have** wird auch als Hauptverb verwendet (**I have a bike. She has a cold.**)

Beachte:

a) Hilfs- und Hauptverb haben die gleichen Formen. **Have** kann alle Zeiten bilden (siehe III.1.1).

b) Hilfs- und Hauptverb gestatten die gleichen Verkürzungen in positiven und negativen Sätzen: **I/you/we/they've waited; he/she/it's waited. I/you/he/she/it/we/they'd listened. I/you/we/they haven't, he/she/it hasn't. I/you/he/she/it/we/they hadn't.**

c) **Have** (als Hauptverb) = **Have got**

Do you	have	a bike?	= Have	you got	a bike?
I	don't have	any time.	= I	haven't got	any time.

2.3 Modale Hilfsverben (Modal Auxiliaries)

Can, may, shall, will, must, needn't, ought to heißen modale Hilfsverben, weil mit ihnen Fähigkeiten, Möglichkeiten, Erlaubnis, Verbot oder Verpflichtung ausgedrückt werden können. (Zur Stellung im Satz siehe I.1)

They	can't	speak English.
Last week we	could	swim in the lake.
He explained why he	had not been able to	learn French.
He hopes his son	will be able to	learn it.

Can *(present tense)*, **could** *(past tense)* drücken hier Fähigkeiten aus. Perfekt, Plusquamperfekt und Futur sind mit der Ersatzform **be able to** zu bilden, die auch im Präsens oder Präteritum verwendet werden kann. (**They are able to speak English. We were able to swim...**).

Perhaps we **could** leave now? = Vielleicht könnten wir jetzt aufbrechen?
Can I borrow your bike? = Kann ich dein Fahrrad borgen?
Couldn't I borrow your bike? = Könnte ich nicht dein Fahrrad borgen?

Can/could können in einem Vorschlag „Möglichkeit" signalisieren oder um Erlaubnis fragen. **Could** ist die höflichere Form.

You **may** visit us tomorrow.
They said I **might** visit them tomorrow.
May we go to the cinema tonight?
We **weren't allowed to** go last night.
He said children **had** not **been allowed to** play on Sundays in those days.

May (= *dürfen*) drückt „Erlaubnis" aus. Mit Ausnahme des *past tense* in der indirekten Rede werden alle Zeiten außer Präsens mit der Ersatzform **be allowed to** gebildet.
May ist höflicher bei Fragen um Erlaubnis als **can**: **May I (Can I) have your pen?**

You **may not** leave yet.
It **might** be a good idea to phone her first.

May not/not to be allowed to = Verweigerung einer Erlaubnis.
Might (= *könnte*) kann wie **could** eine Möglichkeit vorschlagen.

Shall we meet at 8 o'clock?
Should I bring my record player?
You **should** ring your parents at once.
We **shouldn't** have stayed so long.

Shall/should in Fragen = *soll/sollte*

Should (= *sollte*) wird in Ratschlägen verwendet.

There **will** be rain tomorrow.
They said there **would** be rain tomorrow.
It **wouldn't** have happened if they had been more careful.

Will dient der Bildung des Futurs (siehe III.1.1). **Would** kann in indirekter Rede als *past tense* von **will** erscheinen. Im Hauptsatz von **if**-Sätzen bedeutet es hingegen *würde* oder *wäre* (siehe II.2.3).

I **must** be on time today.
I **had to** look after my little brother yesterday.
We **will have to** learn this poem, too.

Die Ersatzform für **must** (= *müssen*) ist in allen Zeiten (auch dem Präsens) **have to**.
Must erscheint nur im Präsens (ganz selten im Präterium: in indirekter Rede).

We **must** go to London today,
but we **needn't** get there before 9 o'clock in the evening.

= Wir **müssen** heute nach London fahren, aber wir **brauchen nicht** (= *müssen nicht*) vor 9 Uhr abends ankommen.
⟶ IV 6

Nicht brauchen oder *nicht müssen* wird im Englischen mit **needn't** (gegenüber *müssen* = **must**) ausgedrückt. Bei der Ersatzform **have to** entsprechen sich positive und verneinte Form direkt: **I have to be on time but I don't have to arrive before 6 o'clock.**
(Ich muß rechtzeitig da sein, aber ich brauche nicht (muß nicht) vor 6 Uhr eintreffen.)

You **mustn't** leave the door open.
We **mustn't** forget our tickets.

Mustn't = *nicht dürfen* drückt ein starkes Verbot oder eine starke Ermahnung aus.

You **ought to** ring up your parents.
You **ought not to** tell her about it.

Ought to drückt eine Verpflichtung aus. ⟶ IV 2

I	'm supposed to	leave by 10.
They	were supposed to	keep their helmets on.
He	's not supposed to	park there.

Am/is/are/was/were + supposed to werden auch verwendet, um Verpflichtungen, Ermahnungen oder Verbote auszudrücken.
⟶ IV 4

Beachte:

a) Modale Hilfsverben haben im Gegensatz zu Hauptverben kein **-s** in der 3. Person Singular (She **can** sing. – She sings.).

b) Modale Hilfsverben bilden Frage und Verneinung *ohne* **do** (**Can** you come? – I **can't**.).

c) Das Hauptverb wird mit Ausnahme von **ought to** immer ohne **to** angeschlossen (She **can sing**. – She **wants to sing**.).

d) In den anderen Zeiten als Präsens oder Präteritum müssen Ersatzformen herangezogen werden.

III.3 Adverbien (Adverbs)

(Zur Satzstellung der Adverbien siehe I.4.)

She sang beautifully , but I could hardly hear anything.
The children quickly crossed the street.
They almost missed the train.
Did they really lose their tickets?

Die Bedeutung eines Verbs kann durch Adverbien in mancherlei Hinsicht modifiziert werden: **beautifully, quickly** sind Adverbien der Art und Weise *(Adverbs of Manner)*, d. h. sie geben an, wie die Handlung ausgeführt wurde oder wie ein Ereignis sich vollzog. **Hardly, almost** geben eine Intensität oder einen Grad an *(Adverbs of Intensity or Degree)*. Wie im Deutschen spielen die Bedeutungen der Adverbien eine Rolle bei der Abwägung, Verstärkung oder Abmilderung einer Bemerkung.

IV. Der Nominalteil

IV.1 Das Nomen oder Substantiv (The Noun)

Formen des nouns:

1.1 Singular- und Pluralformen

Singular	Plural		
	[s]	[z]	[ɪz]
one shirt	2 shirts		
a month	six months		
one dog		two dogs	
one shoe		a pair of shoes	
a sandwich			a few sandwiches
a box			some boxes
one page			ten pages

Der Plural von Substantiven wird in der Regel durch Anhängen von **-s** an die Singularform gebildet.

Nach Zischlauten [s, z, ʃ, ʒ, tʃ, dʒ] wird **-es** (Aussprache [-ɪz]) angefügt (falls der Singular nicht schon auf stummes **-e** endet).

Aussprache: [s] nach stimm*losen* Konsonanten [p, t, k, f, θ]
[z] nach stimm*haften* Konsonanten, wie [b, g, m,...] und Vokalen
[ɪz] nach Zischlauten [s, z, ʃ, ʒ, tʃ, dʒ]

Besonderheiten der Schreibung:

our countr**y**	- most countr**ies**	**-y** nach Konsonant wird zu **-ie**.
my kni**fe**	- our kni**ves**	Substantive auf **-lf, -fe** sowie **thief, loaf** enden
a shel**f**	- two shel**ves**	im Plural auf **-ves** [vz].
a thie**f**	- some thie**ves**	
a potat**o**	- a pound of potat**oes**	Einige Wörter auf **-o** haben die Pluralendung **-es** (nicht jedoch
a her**o**	the her**oes** of the Western	Wörter neueren Ursprungs wie **piano, photo, radio**).

Unregelmäßige Pluralformen:

man	- men	
woman	- women	Einige Substantive haben eine unregelmäßige Pluralform
child	- children	(Pluralbildung durch Umlaut: vgl. *Fuß - Füße*).
mouse	- mice	
foot	- feet	
tooth	- teeth	
a fish	- a lot of fish	Einige wenige Substantive haben die gleiche Form in Singular
a sheep	- a lot of sheep	und Plural.

1.2 s-Genitiv (s-Genitive) und of-Genitiv (of-Genitive)

Der **s**-Genitiv ist die einzige Kasusform des Nomens, die im Englischen noch durch eine Endung markiert ist.
Sie wird in erster Linie verwendet, um *Besitz oder Zugehörigkeit* bei Personen (und manchmal bei Tieren) auszudrücken.

Form:	The	boy's	books	Singular:	' + s
	The	boys'	books	Plural:	'
	The	children's	books	unregelm. Plural:	' + s
		James's [ɪz]	books	bei Vornamen auf -s:	' + s

Die *Aussprache* der **s**- Endung richtet sich nach dem vorangehenden Laut, wie beim Plural der Substantive (vgl. IV. 1.1).
Der **s**-Genitiv kann als Antwort allein, ohne das Bezugswort stehen:

Whose book is this? - It's | my friend's.
| John's.

Beachte:

Der **s**-Genitiv wird auch bei Zeitangaben wie **an hour's walk**, **today's programme** verwendet.

of-Genitiv (**of**-Genitive)

Handelt es sich bei dem Bezugswort nicht um eine Person (**my father's car**) bzw. ein Tier (**my dog's name is Jake**), so wird der **of**-Genitiv verwendet:

London is the capital of Great Britain .

Can you see the number of the bus ?

1.3 Arten des Substantivs (Kinds of Noun)

Bei einigen Gruppen von Substantiven weicht der englische Sprachgebrauch vom deutschen ab:

Substantive, die *nur im Singular* gebraucht werden:

a) Substantive für nicht-zählbare Begriffe *(abstract uncountables):*

News has just come in that the building is on fire.

Can you give me some advice ? (= *einen Rat oder ein paar Ratschläge*)

You can ask for information over there.

Bei solchen Substantiven steht das Verb *im Singular.* Sie haben *keine* Pluralform und können nicht mit dem unbestimmten Artikel **a/an** oder Zahlwörtern verbunden werden.

Substantive, die *nur im Plural* gebraucht werden:

b) Sammelbegriffe wie **clothes** *(Kleidung)* und **goods** *Ware,-n)*

Clothes are quite expensive here.

(Kleidung ist hier ziemlich teuer.)

c) Wörter für Gegenstände, die aus zwei gleichartigen Teilen bestehen *(pair nouns)* wie **trousers, jeans, shorts, glasses, scissors**, u. a. :

Have you got the scissors ? – Yes. **They are** in my bag.

(Hast Du die Schere? – Ja. Sie ist in meiner Tasche.)

Those trousers are nice, aren't they?

(Diese Hose ist hübsch, nicht?)

I need two pairs of glasses .

(Ich brauche zwei Brillen.)

Bei diesen *pair nouns* stehen das Verb und Pronomen, die sich auf sie beziehen, stets *im Plural.* Wenn wir diese Gegenstände zählen, verwenden wir **two** (**three** etc.) **pairs of** . . . ⟶ IV 1, IV 6

d) Wörter für Gruppenbezeichnungen *(group nouns)*

Police have pushed the crowd back.

My family are all tall.

Wörter wie **police** und **family** beziehen sich auf eine Gruppe, die als Vielheit, als Summe von Einzelpersonen aufgefaßt wird. Sie werden daher als Plural gebraucht.
Wenn aber die Familie als Einheit gemeint ist, wird **family** als Singular gebraucht.

⟶ **IV 1**

IV.2 Der Artikel (The Article)

2.1 Der unbestimmte Artikel (The Indefinite Article)

[ə]	[ən]
a man	an old man
a big apple	an apple

Der unbestimmte Artikel lautet im Englischen:

a   vor Konsonanten
an   vor Vokalen (beim Sprechen mit dem folgenden Wort verbunden)

Mr Rice is a mechanic.

I've been waiting for half an hour.
What a pity.
We go to school five days a week.
How much are these apples? – 60 p a pound.

Im Unterschied zum Deutschen steht der unbestimmte Artikel bei *Berufsbezeichnungen*.

Nach **half**, **quite** *(ziemlich)*, **such** und dem Ausruf **what a...** wird der unbestimmte Artikel nachgestellt.

Bei Maß- und Zeitangaben wird der unbestimmte Artikel im Sinne von „pro" gebraucht *(5 x pro Woche, in der Woche; 60 p pro Pfund)*.

2.2 Der bestimmte Artikel (The Definite Article)

Der bestimmte Artikel **the** (Aussprache vor Vokalen [ðɪ]) wird im Englischen weniger häufig gebraucht als im Deutschen.
Er steht vor allem, wenn Personen, Dinge und Sachverhalte näher bestimmt und gegen andere abgegrenzt werden sollen.

a)   Dinner is ready, please.
     Summer can be rather warm in Scotland.

     aber:
     The dinner we had yesterday was really excellent.
     The summer of 1980 was rather cool.

Substantive, die Jahreszeiten, Monate, Wochentage und Mahlzeiten bezeichnen, stehen im allgemeinen *ohne* Artikel.

Nur wenn sie näher bestimmt sind (z. B. durch **of**-*phrase* oder Relativsatz), wird der bestimmte Artikel gesetzt.

b)   We go to school from Monday to Friday.
     School begins at 8 o'clock.
     Are you going to church now?
     She's in hospital at the moment.

     aber:
     The school I go to is a very big building.
     Where is **the church** ? (= the building)

Bei **school**, **church**, **hospital** wird der Artikel nicht verwendet, wenn die Institution gemeint ist (z. B. der Unterricht).

c)   People were blocking the roads.
     Most people were rescued by the firemen.

     Both (the) brothers had disappeared.
     All the money was gone.

People (= *die Leute*) wird stets ohne Artikel gebraucht.
Vor **most** im Sinne von *die meisten* steht ebenfalls kein Artikel.

Bei **both** und **all** (*das ganze...*, *die ganzen* etc.) wird der Artikel nachgestellt. Bei **both** wird er meist weggelassen.

IV.3 Das Adjektiv (The Adjective)

3.1

The Wests have a `new` house. It's `big` and `modern`.

The film was `rather boring`.
An `extremely interesting` book.

Adjektive stehen vor einem Nomen oder nach einer Form von **to be**.

Adjektive können selbst näher bestimmt sein:
- durch Adverbien wie **very, quite, rather, so, too**
- durch abgeleitete Adverbien auf **-ly**.

3.2 Das Adjektiv als Nomen (The Adjective Used as Noun)

a) `The poor` need our help.
The relatives of `the injured` were informed.
`The dead` were buried.
I didn't know `the English` were like that.

Im Englischen kann man Adjektive nur dann wie ein Nomen gebrauchen (mit dem bestimmten Artikel, aber ohne Plural-endung), wenn damit eine Gesamtheit gemeint ist: *die Armen, alle Armen, alle Verletzten/Toten im Unfall*.

In dieser Weise werden auch Nationalitätsadjektive wie **English** und **French** gebraucht.

b) `30 injured people` were taken to hospital. (= 30 Verletzte ...)
They found three dead people. (= 3 Tote)

Wenn eine Gruppe von Einzelnen gemeint ist, muß das Adjektiv mit einem Nomen wie **people, men, women** verbunden werden.

c) Das Adjektiv mit dem Stützwort **one** (Adjective + *prop word* **one**)
This sweater is too expensive. Can I have a cheaper `one`?
Do you want the green apples? - No, the red `ones`.

Damit man ein Nomen nicht wiederholen muß, wird es durch **one** (Singular) bzw. **ones** (Plural) ersetzt.

Das Adjektiv kann nicht wie im Deutschen allein stehen.

3.3 Das Adjektiv nach den Verben feel, look, sound, smell etc.

We `felt` quite `happy`.
He `is looking sad`.
That `sounds interesting`.
That `smells good`.

Nach Verben, die einen Zustand bzw. eine Eigenschaft aus-drücken (und keine Tätigkeit) - **feel, look, sound, smell** -, steht ein Adjektiv (kein Adverb).

3.4 Steigerung der Adjektive (Comparison of Adjectives)

Grundform (Positive)	Komparativ (Comparative)	Superlativ (Superlative)
Bob's room is `small`.	Mike's room is `smaller`.	Tim's room is `smallest`.
Berlin is `big`.	London is `bigger`.	New York is `biggest`.
A cat is `easy` to keep.	A guinea pig is `easier` to keep.	A mouse is `easiest` to keep.
Mike's bike was `expensive`.	Bob's motorbike was `more expensive`.	Mr Hunt's car was `most expensive`.

1-silbige Adjektive sowie 2-silbige auf **-y** (außerdem *clever, simple, narrow*) steigern auf **-er, -est**.

Schreibregeln:

Verdoppelung des Endkonsonanten nach kurzem betonten Vokal.

Wechsel von **-y** zu **-i**.

Alle übrigen Adjektive (die meisten zwei-silbigen und alle mit mehr als 2 Silben) steigern mit **more, most**.

Unregelmäßige Steigerungsformen:

good	better	best
bad	worse	worst
much	more	most
little (= wenig)	less	least
far	further/farther	furthest/farthest

3.5 Vergleiche in Sätzen (Sentences with Comparison)

Wales is	**as**	interesting		**as**	Scotland.
Holiday camps are	cheap **er**			**than**	hotels.
They can be	**more**	exciting		**than**	hotels.
Youth hostels are	**not as**	expensive		**as**	hotels.
(= They are	**less**	expensive		**than**	hotels.)

IV.4 Das Adverb (The Adverb)

4.1 Adverbien dienen, wie ihr Name andeutet, zur näheren Bestimmung von
- Verben **(He listened quietly)**, jedoch auch von
- Adjektiven **(an extremely interesting book)** und anderen Adverbien **(you're rather late)**,
- ja sogar von ganzen Sätzen **(Frankly, I didn't tell anyone.** Siehe I.4, III.3, IV.3.1)

Arten der Adverbien:

Entsprechend ihrer Funktion im Satz kann man unterscheiden:
- Adverbien des Ortes und der Zeit *(Adverbs of Place and Time)* wie **inside, yesterday**
- Häufigkeitsadverbien *(Adverbs of Frequency)* wie **sometimes, often, never**
- Adverbien des Grades *(Adverbs of Degree)*, die verstärken oder abschwächen, wie **rather, quite, very**
- Adverbien der Art und Weise *(Adverbs of Manner)*, die angeben, *wie* etwas geschieht, wie **quietly, nervously, quickly, fast**
- Satzadverbien *(Sentence Adverbials)*, die einen ganzen Satz modifizieren, wie **unfortunately, frankly (Unfortunately he didn't come.).**

(Zur *Stellung* dieser verschiedenen Adverb-Arten im Satz siehe I.4.)

4.2 Form der Adverbien der Art und Weise

a) A **quiet** man: he listened **quietly** .
   A **careful** driver: he drives **carefully** .
   A **happy** boy: he laughed **happily** .

Die meisten Adverbien der Art und Weise werden von Adjektiven abgeleitet, indem man **-ly** anfügt. Dabei wird **-y** nach Konsonant zu **-i**.

b) A **fast** train : the train ran **fast** .
   A **hard** worker : he works **hard** .
   An **early** train : the train arrived **early** .
   A **late** train : the train arrived **late** .

Einige Adverbien der Art und Weise haben die gleiche Form wie das entsprechende Adjektiv: **fast** und **hard** (nicht zu verwechseln mit **hardly** = *kaum*).

c) Das Adverb zu **good** lautet **well**:
   She is **good** at painting: she paints very **well** .

d) Nach **feel, look, smell, sound** steht ein Adjektiv:
   It **looks good** . (Siehe IV.3.3)

4.3 Steigerung der Adverbien (Comparison of Adverbs)

a) They speak more clearly than Americans.
I can understand them most easily .

Adverbien mit der Endung **-ly** steigern mit **more** *(comparative)* und **most** *(superlative)*.

b) He walked faster than I did.
She jumped higher than all the others.
Jack jumped farther than John.

Adverbien mit der gleichen Form wie Adjektive steigern auch wie diese. (Siehe IV. 4.2)

c) *Unregelmäßige Steigerung:*

    well   –   better   –   best
    badly –   worse   –   worst
    early –   earlier –   earliest

(**-ly** ist hier nicht Endung, sondern Teil des Wortes.)

⟶ IV 4

IV.5 Die Pronomen und Mengenangaben (The Pronouns and Quantifiers)

5.1 Die Personalpronomen (The Personal Pronouns)

a)

Subjektform: *(subject case)*	I	you	he	she	it	we	you	they
Objektform: *(object case)*	me	you	him	her	it	us	you	them

Das Personalpronomen hat im Englischen nur 2 Formen: eine Subjektform *(subject case)* und eine Objektform *(object case)*.

b) He likes her very much.
He gave her a nice present.

Daher vertritt die Objektform sowohl das *direkte* Objekt (er mag *sie*) wie das *indirekte* (er machte *ihr* ein Geschenk).

c) Zur Stellung der Personalpronomen als Objekte im Satz siehe I.1.

5.2 Die Possessivpronomen (The Possessive Pronouns)

I must repair my bike.
Can you repair your bike?
He cleans his car once a week.
She likes her pet.
It is a hamster and its name is Jerry.
We must do our homework.
Have you done your homework, Tom and Peter?
They're proud of their skates.

a) Tim broke his leg.
(Tim hat sich *den* Fuß gebrochen.)
He lifted his arm. (... *den* Arm)
Please, take your cap off. (*die* Mütze)

Die Possessivpronomen werden im Englischen häufiger verwendet:
Sie stehen bei Körperteilen und Kleidungsstücken, wo wir im Deutschen den Artikel verwenden.

b) I've got `my own` room.
    Have you got a room `of your own` ?

Die Possessivpronomen können durch **own** verstärkt werden. (**own** kann nicht unmittelbar nach dem Artikel stehen: vgl. *ein* eigenes Zimmer).

c) My birthday is on the 27th.
    And when is `yours` ?
         Oh, `mine` is next Sunday.
    Formen: **mine, yours, his, hers,**
            ours, yours, theirs
    She's an old friend `of mine` .

Die substantivisch gebrauchten Possessivpronomen beziehen sich auf ein vorhergenanntes Nomen.
Sie unterscheiden sich in der Form von den adjektivisch gebrauchten Possessivpronomen (mit Ausnahme von **his**).

Wir gebrauchen die substantivischen Possessivpronomen auch in einer nachgestellten **of**-Fügung, besonders wenn wir über Freunde u. ä. sprechen. ⟶ **IV 2**

5.3 Die Pronomen mit self/-selves (The self-pronouns)

Die Formen dieser **self**-*pronouns* sind:

myself, yourself, himself, herself, itself, ourselves, yourselves, themselves.

Sie werden in zwei Funktionen verwendet:

a) zur Hervorhebung und Betonung *(Intensifiers)*
    Mr West washes his car `himself` .
    (Er   wäscht sein Auto selbst.)

    We did   it `ourselves` .
    (Wir haben es   selber gemacht.)

b) als Reflexivpronomen *(Reflexive Pronouns)*:
    May I introduce `myself` ?
    (Darf ich   mich   vorstellen?)

    The pupils wrote about `themselves` .
    Sie schrieben über   sich.)

Die **self**-Pronomen werden reflexiv gebraucht, wenn sich die Aussage eines Satzes auf das Subjekt zurückbezieht.

In the morning I wash, brush my teeth and dress..
(ich wasche *mich*, ..., ziehe *mich* an ...)

Im Englischen gebraucht man die Reflexivpronomen sparsamer als im Deutschen. Wenn klar ist, daß sich das Verb auf das Subjekt zurückbezieht, steht kein Reflexivpronomen.

I can't **remember** his name.
(= ich kann *mich* nicht ... erinnern)
We **met** at the youth club.
(= wir trafen *uns* ...)

Häufige Fälle, in denen das Englische im Unterschied zum Deutschen *kein* Reflexivpronomen verwendet, sind vor allem **remember** und **meet**.

5.4 Die reziproken Pronomen each other/one another (The Reciprocal Pronouns)

Alan and David helped each other.
one another.

(Alan und David halfen sich (gegenseitig).
einander.)

Die Pronomen **each other** und **one another** drücken eine wechselseitige (reziproke) Beziehung zwischen Personen aus.
Die beiden Pronomen sind austauschbar.

Beachte:

The two girls are looking at themselves.

(Die beiden Mädchen schauen sich an.)

(= jede sich selbst)

The two girls are looking at each other.
one another.

(Die beiden Mädchen schauen sich an.)

(= einander!)

(= reflexiv)

(= reziprok)

5.5 Die Demonstrativpronomen (The Demonstrative Pronouns)

this book (here)   that book (there)
these books (here)   those books (there)

Which book do you want?
This one or that one?

What's this ?
that ? It's my new dictionary.

Do you know that man over there?
When did that happen?

This/that (Singular) und **these/those** (Plural) weisen auf Personen und Gegenstände hin.

This und **that** werden verwendet, um einen Gegensatz oder eine Auswahl anzuzeigen.

Bei räumlicher und zeitlicher Nähe werden **this (these)** oder **that (those)** gebraucht.

Bei räumlicher oder zeitlicher Entfernung vom Sprecher werden nur **that/those** gebraucht.

5.6 Die Relativpronomen (The Relative Pronouns)

Die Relativpronomen (**who/that** für Personen; **which/that** für Gegenstände und Sachverhalte; **whose** für Personen und Sachen) leiten wie im Deutschen Relativsätze ein (siehe II.3).

5.7 Das Pronomen one (The Pronoun one)

a) Das Pronomen **one** nach Adjektiven:
   Do you want a big tin or just a small one ?
   What about these red apples?
   No, I'd rather have those green ones .

Um den Namen eines Gegenstands oder einer Person nicht wiederholen zu müssen, gebraucht man nach Adjektiven **one**, im Plural **ones**. (Siehe IV.3.2c)

b) Which (one) do you want, this one or that one ?
   I think I'll take this one .

One wird oft auch nach dem Fragewort **which** und nach Demonstrativpronomen verwendet.

5.8 Some, any und ihre Zusammensetzungen (Some, Any and Their Compounds)

a) We need `some` sugar and `some` oranges for the fruit salad.

Some und **any** stehen vor zählbaren Begriffen (wie **oranges**) und nicht-zählbaren Begriffen (wie **sugar**), um eine nicht genau bestimmte Menge anzuzeigen.
Some steht in bejahten Aussagesätzen (a).

b) We haven't got `any` oranges.
Is there `any` sugar left?

Any steht in verneinten Sätzen und Fragen (b).

c) Can I have `some` more tea, please?
Certainly. Would you also like `some` biscuits?
No, thank you, I don't want `any` now.

Some wird auch in Sätzen verwendet, die der *Form* nach Fragen sind, bei denen es sich aber eigentlich um (höfliche) Bitten bzw. Angebote handelt.
Der Sprecher geht davon aus, daß das Angesprochene vorhanden ist.

d) There's `somebody` on the telephone for you.
I don't know `anybody` I could ask.
We need `something` (cold) to drink.
Is there `anything` left in the fridge?

Some und **any** stehen vor einem Substantiv bzw. sie beziehen sich auf ein vorhergenanntes. Sonst werden die zusammengesetzten Formen verwendet:

- **Somebody/anybody**, wenn wir von Personen sprechen (= **someone/anyone**)
- **Something/anything**, wenn wir von Gegenständen oder Sachverhalten sprechen.

Der Gebrauch der **some**- bzw. **any**-Formen entspricht dem unter *a – c* Gesagten.

5.9 No und seine Zusammensetzungen (No and its Compounds)

a) There's `no` money left. (= There isn't any money left.)
There are `no` eggs in the fridge. (= There aren't any eggs . . .)

No entspricht **not . . . any**. Es gibt der Äußerung stärkeren Nachdruck; daher sind die **not . . . any**-Formen üblicher.

b) There's `nobody` `(no one)` in the office.
We can do `nothing` . (= we can't do anything).

Nobody/no one beziehen sich auf Personen (= *niemand, keiner*).
Nothing (= **not . . . anything**) bezieht sich auf Gegenstände (= *nichts*).

5.10 Every und seine Zusammensetzungen; each

a) We go on an outing `every` term.
`Each` class can decide on where to go.
`Each` of us will need a ticket.

b) Is `everybody` `(everyone)` ready to start?
I think we've got `everything` now.

Dem deutschen *jeder* entsprechen im Englischen **every** oder **each**. **Every** bedeutet „praktisch alle", „jeder ohne Ausnahme".
Each bezeichnet mehr jeden einzelnen. **Each** *muß* stehen, wenn eine *of-phrase* folgt.
Everybody (= **everyone**) für Personen und **everything** für Sachen werden nur substantivisch gebraucht.
Everything darf in dieser Position *nicht* durch **all** ersetzt werden (deutsch: wir haben *alles*; englisch: **we've got everything**).

5.11 Much/many/a lot of/plenty of

How `much` money have you got? –
I'm afraid I haven't got very `much`.

How `many` tomatoes do we need? –
I don't think we need very `many`.

We'll need `a lot of` bread.
We'll need `plenty of` bread.
We've got `plenty of` tomatoes.
We've got `a lot of` tomatoes.

Much/many werden vor allem in Fragen und verneinten Sätzen verwendet, und zwar: **much** bei Substantiven, die nicht zählbar sind *(mass nouns)*;

many bei Substantiven, die zählbar sind und im Plural stehen *(count nouns, plural)*.

A lot of und **plenty of** werden vor allem in bejahten Sätzen verwendet, und zwar vor zählbaren und nicht-zählbaren Begriffen. Im gesprochenen Englisch heißt es auch **lots of**.

5.12 A little/a few

Do you take milk in your tea? –
Just `a little`. *(Nur ein bißchen.)*

We've only got `a few` bottles of Coke.
(Wir haben nur ein paar Flaschen Cola.)

I have `n't` got `much` time.
(Ich habe wenig Zeit.)

A little wird bei Substantiven verwendet, die nicht zählbar sind *(mass nouns)*. Es steht sehr oft zusammen mit **just** oder **only**.

A few wird bei Substantiven verwendet, die zählbar sind und im Plural stehen.

Um eine geringe Anzahl oder Menge auszudrücken, verwendet man jedoch üblicherweise **not many** bzw. **not much**.

VOCABULARY

Im Fettdruck erscheinen alle in diesem Band neu eingeführten Wörter und Wendungen, die die Schüler aktiv beherrschen sollen.
Im Magerdruck erscheinen Wörter und Wendungen, die
a) hier nur erläutert werden (die Schüler brauchen sie nicht aktiv zu beherrschen);
b) zum Zusatzlernangebot gehören (mit EXTRA bezeichnete Teile);
c) den Zusammenhang zeigen, in dem ein anderes Wort gebraucht wird.
Die neuen Wörter der Geschichte „The Glove" in Unit 9 sind in diesem Vocabulary nicht angegeben.
BE = British English
AE = American English
n. = noun
v. = verb
adj. = adjective
adv. = adverb
sing. = singular
pl. = plural

UNIT 1 FIRE!

fire ['faɪə] — Feuer
skyscraper ['skaɪˌskreɪpə] — Wolkenkratzer
Chicago [ʃɪ'kɑːgəʊ]
downtown (AE) ['daʊn'taʊn] — in die (der) Innenstadt
in downtown Chicago — in der Innenstadt von Chicago

"Here is the News"
here is the news — *hier:* Wir bringen Nachrichten/Sie hören Nachrichten

Listening (page 2)
radio report — Radioreportage, Bericht
get (got, got) — *hier:* verstehen, herausbekommen
the main [meɪn] — der, die, das wichtigste
fact [fækt] — Tatsache, Punkt
notes [nəʊts] — Notizen
separate ['seprət] — extra, gesondert
a sheet of paper [ʃiːt] — ein Blatt Papier

Did you get it? (page 2)
First Report
1 **be on fire** — brennen, in Brand sein
if — *hier:* ob
2 **situation** [ˌsɪtjʊ'eɪʃn] — Situation
worse [wɜːs] — schlechter, verschlechtert

spread (spread, spread) [spred, spred, spred] — sich ausbreiten
helicopter ['helɪkɒptə] — Hubschrauber
fireman ['faɪəmən] — Feuerwehrmann
properly ['prɒpəlɪ] — richtig, gründlich
fire truck (AE) [trʌk], fire engine (BE) ['endʒɪn] — Feuerwehrauto
get to — *hier:* hinkommen, erreichen
3 cause (v.) [kɔːz] — verursachen

Second Report
information [ˌɪnfə'meɪʃn] — Information
rescue (v.) ['reskjuː] — retten
trapped [træpt] — *hier:* eingeschlossen
plan (v.) (to do) [plæn] — planen, vorhaben (zu tun)
neighboring (AE), neighbouring (BE) ['neɪbərɪŋ] — benachbart

Third Report
on the next day — am darauffolgenden Tag
helicopter ['helɪkɒptə] — Hubschrauber
complete [kəm'pliːt] — vervollständigen
summary ['sʌmərɪ] — Zusammenfassung
roof [ruːf] — Dach
seriously (injured) ['sɪərɪəslɪ] — schwer (verletzt)
according to [ə'kɔːdɪŋ] — wie... sagte, ...zufolge
according to (the news) — wie (in den Nachrichten) gemeldet
under control [kən'trəʊl] — unter Kontrolle

Using the language (page 3)
someone = somebody ['sʌmwʌn] — jemand
like this — so, wie folgt, folgendermaßen
most people — die meisten Leute

Reading (page 4)
extracts (from) ['ekstrækts] — Auszüge (aus)
1 *the Victory Building* ['vɪktərɪ]
in downtown Chicago — in der Innenstadt von Chicago
out of control — außer Kontrolle
spread (spread, spread) [spred, spred, spred] — sich ausbreiten
office worker ['wɜːkə] — Büroangestellter
leave work — *hier:* das Büro verlassen, nach Hause gehen
news has just come in — *hier:* soeben erhalten wir die Nachricht
fire chief [tʃiːf] — Feuerwehrhauptmann
Amos Dixon ['eɪməs 'dɪksn]
request (help) [rɪ'kwest] — (Hilfe) erbitten
break out (broke, broken) — ausbrechen
the fire broke out — das Feuer brach aus
fire truck (AE) [trʌk] — Feuerwehrauto
burn (burnt, burnt) [bɜːn, bɜːnt, bɜːnt] — (ab)brennen
burning ['bɜːnɪŋ] — in Flammen stehend
2 down here — hier unten
fight (fought, fought) [faɪt, fɔːt, fɔːt] — (be)kämpfen
high [haɪ] — hoch
high wind(s) — Windbö, Sturmbö

because of	wegen	flame [fleɪm]	Flamme	4 ... **before** (*nachgestellt*)	vorher
serious [ˈsɪərɪəs]	ernst(zunehmen), gefährlich	**seriously injured** dead [ded]	schwer verletzt *hier*: die Toten	**put out** **put out the fire**	ausmachen das Feuer löschen
a hard job	*hier*: ein schweres Stück Arbeit	the number of dead **as**	die Zahl der Toten weil, da	**rest** (n.) [rest] **scene** [siːn]	Pause Schauplatz, Ort des Geschehens
everyone [ˈevrɪwʌn] = everybody	jedermann	could be as high as 50 fire fighter [ˈfaɪə ˈfaɪtə]	könnte bei 50 liegen Feuerwehrmann	**explode** [ɪkˈspləʊd]	explodieren
urgent [ˈɜːdʒənt]	dringend	push [pʊʃ]	schieben	**rush** (v.) [rʌʃ]	*hier*: rasen
message [ˈmesɪdʒ]	Meldung, Nachricht	push back	*hier*: zurückdrängen	**Using the language (page 8)**	
urgent message	dringende Durchsage	scene [siːn] collapse [kəˈlæps]	Schauplatz einstürzen, zusammenbrechen	1 **sentence** [ˈsentəns]	Satz
repeat [rɪˈpiːt]	wiederholen	press conference	Pressekonferenz	2 **luckily** [ˈlʌkɪlɪ]	glücklicherweise, zum Glück
enter [ˈentə] **central** [ˈsentrəl]	betreten zentral; -zentrum	[pres ˈkɒnfərəns] mayor [ˈmeə]	Bürgermeister	(**un**)**fortunately** [ʌnˈfɔːtʃnətlɪ]	(un)glücklicherweise
district [ˈdɪstrɪkt] central district	Bezirk Innenstadtbereich	**hold** (**held, held**) [həʊld, held, held]	(ab)halten	**By the way (page 9)**	
stand-still [ˈstændstɪl] come to a stand-still	Stillstand zum Stillstand kommen	*Maple Grand Hotel* [ˈmeɪpl ɡrænd həʊˈtel] **president** [ˈprezɪdənt]	Präsident	**tape** [teɪp] *Spain* [speɪn] *Manchester United*	Tonband Spanien
3 **story** (AE) (*pl.*: stories), **storey** (BE) (*pl.*: storeys) [ˈstɔːrɪ]	Etage, Stockwerk	fire department (AE) [dɪˈpɑːtmənt] fire brigade (BE) [brɪˈɡeɪd]	Feuerwehr	[ˈmæntʃɪstə juːˈnaɪtɪd] refer to [rɪˈfɜː]	sich beziehen auf
fully computerized [ˈfʊlɪ kəmˈpjuːtəraɪzd]	voll durch Computer gesteuert	**Looking at the language (page 5)**		**Extra: Some Facts about Chicago (page 9)**	
system [ˈsɪstəm]	System	following [ˈfɒləʊɪŋ]	folgend(e, er, es)	1 *Chicago* industrial centre	Industriezentrum
immediate [ɪˈmiːdjət] **warning** [ˈwɔːnɪŋ]	sofort, umgehend Warnung	heading [ˈhedɪŋ]	Kategorie, Rubrik, Obertitel	[ɪnˈdʌstrɪəl] **port** [pɔːt]	Hafen
automatically [ˌɔːtəˈmætɪkəlɪ]	automatisch	compare [ˈkɒmpeə] statement [ˈsteɪtmənt]	vergleichen Aussage, Feststellung	inland port [ˈɪnlənd] bank [bæŋk]	Binnenhafen *hier*: Ufer des Sees
go wrong	schiefgehen, nicht klappen	make a statement	eine Erklärung abgeben	*Lake Michigan* [leɪk ˈmɪʃɪɡən]	
4 **the worst** [wɜːst]	der, die, das schlimmste	**immediately** [ɪˈmiːdjətlɪ] Chicago Fire Dept.	sofort, auf der Stelle = Chicago Fire	total [ˈtəʊtl] population [ˌpɒpjʊˈleɪʃn]	gesamt, Gesamt- Bevölkerung
U.S. (= The United States) [juːˈes]	die Vereinigten Staaten	**smoke** (n.) [sməʊk]	Department Rauch	million [ˈmɪljən] a third of [θɜːd]	Million ein Drittel von
history [ˈhɪstərɪ] **member** [ˈmembə] **staff** [stɑːf]	Geschichte Mitglied Personal, Belegschaft	**inform** [ɪnˈfɔːm] **event** [ɪˈvent] **result** [rɪˈzʌlt]	informieren Ereignis Ergebnis, Resultat	associate [əˈsəʊʃɪeɪt]	verbinden, in Zusammenhang bringen
cleaning staff	„Putzkolonne", Gebäudereinigung	**official** [əˈfɪʃl]	offiziell; *hier*: öffentlich	**underworld** [ˈʌndəwɜːld] violence [ˈvaɪələns]	Unterwelt Gewalt(tätigkeit)
trap [træp]	(in einer Falle) fangen, einschliessen	official statement	öffentliche Erklärung	world [wɜːld] in the world	Erde, Welt auf der Welt
trapped	eingeschlossen	**Focus on Grammar (page 6)**		a great deal of [diːl] destroy [dɪˈstrɔɪ]	ein großer Teil zerstören
cause (n.) [kɔːz] **failure** [ˈfeɪljə]	Ursache, Grund Versagen, Störung, Ausfall	notice (v.) [ˈnəʊtɪs]	bemerken	2 *Munich* [ˈmjuːnɪk] war [wɔː]	Krieg
alarm system [əˈlɑːm]	Alarmanlage, Alarmsystem	**Can you do it? (page 6)**		museum [mjuːˈzɪəm]	Museum
huge [hjuːdʒ]	riesig	1 you go on	du bist an der Reihe	**Focus on grammar (page 10)**	
neighboring building (AE)	Nachbargebäude	**badly hurt** burn, burned, burned	schwer verletzt (ver)brennen	question word	Fragewort
sightseer [ˈsaɪtsɪə] **prevent** [prɪˈvent]	*hier*: Schaulustige(r) (ver)hindern	(AE) **burn (burnt, burnt) (BE)**		1 listening text compare [kɒmˈpeə]	Hörtext vergleichen
use (n.) [juːs] the use of	Gebrauch, Einsatz den Einsatz von	passenger [ˈpæsɪndʒə] aeroplane [ˈeərəpleɪn]	Passagier, Fahrgast Flugzeug	in writing whom [huːm]	in der Schriftsprache wen
evacuate [ɪˈvækjʊeɪt]	evakuieren, (von Bewohnern) räumen	2 **imagine** [ɪˈmædʒɪn] **slightly injured** [ˈslaɪtlɪ]	sich (etwas) vorstellen leicht verletzt	2 statement	Aussage, Feststellung
mind (n.) [maɪnd] the question in everybody's mind is	Sinn, Bewußtsein jeder stellt sich die Frage	3 the injured ambulance [ˈæmbjʊləns]	die Verletzten Krankenwagen	**Focus on grammar (page 11)**	
5 **last night**	gestern abend	bury [ˈberɪ] inform [ɪnˈfɔːm]	beerdigen, begraben informieren	1 **whose** [huːz] possession [pəˈzeʃn]	dessen, deren Besitz
roof [ruːf] **despite** [dɪˈspaɪt]	Dach trotz	example [ɪɡˈzɑːmpl]	Beispiel	2 afterwards [ˈɑːftəwədz]	anschließend, danach

Can you do it? (page 12)

1. sentence — Satz
   die (v.) [daɪ] — sterben
2. rewrite [ˌriːˈraɪt] — noch einmal schreiben
   bold print [bəʊld prɪnt] — Fettdruck
   become (became, become) [bɪˈkʌm, bɪˈkeɪm, bɪˈkʌm] — werden
   send for someone — jemanden holen lassen
   badly damaged — stark beschädigt, stark zerstört
   rescue from the smoke — aus dem Rauch retten (holen)

Looking at the language (page 12)

note (on something) — Bemerkung, Anmerkung
difference [ˈdɪfrəns] — Unterschied
expression [ɪkˈspreʃn] — Ausdruck
spell (spelt, spelt) [spel, spelt, spelt] — buchstabieren
spelling [ˈspelɪŋ] — das Buchstabieren
pronounce [prəˈnaʊns] — aussprechen
pronunciation [prəˌnʌnsɪˈeɪʃn] — Aussprache
look up — nachschlagen
torch [tɔːtʃ] — Taschenlampe
address [əˈdres] — Adresse
either [ˈaɪðə] — entweder

Extra: Inferno Girl Plans Wedding (page 13)

inferno [ɪnˈfɜːnəʊ] — Hölle
plan (v.) [plæn] — planen, vorhaben
wedding [ˈwedɪŋ] — Heirat
The World Tribune [wɜːld ˈtrɪbjuːn]
Trib = Tribune
exclusive [ɪkˈskluːsɪv] — exklusiv, Sonder-, Extra-
Sandra Casey [ˈsændrə ˈkeɪsɪ]
Peter O'Shaugnessy [ˈpiːtə əʊˈʃɔːnɪsɪ]
Victory Tower [ˈvɪktərɪ ˈtaʊə]
marry [ˈmærɪ] — heiraten
boss [bɒs] — Chef
Gregory Jones [ˈgregərɪ dʒəʊnz]
courage [ˈkʌrɪdʒ] — Mut
Bartholomew [bɑːˈθɒləmjuː]
stroke (v.) [strəʊk] — streicheln
dream (dreamed, dreamed) (AE), dream (dreamt, dreamt) (BE) [driːm, dremt, dremt] — träumen
notice (v.) [ˈnəʊtɪs] — bemerken
we are … serious about each other — wir meinen es ernst mit einander
Victory and Mutual [ˈmjuːtʃʊəl] — (Name einer Versicherungsgesellschaft)
dollar [ˈdɒlə] — Dollar
cleaning woman — Putzfrau

Meryl Johnson [ˈmerɪl ˈdʒɒnsn]
drop [drɒp] — fallen lassen
cigarette [ˌsɪgəˈret] — Zigarette
waste basket (AE) [weɪst ˈbɑːskɪt] — Papierkorb
wastepaper basket (BE) [ˌweɪstˈpeɪpəˌbɑːskɪt]
set (set, set) [set] — setzen
set fire to something — etwas in Brand setzen
race (v.) [reɪs] — rasen
somehow [ˈsʌmhaʊ] — irgendwie
brave [breɪv] — tapfer
proud (of) [praʊd] — stolz (auf)
real proud of (umgangssprachlich für: really proud of) — wirklich sehr stolz auf
rescue (n.) [ˈreskjuː] — Rettung
reach [riːtʃ] — erreichen
search something for [sɜːtʃ] — etwas durchsuchen nach
do a great job — gute Arbeit leisten, Großartiges leisten
get the facts right/wrong — richtige/falsche Angaben machen
account [əˈkaʊnt] — *hier:* Bericht
phrase [freɪz] — (Rede)wendung, Ausdruck

Using the language (page 14)

imagine [ɪˈmædʒɪn] — sich etwas vorstellen

UNIT 2 BREAKING UP

break up (broke, broken) — auseinanderbrechen, -gehen

Sally's Diary

Sally [ˈsælɪ]

Reading (page 15)

1. *Roger* [ˈrɒdʒə]
   along [əˈlɒŋ] — entlang
   Yorkshire [ˈjɔːkʃə]
   Tillot's [ˈtɪləts]
   sheep (pl.: sheep) [ʃiːp, ʃiːp] — Schaf, Schafe
   lamb [læm] — Lamm
   look forward to [ˈfɔːwəd] — sich freuen auf
   love (v.) [lʌv] — lieben
   for five months — seit fünf Monaten
   get + adj. — werden
   moody [ˈmuːdɪ] — trübsinnig
   get moody — traurig, trübsinnig werden, schlechte Laune bekommen
   cheer up [ˈtʃɪərʌp] — aufheitern, in gute Laune versetzen
   perfectly [ˈpɜːfɪktlɪ] — völlig, vollkommen

   suited to each other [ˈsuːtɪd] — zueinander passend
2. a bit [əˈbɪt] — ein wenig, ein bißchen
   usual [ˈjuːʒʊəl] — gewöhnlich, normalerweise
   shout at someone [ʃaʊt] — jemanden anschreien
   it's not like him — es sieht ihm nicht ähnlich
   before (nachgestellt) — vorher, früher
   anyway [ˈenɪweɪ] — egal, wie dem auch sei
   Freaks [friːks]
   cheer up — bessere Laune bekommen
   later on — später
   still [stɪl] — *hier:* jedoch, trotzdem
   friendship [ˈfrendʃɪp] — Freundschaft
   autumn [ˈɔːtəm] — Herbst
   since [sɪns] — seit
   such [sʌtʃ] — solch, so
3. *Liz Forman* [lɪz ˈfɔːmən]
   go past — vorbeigehen, -fahren
   café [ˈkæfeɪ] — Café
   go mad [mæd] — verrückt werden
   a friend of mine — ein Freund von mir
   it's no use worrying — es hat keinen Sinn, sich Sorgen zu machen
   all evening — den ganzen Abend
   stupid [ˈstjuːpɪd] — blöd, dumm
   smile (n.) [smaɪl] — Lächeln
4. *Grandma* [ˈgrænmɑː] = Grandmother — Großmutter
   stairs (pl.) [steəz] — Treppe
   ring someone up (rang, rung) [rɪŋ, ræŋ, rʌŋ] — jemanden anrufen
   childish [ˈtʃaɪldɪʃ] — kindisch
   you've got a cheek [tʃiːk] — du bist unverschämt, frech
   put the phone down — den Hörer auflegen
   spit (spat, spat) [spɪt, spæt, spæt] — spucken
5. not … after all — *hier:* doch nicht
   miserable [ˈmɪzərəbl] — unglücklich
   Joan [dʒəʊn]
   not … any more — nicht mehr
   study [ˈstʌdɪ] — *hier:* lernen
   he's got to study — er muß lernen
   quite a long time — eine ganz schön lange Zeit
   get bored — sich langweilen
   though (nachgestellt) [ðəʊ] — allerdings, in der Tat
   be in love with someone — in jemanden verliebt sein
   I'm in love with him — ich liebe ihn
   he's still fond of me [fɒnd] — er mag mich noch immer
   wait and see — mal abwarten
   it's not worth … ing [wɜːθ] — es lohnt sich nicht
   even — *hier:* sogar
   you ought to forget it [ɔːt] — du solltest es vergessen

1 relationship [rɪˈleɪʃnʃɪp]   Verhältnis, Beziehung
   develop [dɪˈveləp]   entwickeln
2 behaviour [bɪˈheɪvjə]   Verhalten, Benehmen
   I have no idea   mir fällt nichts ein
   I don't really care [keə]   mir ist es eigentlich egal

Did you get it? (page 18)
summary [ˈsʌmərɪ]   Zusammenfassung
complete [kəmˈpliːt]   vervollständigen
by   an, entlang
time   *hier:* Mal
for the first time   zum erstenmal

Can you do it? (page 18)
2 ask for   fragen nach, bitten um
3 don't worry   mach dir keine Gedanken

Looking at the language (page 19)
expression [ɪkˈspreʃn]   Ausdruck
structure [ˈstrʌktʃə]   Struktur
niece [niːs]   Nichte
nephew [ˈnevjuː]   Neffe

Can you do it? (page 19)
2 correct (adj.) [kəˈrekt]   korrekt, richtig

Focus on grammar (page 20)
1 since   seit
   for   seit
   end   enden, zu Ende gehen
   be careful   Vorsicht! Sei vorsichtig!
2 a period of time [ˈpɪərɪəd]   (Zeit-)spanne, Periode
   a point of time [pɔɪnt]   (Zeit-)punkt
   certain   bestimmt, gewiß

Can you do it? (page 21)
1 Christmas [ˈkrɪsməs]   Weihnachten
2 partner [ˈpɑːtnə]   Partner

Using the language (page 21)
2 make up a dialogue [ˈdaɪəlɒg]   einen Dialog erfinden
   member   Mitglied
   certain [ˈsɜːtn]   bestimmt, gewiß

Giving Advice
advice [ədˈvaɪs]   Rat(-schlag), Tip

Looking at the language (page 22)
you ought to [ˈɔːtʊ]   du solltest
it's no use …ing [juːs]   es hat keinen Sinn
it's not worth …ing [wɜːθ]   es lohnt sich nicht

By the way (page 22)
You ought not to   du solltest nicht

Can you do it? (page 22)
2 continue [kənˈtɪnjuː]   weitermachen

Using the language (page 23)
2 act out [ækt]   als Szene spielen, etwas darstellen
   someone else [els]   jemand anders
   nasty [ˈnɑːstɪ]   gehässig, ungezogen

An Argument
Looking at the language (page 24)
conversation [ˌkɒnvəˈseɪʃn]   Unterhaltung, Gespräch
cause (v.) [kɔːz]   verursachen
at least [ətˈliːst]   mindestens
write down   auf-, hinschreiben
over [ˈəʊvə]   über, mehr als
oh, goodness [ˈgʊdnɪs]   ach du meine Güte
completely [kəmˈpliːtlɪ]   völlig, ganz und gar
date [deɪt]   *hier:* Verabredung
I'll come over   ich komme vorbei
all afternoon   den ganzen Nachmittag
Oh, stop it!   Hör bloß auf!
I suppose [səˈpəʊz]   vermutlich
be in trouble   in Schwierigkeiten sein
selfish [ˈselfɪʃ]   selbst-, eigensüchtig
that's a joke, that is [dʒəʊk]   das soll wohl ein Witz sein
instead [ɪnˈsted]   statt dessen

Listening (page 24)
tape   Tonband
this time   dieses Mal, diesmal
avoid [əˈvɔɪd]   (ver)meiden

Focus on grammar (page 25)
action [ˈækʃn]   Handlung, Aktion

Can you do it? (page 26)
2 phrase [freɪz]   Rede(wendung)

Using the language (page 26)
2 dialogue   Dialog
   tense [tens]   Zeit
   bracket [ˈbrækɪt]   Klammer
   in brackets   in Klammern
   suitable [ˈsuːtəbl]   passend
   Jean [dʒiːn]
   as a matter of fact [fækt]   tatsächlich, in der Tat, um ehrlich zu sein

Avoiding Confrontations
avoid [əˈvɔɪd]   vermeiden
confrontation [ˌkɒnfrʌnˈteɪʃn]   Konfrontation; *hier:* Streit, Auseinandersetzung

Listening (page 27)
develop into [dɪˈveləp]   sich zu etwas entwickeln
provoking [prəˈvəʊkɪŋ]   verletzend

remark (n.) [rɪˈmɑːk]   Bemerkung
suggest [səˈdʒest]   vorschlagen
reaction [rɪˈækʃn]   Reaktion

Using the language (page 27)
chart [tʃɑːt]   Tabelle, Übersicht
below [bɪˈləʊ]   darunter, *hier:* unten
arrange [əˈreɪndʒ]   sich verabreden, ausmachen
roller skates [ˈrəʊlə skeɪts]   Rollschuhe
accuse someone [əˈkjuːz]   jemanden beschuldigen, anklagen
deny [dɪˈnaɪ]   abstreiten, verneinen
admit [ədˈmɪt]   zugeben
explain [ɪkˈspleɪn]   erklären
refuse [rɪˈfjuːz]   ablehnen, sich weigern
nonsense [ˈnɒnsəns]   Unsinn, Blödsinn
forgive (forgave, forgiven) [fəˈgɪv, fəˈgeɪv, fəˈgɪvn]   verzeihen
smoke (v.) [sməʊk]   rauchen
spill (spilt, spilt) [spɪl, spɪlt, spɪlt]   verschütten, auskippen
beer [bɪə]   Bier

How Will it End?
end (v.)   enden

Using the language (page 29)
Frank [fræŋk]
sweet [swiːt]   süß, niedlich
look forward to [ˈfɔːwəd]   sich freuen auf
by the way   übrigens
Jennifer [ˈdʒenɪfə]
Sonya [ˈsɒnjə]
Sarah [ˈseərə]
dance [dɑːns]   tanzen
I wonder [ˈwʌndə]   ich frage mich, ich wüßte gern
ending   Schluß

UNIT 3
IT'S WORTH VISITING WALES
it's worth   es lohnt sich
Wales [weɪlz]

The Holiday of a Lifetime
think of …ing   daran denken, etwas zu tun
brochure [ˈbrəʊʃə]   Broschüre, Prospekt
holiday camp   Ferienlager

Reading (page 30)
lifetime [ˈlaɪftaɪm]   Leben
Camp Cymraig [ˈkʌmraɪg]
adventure [ədˈventʃə]   Abenteuer
attract [əˈtrækt]   anziehen, anlocken
guest [gest]   Gast, Besucher

at least [ətˈliːst]	mindestens
offer (v.) [ˈɒfə]	anbieten
attractive [əˈtræktɪv]	attraktiv, ansprechend
train [treɪn]	ausbilden
fully trained	hervorragend ausgebildet
staff [stɑːf]	Personal
a variety of [vəˈraɪətɪ]	eine Vielfalt von
social [ˈsəʊʃl]	gesellig
opportunity [ˌɒpəˈtjuːnətɪ]	Möglichkeit, Gelegenheit
England [ˈɪŋglənd]	
Ireland [ˈaɪələnd]	
Scotland [ˈskɒtlənd]	
magnificent [mægˈnɪfɪsnt]	großartig
mountain [ˈmaʊntɪn]	Berg
unique [juːˈniːk]	einzigartig
money-back guarantee [ˈmʌnɪbæk gærənˈtiː]	garantierte Geldrückerstattung
satisfied (with) [ˈsætɪsfaɪd]	zufrieden (mit)
include [ɪnˈkluːd]	einschließen, beinhalten
canoeing [kəˈnuːɪŋ]	Kanufahren
sailing [ˈseɪlɪŋ]	Segeln
water skiing [ˈskiːɪŋ]	Wasserski fahren
rock climbing [ˈklaɪmɪŋ]	Bergsteigen
caving [ˈkeɪvɪŋ]	Höhlenwandern
mountain walking	Bergwandern
pony trekking [ˈpəʊnɪ ˈtrekɪŋ]	Ponyreiten
wind surfing [ˈsɜːfɪŋ]	Windsurfen
Penscynor Bird Gardens [pensˈkʌnɔːr]	
historic [hɪˈstɒrɪk]	historisch
Pembroke [ˈpembrʊk]	
Caerphilly [kɑːˈfɪlɪ]	
Gower [ˈgaʊə]	
Brecon Beacons [ˈbrekən ˈbiːkənz]	
national [ˈnæʃənl]	national
Dan-yr-Ogof [ˈdænər ˈɒgɒv]	
be tired of something [ˈtaɪəd]	einer Sache überdrüssig sein
be tired of ...ing	satt haben, etwas zu tun
sightseeing [ˈsaɪtsiːɪŋ]	Besichtigung von Sehenswürdigkeiten
relax [rɪˈlæks]	faulenzen, sich entspannen
join in [dʒɔɪn]	sich anschließen, beteiligen
indoor [ˈɪndɔː]	in einem Gebäude, nicht im Freien
musical evening [ˈmjuːzɪkl]	Musikabend
international [ɪntəˈnæʃənl]	international
country dancing	Volkstanz
electronic [ˌɪlekˈtrɒnɪk]	elektronisch
jukebox [ˈdʒuːkbɒks]	Musikbox, -automat
photography [fəˈtɒgrəfɪ]	Fotografie
arts and crafts [ɑːts ənd krɑːfts]	Kunst(-hand)werk
be keen on something [kiːn]	etwas sehr gern haben
be keen on ...ing	etwas sehr gern tun
company [ˈkʌmpənɪ]	Gesellschaft
head office [hed ˈɒfɪs]	Hauptgeschäftsstelle
Cardiff [ˈkɑːdɪf]	
information [ˌɪnfəˈmeɪʃn]	Information, Auskunft
application form [ˌæplɪˈkeɪʃn fɔːm]	Anmeldeformular
Heol [ˈhəɒl]	walisisch: Straße

Did you get it? (page 32)
1 special [ˈspeʃl]	besonder(e, er, es)
attraction [əˈtrækʃn]	Anziehungspunkt, Reiz

Using the language (page 32)
dream (dreamt, dreamt) [driːm, dremt, dremt]	träumen

What Are Your Interests?
interest [ˈɪntrɪst]	Interesse

Looking at the language (page 33)
plan (v.) [plæn]	planen, vorhaben
be fond of ...ing [fɒnd]	sehr gern etwas tun
look forward to ...ing [ˈfɔːwəd]	sich freuen darauf, etwas zu tun

Focus on grammar (page 33)
thank someone for ...ing	jemandem danken, daß er...

Can you do it? (page 34)
fill in [fɪl]	ausfüllen
questionnaire [ˌkwestɪəˈneə]	Fragebogen
code [kəʊd]	Code(wort), Schlüssel(wort)
badminton [ˈbædmɪntən]	Federballspiel
classical [ˈklæsɪkl]	klassisch
comedy [ˈkɒmɪdɪ]	(Film-)komödie
cartoon [kɑːˈtuːn]	Karikatur, Zeichentrickfilm
horror film [ˈhɒrə]	Horrorfilm
outdoor [ˈaʊtdɔː]	draußen, im Freien stattfindend
pottery [ˈpɒtərɪ]	Töpferei
athletics [æθˈletɪks]	Leichtathletik
likes and dislikes [laɪks ənd ˈdɪslaɪks]	Neigungen und Abneigungen

Using the language (page 35)
1 above [əˈbʌv]	oben, oberhalb
3 pizza [ˈpiːtsə]	Pizza

Two Letters
Reading (page 36)
1 madam [ˈmædəm]	höfliche Anrede an eine Dame, ohne Namensnennung
reserve [rɪˈsɜːv]	reservieren
yours faithfully (Schlußformel in einem offiziellen Brief) [ˈfeɪθfʊlɪ]	mit freundlichen Grüßen
2 *Pontardawe* [pɒntɑːˈdaʊə]	
Paddington [ˈpædɪŋtən]	
Swansea [ˈswɒnzɪ]	
minibus [ˈmɪnɪbʌs]	Kleinbus
enclose [ɪnˈkləʊz]	beilegen, beifügen
stay (n.) [steɪ]	Aufenthalt
yours sincerely (freundlichere Schlußformel in einem offiziellen Brief) [sɪnˈsɪəlɪ]	viele/herzliche Grüße
director [dɪˈrektə]	Direktor, Leiter

Extra: Welcome to Wales (page 37)
welcome to [ˈwelkəm]	willkommen in...
land [lænd]	Land (geographisch)
Britain [ˈbrɪtn]	(Groß)britannien
beauty [ˈbjuːtɪ]	Schönheit
landscape [ˈlændskeɪp]	Landschaft
forest [ˈfɒrɪst]	Wald
deep [diːp]	tief
valley [ˈvælɪ]	Tal
rocky [ˈrɒkɪ]	felsig
coastline [ˈkəʊstlaɪn]	Küste
sandy [ˈsændɪ]	sandig
be impressed by [ɪmˈprest]	beeindruckt sein von
medieval [meˈdiːvl]	mittelalterlich
dull [dʌl]	langweilig
explore [ɪkˈsplɔː]	erforschen
museum [mjuːˈzɪəm]	Museum
go for rides [raɪdz]	Fahrten machen
steam train [stiːm]	Zug mit Dampflok
eisteddfod (pl. eisteddfodau) [aɪsˈteðvɒd, aɪsˈteðvɒdaɪ]	
Welsh [welʃ]	Waliser(in), walisisch
world [wɜːld]	Welt, Erde
as well	ebenso
Brunel House [bruːˈnel]	
Fitzalan Road [fɪtsˈælən]	

Extra: Wales – a land of castles (page 38)
Caernarfon Castle [kəˈnɑːvən]	
Edward I [ˈedwəd ðə fɜːst]	
according to the story [əˈkɔːdɪŋ]	wie man erzählt, wie erzählt wird
present (v.) [prɪˈzent]	(der Öffentlichkeit) vorstellen, präsentieren
Prince Charles [prɪns tʃɑːlz]	
Pembroke Castle [ˈpembrʊk]	
birthplace [ˈbɜːθpleɪs]	Geburtsort, Geburtshaus
outstanding [ˌaʊtˈstændɪŋ]	herausragend, außergewöhnlich
Welshmen [ˈwelʃmən]	Waliser
British [ˈbrɪtɪʃ]	Brite, britisch
Caerphilly Castle [kɑːˈfɪlɪ]	
fortress [ˈfɔːtrɪs]	Festung
leaning [ˈliːnɪŋ]	schief

Extra: Narrow gauge railways, wildlife parks, caves (page 39)

narrow gauge railway ['nærəʊ geɪdʒ]	Schmalspurbahn
wildlife park ['waɪldlaɪf]	Wildpark
cave [keɪv]	Höhle
unusual [ʌn'ju:ʒʊəl]	ungewöhnlich
for example	zum Beispiel
line [laɪn]	hier: Bahnlinie
in all	insgesamt
steam train [sti:m]	Zug mit Dampflok
speciality [ˌspeʃɪ'ælətɪ]	Spezialität, Besonderheit
contact (v.) ['kɒntækt]	Kontakt aufnehmen, in Verbindung setzen
Penscynor Wildlife Park [pens'kʌnɔr]	
Cilfrew [kɪl'vrəʊ]	
protect [prə'tekt]	schützen, Schutz bieten
forest ['fɒrɪst]	Wald
variety [və'raɪətɪ]	Vielfalt
throughout the year [θru:'aʊt]	während des ganzen Jahres
play area ['eərɪə]	Spielplatz, Spielgelände
Dan-yr-Ogof ['dænər 'ɔgəv]	
showcave [ʃəʊkeɪv]	Höhle mit Besichtigungsmöglichkeit
be situated ['sɪtjʊeɪtɪd]	gelegen sein
Brecon ['brekən]	
Swansea ['swɒnzɪ]	
guided tour ['gaɪdɪd tʊə]	Besichtigung mit einem Führer
stalagmite ['stæləgmaɪt]	Tropfstein, der von unten nach oben wächst
stalactite ['stæləktaɪt]	Tropfstein, der von oben nach unten wächst

Extra: Arts festivals and eisteddfodau (page 39)

arts festival [ɑ:ts 'festəvl]	Musik- und Theaterfestival
youth [ju:θ]	Jugend
Llangollen [læn'gɒθlən]	
singer ['sɪŋə]	Sänger
musician [mju:'zɪʃn]	Musikant
dancer ['dɑ:nsə]	Tänzer
take part in something	an etwas teilnehmen
impressed (by) [ɪm'prest]	beeindruckt (von)
valley ['vælɪ]	Tal
fishing ['fɪʃɪŋ]	angeln
orchestra ['ɔ:kɪstrə]	Orchester
poetry ['pəʊtrɪ]	Dichtung, Dichtkunst
jazz [dʒæz]	Jazz
exhibition [ˌeksɪ'bɪʃn]	Ausstellung
drama ['drɑ:mə]	Drama
ballet ['bæleɪ]	Ballett
Pembrokeshire ['pembrʊkʃə]	

Some Facts about Wales

fact [fækt]	Tatsache, Angabe

Reading (page 40)

general ['dʒenərəl]	allgemein
Cymru [kʌm'rɪ]	walisischer Name für Wales
mean (v.) [mi:n]	bedeuten, heissen
comradeship ['kɒmrɪdʃɪp]	Kameradschaft
Great Britain [greɪt 'brɪtn]	
area ['eərɪə]	Fläche
square (mile) [skweə]	Quadrat(meile)
capital ['kæpɪtl]	Hauptstadt
main port [meɪn pɔ:t]	wichtigster Hafen eines Landes
population [ˌpɒpjʊ'leɪʃn]	Bevölkerung
landscape ['lændskeɪp]	Landschaft
plateau ['plætəʊ]	Hochebene, Plateau
valley ['vælɪ]	Tal
coastline ['kəʊstlaɪn]	Küste
Snowdonia [snəʊ'dəʊnjə]	
lake [leɪk]	der See
climate ['klaɪmɪt]	Klima
snowfall ['snəʊfɔ:l]	Schneefall
economy [ɪ'kɒnəmɪ]	Wirtschaft
agriculture ['ægrɪkʌltʃə]	Landwirtschaft
forestry ['fɒrɪstrɪ]	Forstwirtschaft
coal mining [kəʊl 'maɪnɪŋ]	Bergbau
culture ['kʌltʃə]	Kultur
traditional [trə'dɪʃənl]	traditionell
of its own	hier: eigenständig
medium ['mi:djəm]	Medium
eisteddfod (pl. eisteddfodau) [aɪs'teðvɒd, aɪs'teðvɒdaɪ]	
cultural ['kʌltʃərəl]	kulturell
event [ɪ'vent]	Ereignis
either ... or ['aɪðə]	entweder ... oder
competition [ˌkɒmpɪ'tɪʃn]	Wettbewerb
literature ['lɪtrɪtʃə]	Literatur
drama ['drɑ:mə]	Drama
art [ɑ:t]	Kunst
meeting place	Treffpunkt
throughout the year [θru:'aʊt]	während des ganzen Jahres

Did you get it? (page 40)

scenery ['si:nərɪ]	Landschaft
thousand ['θaʊznd]	Tausend

Using the language (page 41)

Wales Tourist Board [bɔ:d]	walisisches Fremdenverkehrsamt
address [ə'dres]	Adresse
organization [ˌɔ:gənəˈzeɪʃn]	Organisation, Verband
greeting ['gri:tɪŋ]	Begrüßung, Anrede
introduction [ˌɪntrə'dʌkʃn]	Einleitung
general reason ['dʒenərəl]	hier: eigentlicher Grund, Hauptanliegen
material [mə'tɪərɪəl]	Unterlagen
closing ['kləʊzɪŋ]	Schlußsatz (im Brief)
signature ['sɪgnətʃə]	Unterschrift

UNIT 4
GETTING TO KNOW EACH OTHER

get to know someone	jmdn. kennenlernen

At Camp Cymraig
Listening (page 42)

find out	herausfinden
nationality [ˌnæʃə'nælətɪ]	Nationalität, Staatsangehörigkeit

Did you get it? (page 42)

1 In the Refectory

refectory [rɪ'fektərɪ]	Speisesaal
Rieke	
complain to somebody	sich bei jemandem beklagen

2 In the Bus

get on	sich verstehen
learn about somebody	lernen über jemanden
Monty Python ['mɒntɪ 'paɪθən]	
explain [ɪk'spleɪn]	erklären

3 At the Camp Gate

Utrecht ['ju:trekt, ju:'trekt]	
gate official [geɪt ə'fɪʃl]	Torwächter

4 On the Walk

walk (n.) [wɔ:k]	Spazierweg

Using the language (page 43)

remain [rɪ'meɪn]	bleiben

Looking at the language (page 43)

common ['kɒmən]	gewöhnlich, hier: häufig, allgemein
you might [maɪt]	hier: du hast vielleicht
extract ['ekstrækt]	Auszug, Abschnitt

1 as if | als ob
you look as if | du siehst aus als ob

2 *Kidwelly Castle* [kɪd'welɪ]
Brian ['braɪən]

3
actress ['æktrɪs]	Schauspielerin
travel ['trævl]	reisen
stay	hier: wohnen

Looking at the language (page 43)

compare [kəm'peə]	vergleichen

1 most of us | die meisten von uns
Portuguese [ˌpɔ:tjʊ'gi:z] | portugiesisch, Portugiese, Portugiesin

anyone else	irgendjemand anders
competition [ˌkɒmpɪ'tɪʃn]	Wettkampf, Wettbewerb

2
guide [gaɪd]	(Wander)Führer
chicken ['tʃɪkɪn]	Huhn
boil [bɔɪl]	kochen

3 Australian [ɒˈstreɪljən] australisch, Australier(in)
clear [klɪə] klar

Focus on grammar (page 44)
1 comparison [kəmˈpærɪsn] Vergleich
competition [ˌkɒmpɪˈtɪʃn] Wettbewerb, Wettkampf
add [æd] hinzufügen
by adding hier: durch Anhängen von
comparative [kəmˈpærətɪv] Komparativ
superlative [suːˈpɜːlətɪv] Superlativ
note (v.) [nəʊt] hier: Beachte

Can you do it? (page 45)
2 suitable [ˈsuːtəbl] passend
prize [praɪz] Preis (beim Wettbewerb)
next time das nächste Mal
high jump [haɪˈdʒʌmp] Hochsprung
long jump [lɒŋˈdʒʌmp] Weitsprung
Joan [dʒəʊn]
Sylvia [ˈsɪlvɪə]
she got an A sie hat die Note A bekommen

Using the language (page 45)
member [ˈmembə] Mitglied

Rules Are Rules
rule [ruːl] Regel, Vorschrift

Looking at the language (page 46)
we are supposed to [səˈpəʊzd] wir sollen/müssen
we are not supposed to wir dürfen nicht
sensible [ˈsensəbl] vernünftig
no. (Abkürzung für "number") [ˈnʌmbə] Nr.
So do I. Ich auch.
Nor do I. [nɔː] Ich auch nicht.

By the way (page 46)
be back hier: zurückgekehrt sein
expression [ɪkˈspreʃn] Ausdruck

Can you do it? (page 47)
1 drop [drɒp] fallenlassen, hier: wegwerfen
litter [ˈlɪtə] Abfall
alcohol [ˈælkəhɒl] Alkohol
area [ˈeərɪə] Gelände
smoke (v.) [sməʊk] rauchen
prohibit [prəˈhɪbɪt] untersagen, verbieten
electrical [ɪˈlektrɪkl] elektrisch
equipment [ɪˈkwɪpmənt] Ausrüstung, Gegenstände

park (v.) [pɑːk] parken
moped [ˈməʊped] Moped
car park Parkplatz
by this time spätestens um diese Zeit
2 permission [pəˈmɪʃn] Erlaubnis
ask permission um Erlaubnis bitten

Using the language (page 47)
1 imagine [ɪˈmædʒɪn] sich etwas vorstellen
certain [ˈsɜːtn] bestimmt, gewiß
2 a set of rules eine Serie/Gruppe/Reihe/Anzahl von Regeln

Cool Pen Friends
Reading (page 48)
Cool [kuːl]
pen friend Brieffreund(in)
make friends with Freundschaft schließen mit
Spanish [ˈspænɪʃ] Spanisch
she can't stand …ing sie kann es nicht leiden
photography [fəˈtɒɡrəfɪ] Photographie
Mary Boyle [ˈmeərɪ bɔɪl]
Italian [ɪˈtæljən] italienisch
shy [ʃaɪ] schüchtern
skiing [ˈskiːɪŋ] Skifahren
Want a …? (umgangssprachlich für: Do you want a …?)
likes (n.) Neigungen
dislikes [dɪsˈlaɪks] Abneigungen

Using the language (page 49)
3 description [dɪˈskrɪpʃn] Beschreibung
similar to somebody/ something [ˈsɪmɪlə] ähnlich
above [əˈbʌv] hier: oben

Extra: You Need a Friend (page 49)
Eric Wilmslow [ˈwɪlmzləʊ]
yawn (v.) [jɔːn] gähnen
tooth, teeth [tuːθ, tiːθ] Zahn, Zähne
drawer [ˈdrɔː] Schublade
scissors (pl.) [ˈsɪzəz] Schere
a pair of scissors eine Schere
cut (cut, cut) [kʌt, kʌt, kʌt] schneiden
toenail [ˈtəʊneɪl] Zehennagel
guide [ɡaɪd] Führer
smile (v.) [smaɪl] lächeln
be puzzled [ˈpʌzld] erstaunt, perplex sein
nail [neɪl] (Finger)nagel
out there da draußen
Earth [ɜːθ] Planet Erde
loudspeaker [ˌlaʊdˈspiːkə] Lautsprecher
explain [ɪkˈspleɪn] erklären
feel uncomfortable [ʌnˈkʌmfətəbl] sich unwohl fühlen

explanation [ˌekspləˈneɪʃn] Erklärung
translate [trænˈsleɪt] übersetzen
Ballantarian [ˌbælənˈteɪrɪən]
attraction [əˈtrækʃn] Attraktion, Sehenswürdigkeit
latest attraction neueste Attraktion
interplanetary [ˌɪntəˈplænɪtərɪ] interplanetar, zwischen den Planeten
zoo [zuː] Zoo, Tierpark
creature [ˈkriːtʃə] Wesen, Kreatur
go to sleep schlafen gehen
not ever niemals
behaviour [bɪˈheɪvjə] Verhalten
expect [ɪkˈspekt] erwarten
in fact in der Tat
planet [ˈplænɪt] Planet
intelligent [ɪnˈtelɪdʒənt] intelligent
although [ɔːlˈðəʊ] obwohl
develop [dɪˈveləp] entwickeln
study (v.) [ˈstʌdɪ] studieren
several [ˈsevrəl] einige, eine Reihe von
colony [ˈkɒlənɪ] Kolonie, kleine Ansiedlung

Ballantaria [ˌbælənˈteɪrɪə]
careful sorgfältig
actually [ˈæktʃʊəlɪ] eigentlich
home hier: Heimat
billion [ˈbɪljən] Billion
3 billion drei Billionen
light years Lichtjahre
experiment [ɪkˈsperɪmənt] Experiment, Versuch
critical [ˈkrɪtɪkl] kritisch
stage [steɪdʒ] Stadium, Phase
critical stage kritischer Punkt, kritische Phase
choice [tʃɔɪs] (Aus)wahl
make his choice seine Wahl treffen
however [haʊˈevə] jedoch
furious [ˈfjʊərɪəs] zornig, wütend
mate [meɪt] Kamerad(in); hier: Frau
that's just not possible das ist doch wohl nicht möglich
lady [ˈleɪdɪ] Dame
arrange [əˈreɪndʒ] hier: erzwingen, planen in die Wege leiten
happen naturally [ˈnætʃrəlɪ] von selbst/alleine passieren
kidnap [ˈkɪdnæp] entführen
Jane [dʒeɪn]
while (n.) [waɪl] Weile
after a while nach einer Weile
have something in common [ˈkɒmən] etwas gemeinsam haben
solution [səˈluːʃn] Lösung
project (v.) (on to) [prəˈdʒekt] projizieren, Bilder an die Wand werfen
ocean [ˈəʊʃn] Ozean
this way so, auf diese Weise
saying [ˈseɪɪŋ] Sprichwort, Redensart, Lebensweisheit
naturally hier: von Natur aus
case [keɪs] Fall

in most cases	in den meisten Fällen
the only reason	der einzige Grund
properly ['prɒpəlɪ]	hier: richtig, ganz und gar
think about something	nachdenken über

UNIT 5 A TASTE OF AFRICA

taste (n.) [teɪst]	Geschmack, Kostprobe
Africa ['æfrɪkə]	

Greetings from Mbour

greeting ['gri:tɪŋ]	Gruß
Mbour [əm'bʊə]	
Peter Robinson ['pi:tə 'rɒbɪnsn]	
Liss [lɪs]	
Hampshire ['hæmpʃə]	
The Gambia (oder: Gambia) ['gæmbɪə]	
Easter ['i:stə]	Ostern
Senegal [ˌsenɪ'gɔ:l]	
neighbouring ['neɪbərɪŋ]	benachbart

Reading (page 51)

marvellous ['mɑ:vələs]	herrlich, wunderbar
bored stiff [stɪf]	zu Tode gelangweilt
by	an, bei
by the sea	an der See, am Strand
the only	der (die, das) einzige
frankly ['fræŋklɪ]	offen gesagt
scare [skeə]	erschrecken
strange [streɪndʒ]	fremd, fremdartig
Alan Ross ['ælən]	
Oak Tree Drive [əʊk tri: draɪv]	
Hants	(Abkürzung für Hampshire bei Anschriften)

Reading (page 52)

conversation [ˌkɒnvə'seɪʃn]	Gespräch, Unterhaltung
Malick ['mælɪk]	
Gambian ['gæmbɪən]	Gambianer, gambianisch
fisherman ['fɪʃəmən]	Fischer
Wolof ['wɒlɒf]	
tribe [traɪb]	(Volks)stamm
border ['bɔ:də]	Grenze
artificial [ɑ:tɪ'fɪʃl]	künstlich
colonial times [kə'ləʊnjəl]	Zeiten der Kolonialherrschaft
ridiculous [rɪ'dɪkjʊləs]	lächerlich
actually ['æktʃʊəlɪ]	eigentlich, wirklich
not ... at all	überhaupt nicht ...
pick someone up	jmdn. abholen, mitnehmen
get something repaired	etwas reparieren lassen

Reading (page 53)

change [tʃeɪndʒ]	(sich) (ver)ändern
along [ə'lɒŋ]	entlang
if	ob

Listening (page 54)

get on	auskommen, zurechtkommen
find out	herausfinden, feststellen

Did you get it? (page 54)

danger ['deɪndʒə]	Gefahr
tourism ['tʊərɪzm]	Tourismus
Aissouta [aɪ'su:tə]	

Reading (page 55)

half an hour [ˌhɑ:fən'aʊə]	eine halbe Stunde
surprised [sə'praɪzd]	überrascht
Lamine [lə'mi:n]	
the first time	das erste Mal
drown [draʊn]	ertrinken
suggest [sə'dʒest]	vorschlagen
sleep (n.) [sli:p]	Schlaf
an hour's sleep	eine Stunde Schlaf
afterwards ['ɑ:ftəwədz]	hinterher, nachher, danach
Joal [dʒɔ'ɑ:l]	
Fadiouth [fə'dju:θ]	
mention ['menʃn]	erwähnen
fish [fɪʃ]	Fisch
change one's mind	die Meinung/Ansicht ändern
incredible [ɪn'kredəbl]	unglaublich, nicht zu fassen
scared [skeəd]	erschrocken

Did you get it? (page 55)

Muslim ['mʊslɪm]	Muslim
colony ['kɒlənɪ]	Kolonie
live off something	von etwas leben
pray [preɪ]	beten
alcohol ['ælkəhɒl]	Alkohol

Focus on grammar (page 56)

toothache ['tu:θeɪk]	Zahnschmerzen

Can you do it? (page 57)

scene [si:n]	Szene
2 I suppose [sə'pəʊz]	vermutlich
Bakotu [bækə'tu:]	

Can you do it? (page 58)

come back	zurückkommen
souvenir [ˌsu:və'nɪə]	Andenken, Souvenir

Extra: Something to think about (page 59)

African ['æfrɪkən]	afrikanisch
have on	tragen
European [jʊərə'pi:ən]	europäisch, Europäer
have got on	tragen

Focus on grammar (page 59)

go right in	geh nur rein
command [kə'mɑ:nd]	Befehl

By the way (page 61)

the day before	am Tag vorher

By the way (page 62)

get something repaired	etwas reparieren lassen
mean (meant, meant) [mi:n, ment, ment]	bedeuten, heißen
cut (cut, cut) [kʌt, kʌt, kʌt]	schneiden, abschneiden

Starting a Conversation

conversation	Gespräch, Unterhaltung
way [weɪ]	Weise, Art und Weise
go up to someone	auf jemanden zugehen
ask for something	um etwas bitten
apologize [ə'pɒlədʒaɪz]	sich entschuldigen
comment on something ['kɒment ɒn]	etwas kommentieren, Bemerkungen über etwas machen
introduce [ˌɪntrə'dju:s]	vorstellen

Listening (page 63)

extract ['ekstrækt]	Auszug, Ausschnitt
go on	weiter machen

Using the language (page 64)

whether ['weðə]	ob
accept [ək'sept]	annehmen
refuse [rɪ'fju:z]	ablehnen
explain [ɪk'spleɪn]	erklären

Extra: Pidgin (page 65)

Pidgin ['pɪdʒɪn]	
special ['speʃl]	besonder(er, e, es)
work out	herausbekommen
have a try	versuchen
check [tʃek]	kontrollieren, (über)prüfen
version ['vɜ:ʃn]	Fassung (eines Textes), Version
Standard English ['stændəd]	hochsprachliches Englisch
Portuguese [ˌpɔ:tjʊ'gi:z]	Portugiesisch

Extra: Some Facts about The Gambia (page 66)

interest (v.) ['ɪntrɪst]	interessieren
general ['dʒenərəl]	allgemein
republic [rɪ'pʌblɪk]	Republik
square... [skweə]	Quadrat-
kilometre ['kɪləˌmi:tə]	Kilometer
Banjul	
geography [dʒɪ'ɒgrəfɪ]	Geographie
narrow ['nærəʊ]	schmal, eng
strip [strɪp]	Streifen

side [saɪd]	Seite	tablespoon ['teɪblspu:n]	Eßlöffel	peaceful ['pi:sfʊl]	friedlich
Gambia River ['gæmbɪə 'rɪvə]		oil [ɔɪl]	Öl	northwest [ˌnɔ:θ'west]	nordwestliche Richtung
wide [waɪd]	breit	bowl [bəʊl]	Schüssel	towards [tə'wɔ:dz]	in Richtung auf, nach
enclave ['enkleɪv]	Enklave	sauce [sɔ:s]	Soße	*Broadford* ['brɔ:dfəd]	
generally ['dʒenərəlɪ]	allgemein, im allgemeinen	mix [mɪks]	mischen	steep [sti:p]	steil
		pour [pɔ:]	gießen	**push** [pʊʃ]	schieben
flat [flæt]	flach	cover ['kʌvə]	zudecken, bedecken	uphill [ˌʌp'hɪl]	bergauf
season ['si:zn]	Jahreszeit	leave [li:v]	lassen	late afternoon	am späten Nachmittag
intense [ɪn'tens]	intensiv	refrigerator [rɪ'frɪdʒəreɪtə]	Kühlschrank	**reach** [ri:tʃ]	erreichen
population [ˌpɒpjʊ'leɪʃn]	Bevölkerung	overnight [ˌəʊvə'naɪt]	über Nacht	**disappointed** [ˌdɪsə'pɔɪntɪd]	enttäuscht
inhabitant [ɪn'hæbɪtənt]	Einwohner	fry [fraɪ]	braten		
rural ['rʊərəl]	ländlich	frying pan [pæn]	Bratpfanne	**ride (rode, ridden)** [raɪd, rəʊd, 'rɪdn]	mit dem Fahrrad fahren
Wolof ['wɒlɒf]		rest (n.) [rest]	Rest		
Fulani [fu:'lɑ:ni:]		add [æd]	hinzufügen	haggis ['hægɪs]	Schafwurst
Dyola [daɪ'əʊlə]		gentle, gently ['dʒentl, 'dʒentlɪ]	sanft	earth [ɜ:θ]	Erde
Soninke [sə'nɪŋkə]				what on earth...?	was in aller Welt...?
Senegalese [ˌsenɪgə'li:z]	Senegalese, senegalesisch	cook gently	auf kleiner Flamme kochen	neither... nor... ['naɪðə nɔ:]	weder... noch...
Syrian ['sɪrɪən]	Syrer, syrisch	serve [sɜ:v]	servieren	explain [ɪk'spleɪn]	erklären
Lebanese [ˌlebə'ni:z]	Libanese, libanesisch	rice [raɪs]	Reis	Scottish ['skɒtɪʃ]	schottisch
religion [rɪ'lɪdʒən]	Religion			**early in the morning**	früh am Morgen
majority [mə'dʒɒrətɪ]	Mehrheit, Überzahl	## UNIT 6 OVER THE SEA TO SKYE		**lead (led, led)** [li:d, led, led]	führen
Christian ['krɪstjən]	Christ(in), christlich				
besides [bɪ'saɪdz]	außer	### Reading (page 70)		the road ran along the coast	die Straße verlief an der Küste
official [ə'fɪʃl]	offiziell	**travel** ['trævl]	reisen	flat [flæt]	flach
official language	Amtssprache	*Jill Southwell* [dʒɪl 'saʊθwəl]		cycle ['saɪkl]	radfahren
British ['brɪtɪʃ]	britisch, Brite	...-year-old	...jährige(r)(s)	block [blɒk]	blockieren
colony ['kɒlənɪ]	Kolonie	**schoolgirl** ['sku:lgɜ:l]	Schulmädchen	number ['nʌmbə]	Anzahl
independent [ˌɪndɪ'pendənt]	unabhängig	*Manchester* ['mæntʃɪstə]		sheep dog	Hirtenhund
economy [ɪ'kɒnəmɪ]	Wirtschaft	account [ə'kaʊnt]	Bericht	guide (v.) [gaɪd]	führen
dependent on [dɪ'pendənt]	abhängig von	cycle ['saɪkl]	radfahren	neighbouring ['neɪbərɪŋ]	Nachbar-, angrenzend
peanut ['pi:nʌt]	Erdnuss	cycling holiday	Urlaub mit dem Fahrrad	**field** [fi:ld]	Feld
groundnut ['graʊndnʌt]	Erdnuss			**bed and breakfast**	Übernachtung mit Frühstück
mountainous ['maʊntɪnəs]	bergig, gebirgig	*Isle of Skye* [aɪl əv skaɪ]		telegram ['telɪgræm]	Telegramm
throughout the year [θru:'aʊt]	das ganze Jahr über	### Off the Beaten Track		**wall** [wɔ:l]	Mauer
rain heavily ['hevɪlɪ]	stark regnen	off [ɒf]	abseits von	harbour ['hɑ:bə]	Hafen
million ['mɪljən]	Million	beat (beat, beaten) [bi:t, bi:t, 'bi:tn]	schlagen; *hier:* viel befahren	*Bonnie Prince Charlie* ['bɒnɪ prɪns 'tʃɑ:lɪ]	
foreigner ['fɒrənə]	Ausländer	track [træk]	Weg, Spur	aloud [ə'laʊd]	laut
grow (grew, grown) [grəʊ, gru:, grəʊn]	wachsen	off the beaten track	weg vom Eingefahrenen	read aloud	vorlesen, laut lesen
				battle ['bætl]	Schlacht
### Extra: Project Africa (page 67)		**road** [rəʊd]	Straße	prince [prɪns]	Prinz
encyclopaedia [enˌsaɪkləʊ'pi:dɪə]	Enzyklopädie	**follow** ['fɒləʊ]	folgen, verfolgen; verlaufen	*Flora Macdonald* ['flɔ:rə mək'dɒnəld]	
prepare [prɪ'peə]	vorbereiten	the road followed the coast	die Straße verlief an der Küste	escape [ɪ'skeɪp]	entkommen, entfliehen
### Extra: Chicken Yassa (page 69)		across [ə'krɒs]	über, jenseits	choice [tʃɔɪs]	Wahl
taste (v.) [teɪst]	schmecken	**air** [eə]	Luft	*Kilmuir* [kɪl'mjʊə]	
recipe ['resɪpɪ]	(Koch)rezept	all the way	den ganzen Weg	grave [greɪv]	Grab
ingredients [ɪn'gri:dʒənts]	Zutaten	while (n.) [waɪl]	Weile, (kurze) Zeit	*Glen Brittle* [glen 'brɪtl]	
kilogram ['kɪləʊgræm]	Kilogramm	**get off our bikes**	vom Rad runtersteigen	**in the end**	schließlich, letzten Endes
juice [dʒu:s]	Saft	**look around** [ə'raʊnd]	sich umschauen	**take the bus**	mit dem Bus fahren, den Bus nehmen
lemon ['lemən]	Zitrone	hilly ['hɪlɪ]	hügelig		
onion ['ʌnjən]	Zwiebel	graze [greɪz]	grasen	change for a change	Abwechslung zur Abwechslung
fine [faɪn]	*hier:* klein	distance ['dɪstəns]	Entfernung	Gaelic ['geɪlɪk]	Gälisch, gälisch
chop [tʃɒp]	hacken, schneiden	*Cuillin Hills* ['ku:lɪn]		notice (v.) ['nəʊtɪs]	bemerken
finely chopped	fein geschnitten	atmosphere ['ætməsfɪə]	Atmosphäre	**sign** [saɪn]	Schild, Wegweiser
pepper ['pepə]	Pfeffer	calm [kɑ:m]	ruhig	*Kingsburgh* ['kɪŋzbərə]	
hot pepper	scharfe Pfefferoni			land (v.)	landen
salt [sɔ:lt]	Salz				

have a look	sich etwas anschauen	*Macdonald* [məkˈdɒnəld]		**Useful Tips and Advice for Visitors**
romantic [rəʊˈmæntɪk]	romantisch	*Macleod* [məˈklaʊd]		

have a look — sich etwas anschauen
romantic [rəʊˈmæntɪk] — romantisch
bay [beɪ] — Bucht
king [kɪŋ] — König
lean [liːn] — lehnen
pause [pɔːz] — *hier:* Denkpause
after a moment's pause — nach kurzer Überlegung
baker [ˈbeɪkə] — Bäcker
pass by [pɑːs] — vorbeifahren, vorbeigehen
ride (n.) [raɪd] — Fahrt
among [əˈmʌŋ] — zwischen, unter
van [væn] — Lieferwagen
exhausted [ɪgˈzɔːstɪd] — erschöpft
Trumpan [ˈtrʌmpən]
ruin [ˈruːɪn] — Ruine
surround [səˈraʊnd] — umzingeln
enemy [ˈenəmɪ] — Feind
lock [lɒk] — abschließen, zusperren
set fire to — in Brand setzen
attack [əˈtæk] — angreifen
villager [ˈvɪlɪdʒə] — Dorfbewohner
save [seɪv] — retten
member [ˈmembə] — Mitglied
clan [klæn] — Familie, Sippe, Clan
rescue (n.) [ˈreskjuː] — Rettung
come to someone's rescue — jemandem zur Hilfe kommen
imagine [ɪˈmædʒɪn] — sich vorstellen
such a [sʌtʃ] — solch ein(e), so ein(e)
fascinating [ˈfæsɪneɪtɪŋ] — faszinierend
sail [seɪl] — segeln
Denmark [ˈdenmɑːk] — Dänemark

Did you get it? (page 72)

1 **tour** (n.) [tʊə] — Tour
2 that way — *hier:* so wie es ist (war)
  get to (a place) — in ... ankommen

Extra: Some Background Information (page 73)

background [ˈbækgraʊnd] — Hintergrund
Inner Hebrides [ˈɪnə ˈhebrɪdiːz]
off — *hier:* an
west — westlich
Scotland [ˈskɒtlənd] — Schottland
population [ˌpɒpjʊˈleɪʃn] — Bevölkerung
mainly [ˈmeɪnlɪ] — hauptsächlich
fishing [ˈfɪʃɪŋ] — Fischen
sheep farming [ʃiːp ˈfɑːmɪŋ] — Schafzucht
agriculture [ˈægrɪˌkʌltʃə] — Landwirtschaft
tourism [ˈtʊərɪzm] — Tourismus
main [meɪn] — Haupt-
countryside [ˈkʌntrɪˌsaɪd] — ländliche Gegend, Landschaft
sandy [ˈsændɪ] — sandig
bay [beɪ] — Bucht
rough [rʌf] — rauh; *hier:* schroff, zerklüftet
hilly [ˈhɪlɪ] — hüglig
metre [ˈmiːtə] — Meter

century [ˈsentʃʊrɪ] — Jahrhundert
historical [hɪˈstɒrɪkl] — historisch
Kilmuir [kɪlˈmjuːr]
escape [ɪˈskeɪp] — entkommen, entfliehen
Culloden [kəˈlɒdn]
Charles Edward Stuart [tʃɑːlz ˈedwəd ˈstjuːət]
national [ˈnæʃənl] — national
hero [ˈhɪərəʊ] — Held
grandson [ˈgrænsʌn] — Enkel
James II [dʒeɪmz ðə ˈsekənd]
catholic [ˈkæθəlɪk] — katholisch
be born [bɔːn] — geboren sein
return [rɪˈtɜːn] — zurückkehren
claim [kleɪm] — beanspruchen
throne [θrəʊn] — Thron
defeat [dɪˈfiːt] — besiegen
hide (hid, hidden) [haɪd, hɪd, ˈhɪdn] — (sich) verstecken, verbergen
west of — westlich von
Italy [ˈɪtəlɪ] — Italien
die [daɪ] — sterben
Rome [rəʊm] — Rom
belong to [bɪˈlɒŋ] — gehören zu
succeed [səkˈsiːd] — Erfolg haben

Extra: The Skye Boat Song (page 74)

traditional [trəˈdɪʃənl] — traditionell

A Good Holiday?

Using the language (page 75)

dull [dʌl] — langweilig
tiring [ˈtaɪərɪŋ] — ermüdend

Looking at the language (page 75)

So do/did I. — Ich auch.
Nor do/did I. — Ich auch nicht.
I don't/didn't either. [ˈaɪðə] — Ich auch nicht.

By the way (page 76)

statement [ˈsteɪtmənt] — Aussage
the same way — *hier:* genauso
apply to someone [əˈplaɪ] — für jemanden zutreffen
expression [ɪkˈspreʃn] — Ausdruck
like these — wie diese
positive [ˈpɒzɪtɪv] — positiv
negative [ˈnegətɪv] — negativ
So can/would/am/have I. — Ich auch.
Nor can/would/am/have I. — Ich auch nicht.
I can't/wouldn't/'m not/haven't either. — Ich auch nicht.

Using the language (page 76)

on my own [əʊn] — allein

Useful Tips and Advice for Visitors

useful [ˈjuːsfʊl] — nützlich, praktisch
tip [tɪp] — Tip, Hinweis
advice [ədˈvaɪs] — Ratschläge

Reading (page 76)

needn't + verb [ˈniːdnt] — nicht müssen, nicht brauchen zu
stay [steɪ] — wohnen
reasonable [ˈriːznbl] — preisgünstig, preiswert
guest house — Pension, Gästehaus
recommend [ˌrekəˈmend] — empfehlen
private [ˈpraɪvɪt] — privat
reliable [rɪˈlaɪəbl] — verläßlich
waterproof [ˈwɔːtəpruːf] — wasserdicht
strong [strɒŋ] — stark, fest
anorak [ˈænəræk] — Anorak
spend money on something — Geld für etwas ausgeben
get around — umher reisen
travel around — umher reisen
tour (n.) — Rundfahrt
service [ˈsɜːvɪs] — *hier:* Verbindung
transport [ˈtrænspɔːt] — Transportation
necessary [ˈnesɪsərɪ] — notwendig, nötig

Can you do it? (page 77)

cold [kəʊld] — Erkältung, Schnupfen
get better — besser werden
tooth (*pl.* **teeth**) [tuːθ, tiːθ] — Zahn

Using the language (page 77)

foreigner [ˈfɒrənə] — Ausländer
spring [sprɪŋ] — Frühling

By the way (page 78)

scissors [ˈsɪzəz] — Schere
count [kaʊnt] — zählen

Using the language (page 78)

ski [skiː] — skifahren
the Alps [ðɪ ælps] — die Alpen
illustration [ˌɪləˈstreɪʃn] — Illustration
bra [brɑː] — B. H.
pants (*for girls*) [pænts] — Unterhose
briefs (*for boys*) [briːfs] — Unterhose
vest [vest] — Unterhemd
boot [buːt] — Stiefel
comb [kəʊm] — Kamm
soap [səʊp] — Seife
toothbrush [ˈtuːθbrʌʃ] — Zahnbürste
toothpaste [ˈtuːθpeɪst] — Zahnpasta
glove [glʌv] — Handschuh
cap [kæp] — Mütze
scarf [skɑːf] — Tuch, Schal

Extra: North, East, South, West (page 79)

express [ɪkˈspres] — ausdrücken
direction [dɪˈrekʃn] — Himmelsrichtung
Great Britain [greɪt ˈbrɪtn]
Edinburgh [ˈedɪnbərə]
Liverpool [ˈlɪvəpuːl]
Cardiff [ˈkɑːdɪf]

Birmingham [ˈbɜːmɪŋəm]
main [meɪn] — wichtigste(r), (s)

"Can You Tell Us the Way?"

Looking at the language (page 80)

tour (v.) — umherreisen, umherfahren
railway track — Bahn(gleis)
right across [əˈkrɒs] — geradewegs über
bridge [brɪdʒ] — Brücke
across — über
opposite [ˈɒpəzɪt] — gegenüber
describe [dɪsˈkraɪb] — beschreiben
certainly [ˈsɜːtnlɪ] — natürlich, sicher(lich)
straight down [streɪt] — hinunter

Focus on grammar (page 81)

meaning [ˈmiːnɪŋ] — Bedeutung

Can you do it? (page 82)

1 phone box — Telefonzelle
2 helpful [ˈhelpfʊl] — hilfsbereit
France [frɑːns] — Frankreich

Using the language (page 82)

walk past something — an etwas vorbeigehen

Extra: Rain, Rain ... (page 83)

weather forecast [ˈfɔːkɑːst] — Wettervorhersage
windy [ˈwɪndɪ] — windig

UNIT 7 LOST IN THE CAVES

cave [keɪv] — Höhle
dos and don'ts [duːz ənd dəʊnts] — Verhaltensregeln
watch [wɒtʃ] — Armbanduhr
spare ... [speə] — Ersatz-, Reserve-
battery [ˈbætərɪ] — Batterie
torch [tɔːtʃ] — Taschenlampe
risk [rɪsk] — Risiko, Wagnis, Gefahr
take risks — sich Gefahren aussetzen, Risiken eingehen
difficulty [ˈdɪfɪkəltɪ] — Schwierigkeit
run into difficulties — in Schwierigkeiten geraten
study [ˈstʌdɪ] — studieren
set out — aufbrechen
keep together — zusammenbleiben
trouble [ˈtrʌbl] — Schwierigkeit
run into trouble — in Schwierigkeiten geraten
panic [ˈpænɪk] — in Panik geraten
helmet [ˈhelmɪt] — Helm

A Radio Play

radio play — Hörspiel
recording [rɪˈkɔːdɪŋ] — Tonaufnahme
broadcast [ˈbrɔːdkɑːst] — Sendung im Rundfunk
direct [dɪˈrekt] — Regie führen
cast [kɑːst] — Besetzung, Rollenverteilung
entrance [ˈentrəns] — Eingang
sound (n.) — Geräusch
check [tʃek] — kontrollieren, prüfen
equipment [ɪˈkwɪpmənt] — Ausrüstung
extra [ˈekstrə] — zusätzlich

Did you get it? (page 86)

1 rucksack [ˈrʌksæk] — Rucksack
first aid [fɜːst eɪd] — erste Hilfe
warning [ˈwɔːnɪŋ] — Warnung

2 stalagmite [ˈstæləgmaɪt] — Stalagmite, Tropfsteinsäule
grow (grew, grown) [grəʊ, gruː, grəʊn] — wachsen
rope [rəʊp] — Seil, Tau
ladder [ˈlædə] — Leiter
rope-ladder [ˈrəʊplædə] — Strickleiter
dare [deə] — wagen

3 go on — weitergehen
come straight back [streɪt] — sofort zurückkehren
they might [maɪt] — sie könnten

4 entrance — Eingang
seeping water [ˈsiːpɪŋ] — sickerndes Wasser
shaft [ʃɑːft] — Schacht
underground river [ˈʌndəgraʊnd] — unterirdischer Fluß
confident [ˈkɒnfɪdənt] — zuversichtlich
search party [sɜːtʃ ˈpɑːtɪ] — Such-, Rettungstrupp
study [ˈstʌdɪ] — studieren
route [ruːt] — Weg, Route
way out — Weg nach draußen
arrow [ˈærəʊ] — Pfeil
steep [stiːp] — steil
make it — *hier:* es schaffen
Black Pool [puːl] — Tunnel
tunnel [ˈtʌnl] — abzweigen, sich verzweigen
branch [brɑːntʃ] —
safe [seɪf] — sicher, in Sicherheit

5 sound (n.) — Geräusch
voice [vɔɪs] — Stimme

Using the language (page 88)

character [ˈkærəktə] — Charakter
sensible [ˈsensəbl] — vernünftig

Talking it Over

Reading (page 89)

1 actually [ˈæktʃʊlɪ] — eigentlich, wirklich
crash [kræʃ] — Krach
notice (v.) [ˈnəʊtɪs] — bemerken
low [ləʊ] — niedrig
turn back — umkehren
in case of [keɪs] — im Falle von
insist on doing something [ɪnˈsɪst] — darauf bestehen, etwas zu tun
warden [ˈwɔːdn] — Aufseher, Leiter des Clubzentrums
warn [wɔːn] — warnen
warn someone not to do something — jemanden davor warnen, etwas zu tun
firm [fɜːm] — fest, bestimmt, standhaft
main (thing) — Haupt(sache)

2 support [səˈpɔːt] — unterstützen
responsible [rɪˈspɒnsəbl] — verantwortlich
go straight back [streɪt] — sofort zurückkehren
entrance — Eingang
blame oneself — sich Vorwürfe machen
turn out (all right) — (ganz gut) abgehen

Focus on grammar (page 90)

structure [ˈstrʌktʃə] — Struktur, Sprachmuster
reproach someone for something [rɪˈprəʊtʃ] — jemandem Vorwürfe machen

Can you do it? (page 90)

1 adventure [ədˈventʃə] — Abenteuer
get into trouble — in Schwierigkeiten geraten

2 do (better) in ... — (besser) in ... abschneiden

Using the language (page 91)

1 regret [rɪˈgret] — bedauern
work hard — viel arbeiten
do (badly) in a test — in einer Prüfung (schlecht) abschneiden
get wet — naß werden
catch a cold — sich erkälten
stomach-ache [ˈstʌməkeɪk] — Magenschmerzen
ache [eɪk] — Schmerz(en)

2 try harder — sich mehr Mühe geben

By the way (page 92)

route — Weg, Route
remind someone of something [rɪˈmaɪnd] — jemanden an etwas erinnern

151

Don't Take Risks!
Looking at the language (page 92)

have a talk with someone	eine Besprechung mit jemandem haben
expect [ɪkˈspekt]	erwarten
expect someone to do something	erwarten, daß jemand etwas tut

Can you do it? (page 93)

beginning [bɪˈgɪnɪŋ]	Anfang

Using the language (page 94)

mountaineering [ˌmaʊntɪˈnɪərɪŋ]	Bergsteigen
find out	herausfinden
weather forecast [ˈfɔːkɑːst]	Wettervorhersage
suitable [ˈsuːtəbl]	geeignet, passend, angemessen
mark [mɑːk]	markieren, kennzeichnen
track [træk]	Weg, Spur
ignore [ɪgˈnɔː]	außer Acht lassen, nicht beachten
admit [ədˈmɪt]	zugeben
defend oneself [dɪˈfend]	sich verteidigen
express [ɪkˈspres]	ausdrücken
regret (n.) [rɪˈgret]	Bedauern
deny [dɪˈnaɪ]	leugnen

UNIT 8 NELSON AND "VICTORY"

Nelson [ˈnelsn]	
Victory [ˈvɪktərɪ]	
tour (n.) [tʊə]	Rundfahrt
a number	eine Anzahl
monument [ˈmɒnjʊmənt]	Denkmal
historic [hɪˈstɒrɪk]	historisch
definitely [ˈdefɪnɪtlɪ]	mit Sicherheit, bestimmt
scene [siːn]	Szene
Trafalgar Square [trəˈfælgə]	
column [ˈkɒləm]	Säule
honour [ˈɒnə]	Ehre
in his honour	ihm zu Ehren

A British National Hero

British [ˈbrɪtɪʃ]	britisch
national [ˈnæʃənəl]	national
hero [ˈhiːərəʊ]	Held

Reading (page 96)

Lord [lɔːd]	(britischer Adelstitel)
successful [səkˈsesfʊl]	erfolgreich
admiral [ˈædmərəl]	Admiral
war [wɔː]	Krieg
France [frɑːns]	Frankreich
Napoleon [nəˈpəʊljən]	
victory [ˈvɪktərɪ]	Sieg
battle [ˈbætl]	Schlacht
Nile [naɪl]	Nil

destroy [dɪˈstrɔɪ]	zerstören
fleet [fliːt]	Flotte
Spanish [ˈspænɪʃ]	spanisch, Spanisch
Napoleonic [nəˌpəʊlɪˈɒnɪk]	napoleonisch
invasion [ɪnˈveɪʒn]	Einmarsch
be born [bɔːn]	geboren sein
Burnham Thorpe [ˈbɜːnəm θɔːp]	
marry [ˈmærɪ]	heiraten
Frances Nisbet [ˈfrɑːnsɪs ˈnɪzbɪt]	
Emma Hamilton [ˈemə ˈhæmɪltən]	
shock [ʃɒk]	schockieren
society [səˈsaɪətɪ]	Gesellschaft
Horatia [həˈreɪʃə]	
bullet [ˈbʊlɪt]	Kugel
on board [bɔːd]	an Bord
bury [ˈberɪ]	beerdigen, beisetzen
St Paul's Cathedral [snt ˈpɔːlz kəˈθiːdrəl]	
statue [ˈstætʃuː]	Statue
name sb./sth. after sb./sth.	jmdn./etwas nach jmdm./etwas nennen
meeting [ˈmiːtɪŋ]	Kundgebung
hold (held, held)	*hier:* veranstalten
rest [rest]	sich ausruhen
resting place	Ruheplatz
flagship [ˈflægʃɪp]	Flaggschiff
preserve [prɪˈzɜːv]	erhalten, (auf)bewahren
Portsmouth [ˈpɔːtsməθ]	
flag [flæg]	Flagge
signal [ˈsɪgnl]	Signal
duty [ˈdjuːtɪ]	Pflicht
die [daɪ]	sterben
hit (hit, hit) [hɪt]	hauen; *hier:* treffen

Did you get it? (page 97)

beat (beat, beaten) [biːt, biːt, biːtn]	schlagen, besiegen
invade [ɪnˈveɪd]	einmarschieren in..., einfallen in...
shoot (shot, shot) [ʃuːt, ʃɒt, ʃɒt]	schießen
rest	sich ausruhen

The Battle of Trafalgar
Reading (page 98)

announcer [əˈnaʊnsə]	Rundfunksprecher, Ansager
programme	Sendung
century [ˈsentʃʊrɪ]	Jahrhundert
master [ˈmɑːstə]	Herr, Meister
narrator [nəˈreɪtə]	Erzähler
be at war with	Krieg führen gegen
Bonaparte [ˈbəʊnəpɑːt]	
emperor [ˈempərə]	Kaiser
invade [ɪnˈveɪd]	einmarschieren in..., einfallen in...
Villeneuve [vɪlˈnɜːv]	
port [pɔːt]	Hafen
Cadiz [kəˈdɪz]	

make sure	sicherstellen, sich vergewissern
captain [ˈkæptɪn]	Kapitän
Captain Keats [kiːts]	

Listening (page 98)

take place	stattfinden

Did you get it? (page 99)

although [ɔːlˈðəʊ]	obwohl
pain [peɪn]	Schmerz(en)
cabin [ˈkæbɪn]	Kabine
order [ˈɔːdə]	befehlen
as soon as [suːn]	sobald

Talking about Heroes
Looking at the language (page 99)

case [keɪs]	Fall
meaning [ˈmiːnɪŋ]	Bedeutung
leader [ˈliːdə]	Führer
private [ˈpraɪvɪt]	privat

Using the language (page 100)

2 well-known [ˌwelˈnəʊn]	bekannt
field [fiːld]	*hier:* Bereich
politics [ˈpɒlɪtɪks]	Politik
science [ˈsaɪəns]	Naturwissenschaft
3 look up to somebody	zu jemandem aufschauen
character [ˈkærəktə]	Charakter
admire [ədˈmaɪə]	bewundern
relationship [rɪˈleɪʃnʃɪp]	Beziehung

Do We Need Heroes?
Did you get it? (page 100)

there is something wrong with	etwas stimmt nicht mit
dictator [dɪkˈteɪtə]	Diktator

Quiz: Famous People

quiz [kwɪz]	Quiz

Reading (page 101)

description [dɪˈskrɪpʃn]	Beschreibung
marvellous [ˈmɑːvələs]	herrlich, wunderbar
Verona [vɪˈrəʊnə]	
period [ˈpɪərɪəd]	Zeitabschnitt, Periode
haircut [ˈheəkʌt]	Haarschnitt
musical [ˈmjuːzɪkl]	musikalisch
thin [θɪn]	dünn
make somebody do something	jemanden etwas tun lassen
make somebody laugh	jemanden zum Lachen bringen
walk (n.)	Gang
bowler hat [ˈbəʊlə hæt]	„Melone"
tiny [ˈtaɪnɪ]	winzig
moustache [məˈstɑːʃ]	Schnurrbart
design [dɪˈzaɪn]	entwerfen, gestalten
architect [ˈɑːkɪtekt]	Architekt
Shakespeare [ˈʃeɪkˌspɪə]	

Sir Christopher Wren [sɜː ˈkrɪstəfə ren]
Queen Victoria [kwiːn vɪkˈtɔːrɪə]

On Board the "Victory"

guided tour [ˈgaɪdɪd]	Besichtigung mit Führung
no different	keineswegs anders

Did you get it? (page 102)

guide (n.) [gaɪd]	Führer
sailor [ˈseɪlə]	Matrose, Seemann
electric [ɪˈlektrɪk]	elektrisch
cabin [ˈkæbɪn]	Kabine
dining cabin	Speiseraum
museum [mjuːˈzɪəm]	Museum
musical box	Musikdose
brave [breɪv]	mutig, tapfer
take part in	teilnehmen an
rigging [ˈrɪgɪŋ]	Takelage

Looking at the language (page 103)

tape [teɪp]	Tonband
toilet cabinet [ˈtɔɪlɪt ˈkæbɪnɪt]	Waschraum, -ecke

Focus on grammar (page 103)

fireman [ˈfaɪəmən]	Feuerwehrmann
mainly [ˈmeɪnlɪ]	hauptsächlich
action [ˈækʃn]	Handlung
object [ˈɒbdʒɪkt]	Gegenstand
perform [pəˈfɔːm]	ausführen

Can you do it? (page 104)

prince [prɪns]	Prinz
touch [tʌtʃ]	anfassen, berühren
jewel [ˈdʒuːəl]	Juwel

Using the language (page 104)

introduction [ˌɪntrəˈdʌkʃən]	Einführung
beginning [bɪˈgɪnɪŋ]	Anfang

Extra: Different Accents (page 105)

accent [ˈæksənt]	Akzent
chart [tʃɑːt]	Tabelle
feature [ˈfiːtʃə]	Merkmal, Kennzeichen
speech [spiːtʃ]	Sprache
Standard British English [ˈstændəd]	hochsprachliches Englisch
pronounce [prəˈnaʊns]	aussprechen
Cockney [ˈkɒknɪ]	Cockney, Londoner Dialekt
instead of [ɪnˈsted]	statt, anstatt
Irishman [ˈaɪrɪʃmən]	Ire

Extra: What Were They Told? (page 105)

1 ceiling [ˈsiːlɪŋ]	Zimmerdecke
stow away [stəʊ]	verstauen, wegpacken
hold up	aufrechthalten, stützen
sail [seɪl]	Segel
Texan [ˈteksən]	Texaner

Extra: Interpreting (page 106)

interpret [ɪnˈtɜːprɪt]	dolmetschen
interpreter [ɪnˈtɜːprɪtə]	Dolmetscher

UNIT 9 READING IS FUN

Reading (page 108)

The Glove

scene [siːn]	Szene
jeweller [ˈdʒuːələ]	Juwelier
need something badly	etwas sehr brauchen
fear [fɪə]	Angst
make someone do something	jemanden zwingen oder veranlassen, etwas zu tun

Did you get it? (page 110)

2 business [ˈbɪznɪz]	Geschäft
thief [θiːf]	Dieb
climb [klaɪm]	klettern
fill [fɪl]	füllen
pocket [ˈpɒkɪt]	Tasche
police station	Polizeirevier

153

DICTIONARY

Das Verzeichnis enthält den Wortschatz dieses Buches sowie den als aktiv verfügbar vorausgesetzten Wortschatz der Bände *English in Action 1 RG*, *English in Action 2 RG* und *English in Action 3 R*.

(BE = British English, AE = American English)

A

a [ə] ein, eine; **five days a week** fünf Tage in der Woche
able ['eɪbl] fähig; **be able to do something** etwas tun können, fähig sein, etwas zu tun
about [ə'baʊt] über, von, ungefähr; **it costs about £ 9** es kostet ungefähr 9 Pfund; **they talk about sport** sie unterhalten sich über Sport; **what about Mike?** wie steht's mit Mike? was ist mit Mike?; **what was it about?** worum ging es?
above [ə'bʌv] oben, oberhalb, über
abroad [ə'brɔːd] im Ausland, ins Ausland
accent ['æksənt] Akzent
accept [ək'sept] annehmen
accident ['æksɪdənt] Unfall
accompany [ə'kʌmpənɪ] begleiten
according to [ə'kɔːdɪŋ] wie ... sagte, ...zufolge; **according to (the news)** wie (in den Nachrichten) gemeldet; **according to the story** wie man erzählt, wie erzählt wird
account [ə'kaʊnt] Bericht
accuse someone [ə'kjuːz] jemanden beschuldigen, anklagen
ache [eɪk] Schmerzen; **stomach-ache** Magenschmerzen
across [ə'krɒs] über, jenseits; **right across** geradewegs über
act out [ækt] als Szene spielen, etwas darstellen
action ['ækʃn] Handlung, Aktion
activity [ək'tɪvətɪ] Tätigkeit, Aktivität
actress ['æktrɪs] Schauspielerin
actually ['æktʃʊəlɪ] eigentlich, wirklich
add [æd] hinzufügen; **by adding** durch Anhängen von
address [ə'dres] Adresse
admiral ['ædmərəl] Admiral
admire [əd'maɪə] bewundern
admit [əd'mɪt] zugeben
adult ['ædʌlt] Erwachsener
advantage [əd'vɑːntɪdʒ] Vorteil
adventure [əd'ventʃə] Abenteuer
advice [əd'vaɪs] Rat (-schlag), Tip
aeroplane ['eərəpleɪn] Flugzeug
afraid [ə'freɪd] ängstlich, furchtsam; **I'm afraid** es tut mir leid

African ['æfrɪkən] Afrikaner, afrikanisch
after ['ɑːftə] nach, nachdem; **after school** nach der Schule; **after that** danach; **not ... after all** doch nicht
afternoon [,ɑːftə'nuːn] Nachmittag; **in the afternoon** am Nachmittag, nachmittags; **this afternoon** heute nachmittag; **good afternoon** guten Tag; **on Monday afternoons** Montag nachmittags
afterwards ['ɑːftəwədz] hinterher, nachher, danach, anschließend
again [ə'gen] wieder
against [ə'genst] gegen; **be against something** gegen etwas sein
age [eɪdʒ] (Lebens)Alter; **at my age** in meinem Alter
ago [ə'gəʊ] vor; **ten months ago** vor zehn Monaten
agree [ə'griː] zustimmen
agriculture ['ægrɪkʌltʃə] Landwirtschaft
air [eə] Luft
airport ['eəpɔːt] Flughafen
alarm system [ə'lɑːm 'sɪstəm] Alarmanlage, Alarmsystem
alcohol ['ælkəhɒl] Alkohol
all [ɔːl] alle, ganz; **all afternoon** den ganzen Nachmittag; **all day** den ganzen Tag; **all evening** den ganzen Abend; **all right** in Ordnung, ja, schön; **all the others** alle anderen; **all the people** alle Leute; **all the time** die ganze Zeit; **all the way** den ganzen Weg; **in all** insgesamt; **not ... at all** überhaupt nicht; **not ... after all** doch nicht; **that's all right** (auf einen Dank) bitte sehr
allow [ə'laʊ] erlauben; **allow somebody to do something** jemandem erlauben, etwas zu tun; **be allowed to do something** etwas tun dürfen
almost ['ɔːlməʊst] fast
alone [ə'ləʊn] allein
along [ə'lɒŋ] entlang; **the road ran along the coast** die Straße verlief an der Küste
aloud [ə'laʊd] laut; **read aloud** vorlesen, laut lesen
already [ɔːl'redɪ] schon, bereits
also ['ɔːlsəʊ] auch
although [ɔːl'ðəʊ] obwohl

always ['ɔːlweɪz] immer
a.m. [eɪ'em] Uhrzeit vor 12 Uhr mittags; **9 a.m.** 9 Uhr vormittags
ambulance ['æmbjʊləns] Krankenwagen
American [ə'merɪkən] Amerikaner, amerikanisch
among [ə'mʌŋ] zwischen, unter
an [æn, ən] ein(e); **an apple** ein Apfel
and [ænd, ənd] und
angry ['æŋgrɪ] verärgert, aufgebracht
animal ['ænɪml] Tier
announcer [ə'naʊnsə] Rundfunksprecher, Ansager
anorak ['ænəræk] Anorak
another [ə'nʌðə] noch ein(e), ein(e) weiter(er, e, es), ein(e) ander(er, e, es); **another boy** ein anderer Junge; **another cup of tea** noch eine Tasse Tee; **one another** einander
answer ['ɑːnsə] (be-)antworten, Antwort
any ['enɪ] irgendein(e), (irgend)welche; **not ... any more** nicht mehr
anybody ['enɪ,bɒdɪ] (irgend) jemand
anyone ['enɪwʌn] (irgend) jemand; **anyone else** irgend jemand anders
anything ['enɪθɪŋ] (irgend) etwas
anyway ['enɪweɪ] egal, wie dem auch sei
apologize [ə'pɒlədʒaɪz] sich entschuldigen
appear [ə'pɪə] erscheinen, auftreten
apple ['æpl] Apfel
application form [,æplɪ'keɪʃn fɔːm] Anmeldeformular
apply to someone [ə'plaɪ] für jemanden zutreffen
April ['eɪprəl] April
architect ['ɑːkɪtekt] Architekt
area ['eərɪə] Gegend, Gebiet, Fläche
argue with someone [ɑː'gjuː] mit jemandem streiten
argument ['ɑːgjumənt] Streit, Auseinandersetzung; **have arguments with someone** mit jemandem streiten
arm [ɑːm] Arm
arrange [ə'reɪndʒ] sich verabreden, ausmachen, erzwingen, planen, in die Wege leiten
arrive [ə'raɪv] ankommen
arrow ['ærəʊ] Pfeil
art [ɑːt] Kunst
artificial [,ɑːtɪ'fɪʃl] künstlich

arts and crafts [,ɑːtsən'krɑːfts] Kunst(Hand)werk
arts festival [,ɑːts 'festəvəl] Musik- und Theaterfestival
as [æz, əz] wie, als, wenn; weil, da; **as if** als ob; **you look as if** du siehst aus als ob; **as old as you** so alt wie du; **as well** ebenso; **as soon as** sobald
ask [ɑːsk] fragen; **ask about** sich erkundigen; **ask for** fragen nach, bitten um; **ask for something** um etwas bitten; **ask questions** Fragen stellen; **ask someone to do something** jemanden bitten, etwas zu tun; **ask the way** nach dem Weg fragen
assistant [ə'sɪstənt] Verkäufer, Ladenhilfe, Assistent
associate [ə'səʊʃɪeɪt] verbinden, in Zusammenhang bringen
at [æt, ət] an, in; **at home** zu Hause; **at last** endlich; **at nine o'clock** um neun Uhr; **at once** sofort; **at school** in der Schule; **at the match** beim Spiel; **at the station** auf dem/am Bahnhof; **at the window** am Fenster; **at least** mindestens; **I'm at Liz's** ich bin bei Liz (zu Hause)
athletics [æθ'letɪks] Leichtathletik
atmosphere ['ætməˌsfɪə] Atmosphäre
attack [ə'tæk] angreifen
attract [ə'trækt] anziehen, anlocken
attraction [ə'trækʃn] Anziehungspunkt, Reiz, Attraktion, Sehenswürdigkeit; **latest attraction** neueste Attraktion
attractive [ə'træktɪv] attraktiv, ansprechend
August ['ɔːgəst] August
aunt [ɑːnt] Tante
Australian [ɒ'streɪlɪən] australisch, Australier(in)
automatically [,ɔːtə'mætɪkəlɪ] automatisch
autumn ['ɔːtəm] Herbst
avoid [ə'vɔɪd] (ver)meiden
away [ə'weɪ] weg, fort
awful ['ɔːfʊl] furchtbar, scheußlich

B

back [bæk] Rücken; Hinter(er, e, es), Rückseite; **be back** zurückgekehrt

sein; **go back** zurückgehen
background [ˈbækgraʊnd] Hintergrund
bad [bæd] schlecht, schlimm, krank
badly [ˈbædlɪ] schlecht; **badly hurt** schwer verletzt; **badly damaged** stark beschädigt, stark zerstört
badminton [ˈbædmɪntən] Federballspiel
bag [bæg] Tasche, Beutel
bake [beɪk] backen
baker [ˈbeɪkə] Bäcker
ball [bɔːl] Ball
ballet [ˈbæleɪ] Ballett
band [bænd] Band, Kapelle
bank [bæŋk] Bank, Sparkasse, Ufer
bar [bɑː] Bar, Tafel; **bar of chocolate** Tafel Schokolade; **snack bar** Snackbar, Imbißstube
basketball [ˈbɑːskɪtbɔːl] Basketball; **basketball court** Basketballplatz
bath [bɑːθ] Bad; **have a bath** ein Bad nehmen, baden, waschen
bathroom [ˈbɑːθrʊm] Badezimmer
battery [ˈbætərɪ] Batterie
battle [ˈbætl] Schlacht
bay [beɪ] Bucht
be (was, were, been) [biː, wɒz, biːn] sein; **be good friends** befreundet sein; **be hungry** Hunger haben
beach [biːtʃ] Strand; **on the beach** am Strand
beat (beat, beaten) [biːt, biːt, biːtn] schlagen, besiegen; **off the beaten track** weg vom Eingefahrenen
beautiful [ˈbjuːtɪfʊl] schön
beauty [ˈbjuːtɪ] Schönheit
because [bɪˈkɒz] weil; **because of** wegen
become (became, become) [bɪˈkʌm, bɪˈkeɪm, bɪˈkʌm] werden
bed [bed] Bett; **bed and breakfast** Übernachtung mit Frühstück; **in bed** im Bett
bedroom [ˈbedrʊm] Schlafzimmer
beer [bɪə] Bier
before [bɪˈfɔː] vor, bevor, vorher, früher; **have you been here before?** warst du schon früher hier?; **before she came to Germany** bevor sie nach Deutschland kam; **the day before yesterday** vorgestern
begin (began, begun) [bɪˈgɪn, bɪˈgæn, bɪˈgʌn] beginnen, anfangen
beginning [bɪˈgɪnɪŋ] Anfang
behave [bɪˈheɪv] sich benehmen
behaviour [bɪˈheɪvjə] verhalten, benehmen
behind [bɪˈhaɪnd] hinter
believe (in) something [bɪˈliːv] (an) etwas glauben
belong to [bɪˈlɒŋ] gehören zu
below [bɪˈləʊ] darunter, unten
besides [bɪˈsaɪdz] außer
best [best] best(er, e, es), am besten; **he is the best swimmer** er ist der beste Schwimmer; **like best** am liebsten haben
better [ˈbetə] besser
between [bɪˈtwiːn] zwischen
bicycle [ˈbaɪsɪkl] Fahrrad

big [bɪg] groß; **bigger** größer
bike [baɪk] Fahrrad; **ride a bike** radfahren
bill [bɪl] Rechnung
billion [ˈbɪljən] Billion; **3 Billion** 3 Billionen
bird [bɜːd] Vogel
birthday [ˈbɜːθdeɪ] Geburtstag; **for his/her birthday** zum Geburtstag
birthplace [ˈbɜːθpleɪs] Geburtsort, Geburtshaus
bit *in*: **a bit** [bɪt, ə bɪt] ein wenig, ein bißchen
black [blæk] schwarz
blackboard [ˈblækbɔːd] (Schul)Tafel
blame oneself [bleɪm wʌnˈself] sich Vorwürfe machen; **blame someone for something** jemanden für etwas tadeln, schelten
block [blɒk] blockieren; **block of flats** Wohnblock
blonde [blɒnd] blond
blouse [blaʊz] Bluse
blue [bluː] blau
board [bɔːd] (Schul)Tafel, Anzeigetafel; **on board** an Bord
boat [bəʊt] Boot
body [ˈbɒdɪ] Körper, Leiche
boil [bɔɪl] kochen
bold print [bəʊld prɪnt] Fettdruck
book [bʊk] Buch
bookshelf [ˈbʊkʃelf] Bücherregal
boot [buːt] Stiefel
border [ˈbɔːdə] Grenze
bored [bɔːd] gelangweilt; **feel bored** Langeweile haben; **bored stiff** zu Tode gelangweilt
boring [ˈbɔːrɪŋ] langweilig
born *in*: **be born** [bɔːn] geboren sein
borrow [ˈbɒrəʊ] (ent)leihen, borgen; **borrow something** sich etwas (aus)borgen
boss [bɒs] Chef
both [bəʊθ] beide
bottle [ˈbɒtl] Flasche
boutique [buːˈtiːk] Boutique
bowl [bəʊl] Schüssel
bowler hat [ˈbəʊlə hæt] "Melone"
box [bɒks] Schachtel, Kasten, Kiste; **phone box** Telefonzelle
boy [bɔɪ] Junge
boyfriend [ˈbɔɪfrend] Freund (eines Mädchens)
bra [brɑː] B. H.
bracket [ˈbrækɪt] Klammer; **in brackets** in Klammern
branch [brɑːntʃ] abzweigen, sich verzweigen
brave [breɪv] mutig, tapfer
bread [bred] Brot
break [breɪk] Pause
break (broke, broken) [breɪk, brəʊk, ˈbrəʊkən] zerbrechen, kaputtmachen; **break out** ausbrechen; **the fire broke out** das Feuer brach aus; **break up** auseinanderbrechen, -gehen
breakfast [ˈbrekfəst] Frühstück; **have breakfast** frühstücken; **bed and breakfast** Übernachtung mit Frühstück
bridge [brɪdʒ] Brücke
briefs [briːfs] Unterhose *(für Jungen)*
bring (brought, brought) [brɪŋ, brɔːt, brɔːt] (her)bringen
British [ˈbrɪtɪʃ] britisch, Brite
broadcast [ˈbrɔːdkɑːst] Sendung im Rundfunk
brochure [ˈbrəʊʃə] Broschüre, Prospekt
broken [ˈbrəʊkən] kaputt
brother [ˈbrʌðə] Bruder
brothers and sisters [ˈbrʌðəz ənd ˈsɪstəz] Geschwister
brown [braʊn] braun
brush [brʌʃ] Bürste, bürsten
build (built, built) [bɪld, bɪlt, bɪlt] (er)bauen; **it was built by...** es wurde von ... gebaut
building [ˈbɪldɪŋ] Gebäude, Bauwerk
bullet [ˈbʊlɪt] Kugel
burn (burnt, burnt) [bɜːn, bɜːnt, bɜːnt] (ab-) (ver)brennen
bury [ˈberɪ] beerdigen, begraben, beisetzen
bus [bʌs] Bus; **on the bus** im Bus; **bus station** Busbahnhof; **bus stop** Bushaltestelle; **busdriver** Busfahrer(in)
business [ˈbɪznɪs] Geschäft
busy [ˈbɪzɪ] fleißig, beschäftigt, arbeitsreich
but [bʌt, bət] aber
buy (bought, bought) [baɪ, bɔːt, bɔːt] kaufen
by [baɪ] bei, an, entlang; **by six o'clock** (spätestens) um/bis sechs Uhr; **by the sea** an der See, am Strand; **by the way** übrigens; **by this time** spätestens um diese Zeit; **go by train** mit dem Zug fahren; **it was built by...** es wurde von ... gebaut
bye [baɪ] auf Wiedersehen

C

cabin [ˈkæbɪn] Kabine
café [ˈkæfeɪ] Café
cage [keɪdʒ] Käfig
cake [keɪk] Kuchen
call [kɔːl] rufen, nennen; **it is called** es heißt
calm [kɑːm] ruhig
camera [ˈkæmərə] Kamera
camp [kæmp] Zeltplatz, Lager; zelten, campen
camp site [kæmp saɪt] Campingplatz
camper [ˈkæmpə] Zeltende(r), Camper(in)
can (could) [kæn, kʊd] können, dürfen
canoeing [kəˈnuːɪŋ] Kanufahren
cap [kæp] Mütze
capital [ˈkæpɪtl] Hauptstadt
captain [ˈkæptɪn] Kapitän
car [kɑː] Auto; **car park** Parkplatz
card [kɑːd] (Spiel)Karte
cardboard [ˈkɑːdbɔːd] Karton, Pappe
care [keə] *in*: **I don't really care** mir ist es eigentlich egal

careful [ˈkeəfʊl] vorsichtig, sorgfältig; **be careful** Vorsicht! sei vorsichtig!
carpet [ˈkɑːpɪt] Teppich
carry [ˈkærɪ] (eine Last) tragen
cartoon [kɑːˈtuːn] Karikatur, Zeichentrickfilm
case [keɪs] Koffer, Fall; **in case of** im Falle von; **in most cases** in den meisten Fällen
cassette recorder [kæˈset rɪˈkɔːdə] Kassettenrekorder
cast [kɑːst] Besetzung, Rollenverteilung
castle [ˈkɑːsl] Burg, Schloß
cat [kæt] Katze
catch (caught, caught) [kætʃ, kɔːt, kɔːt] *in*: **catch a cold** sich erkälten; **catch the bus** den Bus erwischen
Catholic [ˈkæθəlɪk] katholisch
cause (n.) [kɔːz] Ursache, Grund
cause (v.) [kɔːz] verursachen
cave [keɪv] Höhle
caving [ˈkeɪvɪŋ] Höhlenwandern
ceiling [ˈsiːlɪŋ] Zimmerdecke
central [ˈsentrəl] Zentral, -Zentrum; **central district** Innenstadtbereich
centre [ˈsentə] Zentrum; **sports centre** Sportzentrum; **town centre** Stadtmitte
century [ˈsentʃərɪ] Jahrhundert
certain [ˈsɜːtn] bestimmt, gewiß
certainly [ˈsɜːtnlɪ] natürlich, sicher(lich)
chair [tʃeə] Stuhl
chance [tʃɑːns] Gelegenheit, Chance, Möglichkeit
change (v.) [tʃeɪndʒ] (sich) (ver)ändern; **change one's mind** die Meinung/Ansicht andern
change (n.) [tʃeɪndʒ] Wechselgeld; Abwechslung; **for a change** zur Abwechslung
channel [ˈtʃænl] Kanal, Programm
character [ˈkærəktə] Charakter
chart [tʃɑːt] Tabelle, Übersicht
cheap [tʃiːp] billig
check [tʃek] kontrollieren, (über)prüfen
cheek *in*: [tʃiːk] **you've got a cheek** du bist unverschämt/frech
cheer up [tʃɪərˈʌp] aufheitern, in gute Laune versetzen, bessere Laune bekommen
cheese [tʃiːz] Käse
chicken [ˈtʃɪkɪn] Huhn
child [tʃaɪld] Kind
childish [ˈtʃaɪldɪʃ] kindisch
children [ˈtʃɪldrən] Kinder
chips [tʃɪps] Pommes frites
chocolate [ˈtʃɒkəlɪt] Schokolade
chocolates [ˈtʃɒkələts] Pralinen
choice [tʃɔɪs] (Aus)wahl; **make his choice** seine Wahl treffen
choose (chose, chosen) [tʃuːz, tʃəʊz, ˈtʃəʊzn] aussuchen, auswählen
chop [tʃɒp] hacken, schneiden; **finely chopped** fein geschnitten
Christian [ˈkrɪstjən] Christ(in), christlich
Christmas [ˈkrɪsməs] Weihnachten
church [tʃɜːtʃ] Kirche
cigarette [ˌsɪgəˈret] Zigarette
cinema [ˈsɪnəmə] Kino

city ['sɪtɪ] Stadt
claim [kleɪm] beanspruchen
clan [klæn] Familie, Sippe, Clan
class [klɑ:s] Klasse
classical ['klæsɪkl] klassisch
classroom ['klɑ:srʊm] Klassenzimmer
clean (adj.) [kli:n] sauber
clean (v.) [kli:n] säubern, reinigen; **clean something out** etwas ausputzen; **clean up** aufwischen
cleaning staff ['kli:nɪŋ ˌstɑ:f] „Putzkolonne"; Gebäudereinigung
cleaning woman ['kli:nɪŋ ˌwʊmən] Putzfrau
clear [klɪə] klar
clever ['klevə] klug
cliché ['kli:ʃeɪ] Klischee
climate ['klaɪmɪt] Klima
climb [klaɪm] klettern
clock [klɒk] Uhr; **at six o'clock** um sechs Uhr
close [kləʊz] schließen, zumachen; **closed** geschlossen
closing ['kləʊzɪŋ] Schlußsatz (im Brief)
clothes [kləʊðz] Kleider, Kleidung; **clothes shop** Bekleidungsgeschäft
cloudy ['klaʊdɪ] wolkig
club [klʌb] Club
coach [kəʊtʃ] (Reise)Bus
coal [kəʊl] in: **coal mining** Bergbau
coast [kəʊst] Küste
coastline ['kəʊstlaɪn] Küste
coat [kəʊt] Mantel
Cockney ['kɒknɪ] Cockney, Londoner Dialekt
code [kəʊd] Code(Wort), Schlüssel(Wort)
coffee ['kɒfɪ] Kaffee
coin [kɔɪn] Münze
coke [kəʊk] Cola
cold (adj.) [kəʊld] kalt; **I'm cold** mir ist kalt, mich friert
cold (n.) [kəʊld] Erkältung, Schnupfen; **catch a cold** sich erkälten
collapse [kə'læps] einstürzen, zusammenbrechen
collect [kə'lekt] (ein)sammeln, einholen
colonial times [kə'ləʊnjəl taɪmz] Zeiten der Kolonialherrschaft
colony ['kɒlənɪ] Kolonie, kleine Ansiedlung
colour ['kʌlə] Farbe
coloured ['kʌləd] bunt
column ['kɒləm] Säule
comb [kəʊm] Kamm
come (came, come) [kʌm, keɪm, kʌm] kommen; **come along** mitkommen; **come back** zurückkommen; **come home** nach Hause kommen; **come in** hereinkommen, eindringen; **come on los! vorwärts! weiter!; come straight back** sofort zurückkehren; **he comes from Germany** er kommt aus Deutschland; **I'll come over** ich komme vorbei
comedy ['kɒmɪdɪ] (Film-)Komödie
comfortable ['kʌmfətəbl] bequem
comic ['kɒmɪk] Comic-Heft

command [kə'mɑ:nd] Befehl
comment on something ['kɒment] etwas kommentieren, Bemerkungen machen
common ['kɒmən] gewöhnlich, häufig, allgemein; **have something in common** etwas gemeinsam haben
company ['kʌmpənɪ] Gesellschaft
comparative [kəm'pærətɪv] Komparativ
compare [kəm'peə] vergleichen
comparison [kəm'pærɪsn] Vergleich
competition [ˌkɒmpɪ'tɪʃn] Wettkampf, Wettbewerb
complain [kəm'pleɪn] sich beklagen; **complain to somebody** sich bei jemandem beklagen
complete (v.) [kəm'pli:t] vervollständigen
completely [kəm'pli:tlɪ] völlig, ganz und gar
comprehensive school [ˌkɒmprɪ'hensɪv sku:l] (engl.) Gesamtschule
comradeship ['kɒmreɪdʃɪp] Kameradschaft
concert ['kɒnsət] Konzert
conference ['kɒnfərəns] in: **press conference** Pressekonferenz
confident ['kɒnfɪdənt] zuversichtlich
confrontation [ˌkɒnfrən'teɪʃn] Konfrontation, Streit
congratulations [kənˌgrætʊ'leɪʃnz] herzlichen Glückwunsch!
contact (v.) ['kɒntækt] Kontakt aufnehmen, sich in Verbindung setzen
continue [kən'tɪnju:] weitermachen
control [kən'trəʊl] Kontrolle; **out of control** außer Kontrolle; **under control** unter Kontrolle
conversation [ˌkɒnvə'seɪʃn] Gespräch, Unterhaltung
cook [kʊk] kochen; **cooky gently** auf kleiner Flamme kochen
corner ['kɔ:nə] Ecke; **at the corner (of)** an der Ecke (von)
correct (adj.) [kə'rekt] korrekt, richtig
cost [kɒst] kosten
could [kʊd] in: **could be as high as 50** könnte bei 50 liegen; **could you come?** könntest du kommen?; **I couldn't hear** ich konnte nicht hören
count [kaʊnt] zählen
counter ['kaʊntə] Theke, Ladentisch
country ['kʌntrɪ] Land; **country dancing** Volkstanz
countryside ['kʌntrɪsaɪd] ländliche Gegend, Landschaft
courage ['kʌrɪdʒ] Mut
cousin ['kʌzn] Vetter, Kusine
cover ['kʌvə] zudecken, bedecken
cow [kaʊ] Kuh
cowboy ['kaʊbɔɪ] Cowboy
crash [kræʃ] Krach
crazy ['kreɪzɪ] verrückt; **be crazy about** verrückt sein nach
creature ['kri:tʃə] Wesen, Kreatur
critical ['krɪtɪkl] kritisch; **critical stage** kritischer Punkt, kritische Phase
cross [krɒs] (Straße) überqueren

crowd [kraʊd] (Menschen)Menge, Haufen, Verein
crowded ['kraʊdɪd] voll (von), vollgestopft (mit Menschen)
cultural ['kʌltʃərəl] kulturell
culture ['kʌltʃə] Kultur
cup [kʌp] Tasse
cupboard ['kʌbəd] Schrank
curtain ['kɜ:tn] Vorhang
custom ['kʌstəm] Sitte, Gebrauch
cut (cut, cut) [kʌt, kʌt, kʌt] schneiden, abschneiden
cycle ['saɪkl] radfahren
cycling holiday ['saɪklɪŋ 'hɒlədeɪ] Urlaub mit dem Fahrrad

D

dad [dæd] Papa, Vati
damaged ['dæmɪdʒd] beschädigt; **badly damaged** stark beschädigt, stark zerstört
dance [dɑ:ns] tanzen
dancer [dɑ:nsə] Tänzer
danger ['deɪndʒə] Gefahr
dangerous ['deɪndʒərəs] gefährlich
dare [deə] wagen
dark [dɑ:k] dunkel
date [deɪt] Datum, Tag, Verabredung
daughter ['dɔ:tə] Tochter
day [deɪ] Tag; **all day** den ganzen Tag; **five days a week** fünf Tage in der Woche; **one day** eines Tages; **the day before** am Tag vorher; **the day before yesterday** vorgestern
dead [ded] tot; **the number of dead** die Zahl der Toten
deal [di:l] in: **a great deal of** ein großer Teil
dear [dɪə] lieb(er, e, es)
December [dɪ'sembə] Dezember
decide [dɪ'saɪd] (sich) entscheiden
deep [di:p] tief
defeat [dɪ'fi:t] besiegen
defend oneself [dɪ'fend] sich verteidigen
definitely ['defɪnɪtlɪ] mit Sicherheit, bestimmt
deny [dɪ'naɪ] leugnen, abstreiten, verneinen
department [dɪ'pɑ:tmənt] Abteilung; **department store** Kaufhaus
dependent on [dɪ'pendənt] abhängig von
describe [dɪ'skraɪb] beschreiben
description [dɪ'skrɪpʃn] Beschreibung
design [dɪ'zaɪn] entwerfen, gestalten
desk [desk] Schreibtisch, Pult
despite [dɪ'spaɪt] trotz
destroy [dɪ'strɔɪ] zerstören
detective [dɪ'tektɪv] Detektiv
develop [dɪ'veləp] entwickeln; **develop into** sich zu etwas entwickeln
dialect ['daɪəlekt] Dialekt
dialogue ['daɪəlɒg] Dialog; **make up a dialogue** einen Dialog erfinden
diary ['daɪərɪ] Tagebuch

dictator [dɪk'teɪtə] Diktator
dictionary ['dɪkʃənrɪ] Wörterbuch
die [daɪ] sterben
difference ['dɪfrəns] Unterschied
different ['dɪfrənt] verschieden; **different from/to** anders als; **no different** keineswegs anders
difficulty ['dɪfɪkəltɪ] Schwierigkeit; **run into difficulties** in Schwierigkeiten geraten
dining cabin ['daɪnɪŋ 'kæbɪn] Speiseraum
dining-room ['daɪnɪŋrʊm] Eßzimmer
dinner ['dɪnə] (Mittag-, Abend-)Essen (Hauptmahlzeit)
direct [dɪ'rekt] Regie führen
direction [dɪ'rekʃn] Richtung, Anweisung, Himmelsrichtung; **give directions** Wegauskünfte erteilen
director [dɪ'rektə] Direktor, Leiter
dirty ['dɜ:tɪ] schmutzig
disadvantage [ˌdɪsəd'vɑ:ntɪdʒ] Nachteil
disagree with somebody [ˌdɪsə'gri:] nicht derselben Meinung sein wie jemand
disappear [ˌdɪsə'pɪə] verschwinden
disappointed [ˌdɪsə'pɔɪntɪd] enttäuscht
disco ['dɪskəʊ] Diskothek
discuss [dɪ'skʌs] besprechen, diskutieren
discussion [dɪ'skʌʃn] Diskussion
dislikes (n.) [dɪs'laɪks] Abneigungen
distance ['dɪstəns] Entfernung
district ['dɪstrɪkt] Bezirk; **central district** Innenstadtbereich
do (did, done) [du:, dɪd, dʌn] tun, machen; **do (better) in ...** (besser) in ... abschneiden; **do sport** Sport treiben; **do subjects** (Schul)fächer lernen; **do the housework** die Hausarbeit machen; **do the shopping** Einkäufe machen; **do the washing-up** das Geschirr spülen; **do (badly) in a test** in einer Prüfung (schlecht) abschneiden; **do a great job** gute Arbeit leisten; **he does his homework** er macht seine Hausaufgaben; **what can I do for you?** Sie wünschen bitte?; **dos and don'ts** Verhaltensregeln
doctor ['dɒktə] Arzt, Ärztin
dog [dɒg] Hund
doll [dɒl] Puppe
dollar ['dɒlə] Dollar
door [dɔ:] Tür
down [daʊn] hinunter, herunter; **down here** hier unten; **down the street** die Straße hin-, herunter; **straight down** hinunter
downstairs [ˌdaʊn'steəz] die Treppe hinunter
downtown [ˌdaʊn'taʊn] in die (der) Innenstadt; **in downtown Chicago** in der Innenstadt von Chicago
drama ['drɑ:mə] Drama
draw (drew, drawn) [drɔ:, dru:, drɔ:n] zeichnen
drawer ['drɔ:ə] Schublade
dream (dreamt, dreamt) [dri:m, dremt, dremt] träumen
dress [dres] Kleid
drink (n.) [drɪŋk] Getränk

drink (v.) (drank, drunk) [drɪŋk, dræŋk, drʌŋk] trinken
drive (drove, driven) [draɪv, drəʊv, 'drɪvn] fahren; **drive a car** Auto fahren
driver ['draɪvə] Fahrer
drop [drɒp] fallenlassen, wegwerfen
drown [draʊn] ertrinken
dry [draɪ] trocken
dull [dʌl] langweilig
during ['djʊərɪŋ] während, im Laufe
duty ['djuːtɪ] Pflicht

E

each [iːtʃ] jed(er, e, es); **each other** einander
ear [ɪə] Ohr
early ['ɜːlɪ] früh; **early in the morning** früh am Morgen
earth [ɜːθ] Erde; **Earth** Planet Erde; **what on earth...?** was in aller Welt...?
east [iːst] Osten
easter ['iːstə] Ostern
easy ['iːzɪ] leicht, einfach
eat (ate, eaten) [iːt, et, 'iːtn] essen
economy [ɪ'kɒnəmɪ] Wirtschaft
egg [eg] Ei
either ['aɪðə] entweder; **either...or** entweder...oder; **I don't/didn't either** ich auch nicht; **I can't/wouldn't either** ich auch nicht
electric [ɪ'lektrɪk] elektrisch
electrical [ɪ'lektrɪkl] elektrisch
electronic [ˌɪlek'trɒnɪk] elektronisch
else [els] *in:* **anyone else** irgend jemand anders; **anything else?** (sonst) noch etwas?; **someone else** jemand anders; **what else?** was (sonst) noch?
emperor ['empərə] Kaiser
empty ['emptɪ] leer
enclave ['enkleɪv] Enklave
enclose [ɪn'kləʊz] beiliegen, beifügen
encyclopaedia [enˌsaɪkləʊ'piːdjə] Enzyklopädie
end (n.) [end] Ende, Schluß; **in the end** schließlich, letzten Endes, zuletzt
end (v.) [end] enden, zu Ende gehen
ending ['endɪŋ] Schluß
enemy ['enəmɪ] Feind
English ['ɪŋglɪʃ] englisch, Englisch; **he's English** er ist Engländer
enjoy [ɪn'dʒɔɪ] genießen, Gefallen haben an; **enjoy (myself, yourself etc.)** sich amüsieren, sich gut unterhalten
enough [ɪ'nʌf] genug
enter ['entə] betreten
entrance ['entrəns] Eingang
equipment [ɪ'kwɪpmənt] Ausrüstung, Gegenstand
escape [ɪ'skeɪp] entkommen, entfliehen
especially [ɪ'speʃəlɪ] besonders
European [ˌjʊərə'piːən] europäisch, Europäer
evacuate [ɪ'vækjʊeɪt] evakuieren, (v. Bewohnern) räumen
even ['iːvn] sogar; **not even** nicht einmal
evening ['iːvnɪŋ] Abend; **in the evening** am Abend, abends; **on Friday evenings** Freitag abends; **this evening** heute abend
event [ɪ'vent] Ereignis
ever ['evə] je, jemals; **have you ever been there?** bist du schon (ein)mal dort gewesen?; **not ever** niemals
every ['evrɪ] jed(er, e, es)
everybody ['evrɪˌbɒdɪ] jeder(mann)
everyone ['evrɪwʌn] = **everybody** jedermann
everything ['evrɪθɪŋ] alles
exam [ɪg'zæm] Prüfung
example [ɪg'zaːmpl] Beispiel; **for example** zum Beispiel
exciting [ɪk'saɪtɪŋ] aufregend, spannend
exclusive [ɪk'skluːsɪv] exklusiv, Sonder-, Extra-
excuse me [ɪk'skjuːz] entschuldigen Sie (bitte), Verzeihung
exercise ['eksəsaɪz] (körperliche) Bewegung
exercise-book ['eksəsaɪzbʊk] Übungsheft
exhausted [ɪg'zɔːstɪd] erschöpft
exhibition [ˌeksɪ'bɪʃn] Ausstellung
expect [ɪk'spekt] erwarten; **expect someone to do something** erwarten, daß jemand etwas tut
expensive [ɪk'spensɪv] teuer
experience [ɪk'spɪərɪəns] Erlebnis
experiment [ɪk'sperɪmənt] Experiment, Versuch
explain [ɪk'spleɪn] erklären
explanation [ˌekspləˈneɪʃn] Erklärung
explode [ɪk'spləʊd] explodieren
explore [ɪk'splɔː] erforschen
express [ɪk'spres] ausdrücken
expression [ɪk'spreʃn] Ausdruck
extra ['ekstrə] zusätzlich
extract (from) ['ekstrækt] Auszug, Ausschnitt, Abschnitt (aus)
eye [aɪ] Auge

F

face [feɪs] Gesicht
fact [fækt] Tatsache, Angabe, Punkt; **as a matter of fact** tatsächlich, in der Tat; **in fact** in der Tat; **get the facts right/wrong** richtige/falsche Angaben machen
factory/factories ['fæktərɪ] Fabrik
failure ['feɪljə] Versagen, Störung, Ausfall
fair [feə] gerecht, fair
faithfully ['feɪθfʊlɪ] *in:* **yours faithfully** mit freundlichen Grüßen
fall (fell, fallen) [fɔːl, fel, 'fɔːlən] fallen; **fall in love (with)** sich verlieben (in)
family ['fæmɪlɪ] Familie
famous ['feɪməs] berühmt
fan [fæn] Fan, Begeisterte(r), Anhänger(in)
fantastic [fæn'tæstɪk] phantastisch
far [fɑː] weit, fern, entfernt
farm [fɑːm] Bauernhof
fascinate ['fæsɪneɪt] faszinieren; **be fascinated** fasziniert sein
fascinating ['fæsɪneɪtɪŋ] faszinierend
fashion ['fæʃn] Mode
fast [fɑːst] schnell
fat [fæt] dick
father ['fɑːðə] Vater
fault [fɔːlt] Schuld; **it's my fault** ich bin schuld
favourite ['feɪvərɪt] Lieblings...
fear [fɪə] Angst
feature ['fiːtʃə] Merkmal, Kennzeichen
February ['februərɪ] Februar
feed (fed, fed) [fiːd, fed, fed] füttern
feel (felt, felt) [fiːl, felt, felt] sich fühlen; **feel uncomfortable** sich unwohl fühlen
ferry ['ferɪ] Fähre
festival ['festəvl] *in:* **arts festival** Musik- und Theaterfestival
fetch [fetʃ] holen, abholen
few [fjuː] *in:* **a few** ein paar
field [fiːld] Bereich, Feld; **football field** Fußballplatz
fight (fought, fought) [faɪt, fɔːt, fɔːt] (be)kämpfen
fill [fɪl] füllen; **fill in** ausfüllen
film [fɪlm] Film; **there is a film on** es läuft ein Film
find (found, found) [faɪnd, faʊnd, faʊnd] finden; **find out** herausfinden, feststellen
fine [faɪn] klein; **finely chopped** fein geschnitten
fine [faɪn] schön, gut; **I'm fine** es geht mir gut
finger ['fɪŋgə] Finger
fingernails ['fɪŋgəneɪlz] Fingernägel
finish ['fɪnɪʃ] (be)enden
fire ['faɪə] Feuer; **be on fire** brennen, in Brand sein; **set fire to something** etwas in Brand setzen
fire brigade (BE) [brɪ'geɪd] Feuerwehr
fire chief [tʃiːf] Feuerwehrhauptmann
fire department (AE) [dɪ'pɑːtmənt] Feuerwehr
fire engine ['endʒɪn] Feuerwehrauto
fire fighter ['faɪtə] Feuerwehrmann
fire truck (AE) [trʌk] Feuerwehrauto
fireman ['faɪəmən] Feuerwehrmann
firm [fɜːm] fest, bestimmt, standhaft
first [fɜːst] erst(er, e, es), zuerst, als erstes; **first aid** erste Hilfe; **at first** zuerst; **for the first time** zum erstenmal
fish [fɪʃ] Fisch
fisherman ['fɪʃəmən] Fischer
fishing ['fɪʃɪŋ] Fischen, Angeln
flag [flæg] Flagge
flagship ['flægʃɪp] Flaggschiff
flame [fleɪm] Flamme
flat (adj.) [flæt] flach
flat (n.) [flæt] (Etagen)wohnung
fleet [fliːt] Flotte
floor [flɔː] Fußboden, Stockwerk, Etage; **ground floor** Erdgeschoß; **on the first floor** im ersten Stock
flower ['flaʊə] Blume
foggy ['fɒgɪ] neblig
folk music [fəʊk] Folk(Musik)
follow ['fɒləʊ] folgen, verfolgen, verlaufen; **the road followed the coast** die Straße verlief entlang der Küste
following ['fɒləʊɪŋ] folgend(e, er, es)
fond [fɒnd] *in:* **be fond of...ing** sehr gern etwas tun; **he's still fond of me** er mag mich noch immer
food [fuːd] Essen, Nahrung
foot/feet [fʊt, fiːt] Fuß, Füße
football ['fʊtbɔːl] Fußball; **football field** Fußballfeld, Fußballplatz; **football match** Fußballspiel
for [fɔː] seit, für, zu; **for a week** eine Woche (lang); **for breakfast** zum Frühstück; **for example** zum Beispiel; **for five months** seit fünf Monaten; **for a change** zur Abwechslung; **for example** zum Beispiel; **for the first time** zum erstenmal
forecast ['fɔːkɑːst] *in:* **weather forecast** Wettervorhersage
foreigner ['fɒrənə] Ausländer
forest ['fɒrɪst] Wald
forestry ['fɒrɪstrɪ] Forstwirtschaft
forget (forgot, forgotten) [fə'get, fə'gɒt, fə'gɒtn] vergessen
forgive (forgave, forgiven) [fə'gɪv, fə'geɪv, fə'gɪvn] verzeihen
form [fɔːm] Klasse; Formular
fortress ['fɔːtrɪs] Festung
frankly ['fræŋklɪ] offen gesagt
French [frentʃ] Französisch, französisch
fresh [freʃ] frisch
Friday ['fraɪdɪ] Freitag
fridge [frɪdʒ] Kühlschrank
friend [frend] Freund, Freundin; **pen friend** Brieffreund(in); **be (good) friends** befreundet sein; **make friends with** Freundschaft schließen mit; **make friends** Freunde gewinnen
friendly ['frendlɪ] freundlich
friendship ['frendʃɪp] Freundschaft
frightened ['fraɪtnd] erschreckt, erschrocken; **be frightened** sich fürchten, Angst haben
from [frɒm, frəm] von, aus; **from Germany** aus Deutschland; **from six to nine o'clock** von sechs bis neun Uhr
front [frʌnt] vorder(er, e, es), Vorderseite; **in front of** vor
fruit [fruːt] Obst
fry [fraɪ] braten
frying pan ['fraɪɪŋ pæn] Bratpfanne
full (of) [fʊl] voll
fully computerized ['fʊlɪ kəm'pjuːtəraɪzd] voll durch Computer gesteuert
fully trained ['fʊlɪ treɪnd] hervorragend ausgebildet
fun [fʌn] Spaß, Vergnügen
funny ['fʌnɪ] spaßig, lustig
furious ['fjʊərɪəs] zornig, wütend
furniture ['fɜːnɪtʃə] Möbel
future ['fjuːtʃə] Zukunft

G

Gaelic ['geɪlɪk] gälisch, Gälisch
Gambian ['gæmbɪən, -bjən] Gambianer, gambianisch
game [geɪm] Spiel, Wettspiel
games [geɪmz] *Schulfach:* Sport und Spiel
garage ['gærɑːʒ; 'gærɪdʒ] Garage, (Auto-)Werkstatt
garden ['gɑːdn] Garten
gate [geɪt] Tor; **gate official** Torwächter
gauge [geɪdʒ] *in:* **narrow gauge railway** Schmalspurbahn
general ['dʒenərəl] allgemein; **general reason** eigentlicher Grund, Hauptanliegen
generally ['dʒenərəlɪ] allgemein, im allgemeinen
gentle, gently ['dʒentl, -tlɪ] sanft; **cook gently** auf kleiner Flamme kochen
Geography [dʒɪ'ɒgrəfɪ] Geographie
German ['dʒɜːmən] Deutsche(r), deutsch, Deutsch; **he is German** er ist Deutscher; **the Germans** die Deutschen
Germany ['dʒɜːmənɪ] Deutschland
get (got, got) [get, gɒt, gɒt] bekommen, holen, gelangen, verstehen, herausbekommen; **get + adj.** werden; **get around** umher reisen; **get better** besser werden; **get bored** sich langweilen; **get moody** traurig, trübsinnig werden; **get off (the train)** (aus dem Zug) aussteigen; **get off our bikes** vom Rad runtersteigen; **get on** auskommen, zurechtkommen, sich verstehen; **get on (the bus)** einsteigen in (den Bus); **get on well with somebody** gut mit jemandem auskommen; **get to (a place)** in... ankommen, hinkommen, erreichen; **get to know (someone)** jemanden kennenlernen; **get up** aufstehen; **get into trouble** in Schwierigkeiten geraten; **get something repaired** etwas reparieren lassen; **get wet** naß werden; **he can't get in** er kann nicht hineinkommen; **he gets £ 5** er bekommt 5 Pfund; **she got an A** sie hat die Note A bekommen; **get the facts right/wrong** richtige/falsche Angaben machen
girl [gɜːl] Mädchen
girlfriend ['gɜːlfrend] Freundin (eines Jungen)
give (gave, given) [gɪv, geɪv, 'gɪvn] geben
glad [glæd] *in:* **be glad** sich freuen
glass [glɑːs] Glas
glove [glʌv] Handschuh
glue [gluː] Klebstoff, Leim
go (went, gone) [gəʊ, went, gɒn] gehen, fahren; **go ahead!** nur zu!; **go away** weggehen; **go by bus** mit dem Bus fahren; **go by tube** mit der U-Bahn fahren; **go home (for lunch)** (zum Essen) nach Hause gehen; **go mad** verrückt werden; **go on** weitergehen, weiter ma-

chen; **go out** ausgehen; **go right in** geh nur rein; **go shopping** einkaufen; **go swimming (skating)** schwimmen (schlittschuhlaufen) gehen; **go to bed** ins Bett gehen; **go up to someone** auf jemanden zugehen; **go wrong** schiefgehen, nicht klappen; **(let!s) go and see Mike** (laß uns) Mike besuchen; **go for rides** Fahrten machen; **go past** vorbeigehen, -fahren; **go to sleep** schlafen gehen; **I'm going to wash my hair** ich wasche mir die Haare; **you go** Du bist an der Reihe
gold [gəʊld] Gold
good [gʊd] gut; **good morning** guten Morgen; **he is good at swimming** er kann gut schwimmen
goodbye [ˌgʊd'baɪ] auf Wiedersehen
goodness ['gʊdnɪs] *in:* **oh, goodness** ach du meine Güte
grandfather ['grænd,fɑːðə] Großvater
grandma ['grænmɑː] = grandmother
grandmother ['grænˌmʌðə] Großmutter
grandson ['grænsʌn] Enkel
grass [grɑːs] Rasen, Wiese
grave [greɪv] Grab
graze [greɪz] grasen
great [greɪt] groß, großartig, prima; **a great deal of** ein großer Teil
green [griːn] grün
greeting ['griːtɪŋ] Gruß, Begrüßung, Anrede
grey [greɪ] grau
ground floor [graʊnd] Erdgeschoß
groundnut ['graʊndnʌt] Erdnuß
group [gruːp] Gruppe
grow (grew, grown) [grəʊ, gruː, grəʊn] wachsen
guest [gest] Gast, Besucher; **guest house** Pension, Gästehaus
guide (n.) [gaɪd] Führer, (Wander-)Führer
guide (v.) [gaɪd] führen
guided ['gaɪdɪd] *in:* **guided tour** Besichtigung mit einem Führer
guitar [gɪ'tɑː] Gitarre; **play the guitar** Gitarre spielen

H

haggis ['hægɪs] Schafwurst
hair [heə] Haar, Haare
haircut ['heəkʌt] Haarschnitt
half [hɑːf] halb; **half a pound** ein halbes Pfund; **half an hour** eine halbe Stunde; **half past six** halb sieben
ham [hæm] Schinken
hamburger ['hæmbɜːgə] Hamburger
hand [hænd] Hand
hang (hung, hung) [hæŋ, hʌŋ, hʌŋ] hängen
happen ['hæpən] geschehen, passieren; **what's happened to...?** was ist mit... passiert?
happy ['hæpɪ] glücklich
harbour ['hɑːbə] Hafen

hard [hɑːd] schwierig, schwer; **a hard job** ein schweres Stück Arbeit; **try harder** sich mehr Mühe geben; **work hard** viel arbeiten
hat [hæt] Hut; **bowler hat** "Melone"
hate [heɪt] hassen
have (had, had) [hæv, hæd, hæd] haben; **have a bath** baden, ein Bad nehmen; **have a coke** eine Cola trinken; **have a party** eine Party geben; **have eggs for breakfast** Eier zum Frühstück essen; **have got** haben, besitzen; **have got on** tragen; **have on** tragen; **have to do something** etwas tun müssen; **have a talk with someone** eine Besprechung mit jemandem haben; **have a look** sich etwas anschauen; **have a try** versuchen; **he has got a bike** er hat ein Fahrrad; **he has got to work** er muß arbeiten
he [hiː] er
head [hed] Kopf; **head office** Hauptgeschäftsstelle
heading ['hedɪŋ] Kategorie, Rubrik, Obertitel
hear (heard, heard) [hɪə, hɜːd, hɜːd] hören
heavy ['hevɪ] schwer
helicopter ['helɪkɒptə] Hubschrauber
hello [he'ləʊ] Hallo! guten Tag!
helmet ['helmɪt] Helm
help [help] Hilfe, helfen; **help somebody with something** jemandem bei etwas helfen; **can I help you?** womit kann ich dienen?
helpful ['helpfʊl] hilfsbereit
her [hɜː] ihr(e), sie; **her book** ihr Buch; **help her!** hilf ihr!; **I saw her yesterday** gestern sah ich sie
here [hɪə] hier, hierher; **here you are** hier (bitte), bitte sehr; **come here!** komm hierher; **it is here** es ist hier
hero ['hɪərəʊ] Held
hers [hɜːz] ihrer, -es, -e
herself [hɜː'self] sie selbst; **she made the cupboard herself** sie baute den Schrank selbst; **she enjoyed herself** sie vergnügte sich, sie hatte Spaß
hi! [haɪ] hallo! guten Tag!
hide (hid, hidden) [haɪd, hɪd, 'hɪdn] (sich) verstecken, verbergen
high [haɪ] hoch; **high wind(s)** Windbö, Sturmbö; **high jump** Hochsprung
hill [hɪl] Hügel
hilly ['hɪlɪ] hügelig
him [hɪm] ihm, ihn; **help him!** hilf ihm!; **I saw him yesterday** gestern sah ich ihn
himself [hɪm'self] er selbst; **he enjoyed himself** er vergnügte sich, er hatte Spaß; **he made the cupboard himself** er baute den Schrank selbst
his [hɪz] sein(e)
his [hɪz] seiner, -e, -es
historic [hɪ'stɒrɪk] historisch
historical [hɪ'stɒrɪkl] historisch
history ['hɪstərɪ] Geschichte
hit (hit, hit) [hɪt, hɪt, hɪt] hauen, treffen
hobby/hobbies ['hɒbɪ] Hobby

hockey ['hɒkɪ] Hockey
hold (held, held) [həʊld, held, held] (ab)halten, veranstalten; **hold up** aufrechthalten, stützen
hole [həʊl] Loch
holiday ['hɒlɪdɪ, -deɪ] Feiertag, Urlaub; **holiday camp** Ferienlager; **be on holiday** in Urlaub sein; **go on holiday** in Urlaub fahren; **on holiday** im Urlaub
holidays ['hɒlɪdeɪz] Ferien, Urlaub
home [həʊm] Heimat, Wohnung, Haus, das Zuhause von jemandem; **be (at) home** zu Hause sein; **come (go) home** nach Hause kommen (gehen)
homework ['həʊmwɜːk] Hausaufgabe(n); **he does his homework** er macht seine Hausaufgaben
honour ['ɒnə] Ehre; **in his honour** ihm zu Ehren
hope [həʊp] hoffen
horror film ['hɒrə] Horrorfilm
horse [hɔːs] Pferd
hospital ['hɒspɪtl] Krankenhaus
hot [hɒt] heiß; **hot dog** Hot Dog; **hot pepper** scharfe Pfefferoni
hotel [həʊ'tel] Hotel
hour ['aʊə] Stunde; **an hour's sleep** eine Stunde Schlaf; **half an hour** eine halbe Stunde
house/houses [haʊs] Haus; **at my house** bei mir zu Hause; **to my house** zu mir nach Hause
housework ['haʊswɜːk] Hausarbeit; **do the housework** die Hausarbeit machen
how [haʊ] wie; **how are you?** wie geht es dir (euch, Ihnen)?; **how funny!** wie lustig; **how long?** wie lange?; **how many?** wie viele?; **how much is that?** was kostet das?; **how much?** wieviel?; **how to do it** wie man es macht
however [haʊ'evə] jedoch
huge [hjuːdʒ] riesig
hundred ['hʌndrɪd] hundert; **hundreds of** Hunderte von
hungry ['hʌŋgrɪ] hungrig; **I'm hungry** ich bin hungrig, ich habe Hunger
hurry up ['hʌrɪ] beeil dich! mach schnell!; **be in a hurry** es eilig haben, in Eile sein
hurt (hurt, hurt) someone [hɜːt, hɜːt, hɜːt] jemanden verletzen; **hurt (myself, yourself etc.)** sich verletzen; **badly hurt** schwer verletzt

I

I [aɪ] ich; **I'm fine** es geht mir gut; **I'm warm** mir ist warm
ice-cream [ˌaɪs'kriːm] (Speise)Eis
idea [aɪ'dɪə] Idee, Gedanke; **I have no idea** mir fällt nichts ein
if [ɪf] wenn, falls, ob; **if I were you** wenn ich Sie (du) wäre..., an Ihrer (deiner) Stelle; **he asked me if I...** er fragte mich, ob ich...
ignore [ɪg'nɔː] außer Acht lassen, nicht beachten

ill [ɪl] krank
illustration [ˌɪləˈstreɪʃn] Illustration
imagine [ɪˈmædʒɪn] sich vorstellen
immediate [ɪˈmiːdjət] sofort, umgehend
immediately [ɪˈmiːdjətlɪ] sofort, auf der Stelle
important [ɪmˈpɔːtnt] bedeutend, wichtig
impossible [ɪmˈpɒsəbl] unmöglich
impressed (by) [ɪmˈprest] beeindruckt (von); **be impressed by** beeindruckt sein von
in [ɪn] in; **in August** im August; **in bed** im Bett; **in cold weather** bei kaltem Wetter; **in English** auf englisch; **in summer** im Sommer; **in the evening** am Abend, abends; **in the morning** am Morgen, morgens; **he's in the match** er nimmt am Wettkampf teil; **in all** insgesamt
include [ɪnˈkluːd] einschließen, beinhalten
incredible [ɪnˈkredəbl] unglaublich, nicht zu fassen
independent [ˌɪndɪˈpendənt] unabhängig
indoor [ˈɪndɔː] in einem Gebäude, nicht im Freien
industrial centre [ɪnˈdʌstrɪəl] Industriezentrum
inferno [ɪnˈfɜːnəʊ] Hölle
inform [ɪnˈfɔːm] informieren
information [ˌɪnfəˈmeɪʃn] Information, Auskunft
ingredients [ɪnˈgriːdjənts] Zutaten
inhabitant [ɪnˈhæbɪtənt] Einwohner
injured [ˈɪndʒəd] verletzt; **be injured** verletzt werden; **seriously injured** schwer verletzt; **slightly injured** leicht verletzt; **the injured** die Verletzten
inland [ˈɪnlænd] *in:* **inland port** Binnenhafen
inside [ˌɪnˈsaɪd] innerhalb, in
insist on doing something [ɪnˈsɪst] darauf bestehen, etwas zu tun
instead [ɪnˈsted] statt dessen; **instead of** statt, anstatt
instruction [ɪnˈstrʌkʃn] Anweisung
intelligent [ɪnˈtelɪdʒənt] intelligent
intense [ɪnˈtens] intensiv
interest (n.) [ˈɪntrɪst] Interesse
interest (v.) [ˈɪntrɪst] interessieren
interested [ˈɪntrɪstɪd] interessiert; **be interested in** sich interessieren für
interesting [ˈɪntrɪstɪŋ] interessant
international [ˌɪntəˈnæʃnl] international
interplanetary [ˌɪntəˈplænɪtərɪ] interplanetar, zwischen den Planeten
interpret [ɪnˈtɜːprɪt] dolmetschen
interpreter [ɪnˈtɜːprɪtə] Dolmetscher
interview [ˈɪntəvjuː] Interview, befragen, interviewen
interviewer [ˈɪntəvjuːə] Befrager, Interviewer
into [ˈɪntʊ] in ... hinein
introduce [ˌɪntrəˈdjuːs] vorstellen
introduction [ˌɪntrəˈdʌkʃn] Einführung, Einleitung
invade [ɪnˈveɪd] einmarschieren in ...
invasion [ɪnˈveɪʒn] Einmarsch
invitation [ˌɪnvɪˈteɪʃn] Einladung
invite [ɪnˈvaɪt] einladen
Irishman [ˈaɪərɪʃmən] Ire
island [ˈaɪlənd] Insel
it [ɪt] es (er, sie)
Italian [ɪˈtæljən] italienisch
its [ɪts] sein(e)

J

January [ˈdʒænjʊərɪ] Januar
jar [dʒɑː] Glas (mit Verschluß); **a jar of coffee** ein Glas Kaffee
jazz [dʒæz] Jazz
jeans [dʒiːnz] Jeans
jewel [ˈdʒuːəl] Juwel
jeweller [ˈdʒuːələ] Juwelier
job [dʒɒb] Job, Arbeit, Beschäftigung; **do a great job** gute Arbeit leisten; **they've got a lot of jobs** sie haben viel zu tun
jog [dʒɒg] dauerlaufen
jogging [ˈdʒɒgɪŋ] Dauerlaufen, Jogging
join in [dʒɔɪn] sich anschließen, beteiligen
joke [dʒəʊk] *in:* **that's a joke, that is** das soll wohl ein Witz sein
journey [ˈdʒɜːnɪ] Reise
juice [dʒuːs] Saft
jukebox [ˈdʒuːkbɒks] Musikbox, -automat
July [dʒuːˈlaɪ] Juli
jump [dʒʌmp] springen; **high jump** Hochsprung; **long jump** Weitsprung
June [dʒuːn] Juni
just [dʒʌst] nur, bloß, gerade; **I have just come** ich bin gerade/eben gekommen; **they were just like...** sie waren genauso wie...

K

keen [kiːn] *in:* **be keen on something** etwas sehr gern haben; *in:* **be keen on...ing** etwas sehr gern tun
keep [kiːp] (be)halten; **keep together** zusammenbleiben
key [kiː] Schlüssel
kidnap [ˈkɪdnæp] entführen
kill [kɪl] umbringen, töten
kilogram [ˈkɪləʊgræm] Kilogramm
kilometre [ˈkɪləʊˌmiːtə] Kilometer
kind [kaɪnd] Sorte, Art, Typ; **all kinds (of)** jede Art (von); **what kind of music?** welche Art Musik? was für Musik?
king [kɪŋ] König
kiss [kɪs] Kuß
kitchen [ˈkɪtʃɪn] Küche
know (knew, known) [nəʊ, njuː, nəʊn] wissen, kennen

L

ladder [ˈlædə] Leiter
lady [ˈleɪdɪ] Dame
lake [leɪk] See
lamb [læm] Lamm
land (v.) [lænd] landen
land (n.) [lænd] Land *(geographisch)*
landscape [ˈlændskeɪp] Landschaft
language [ˈlæŋgwɪdʒ] Sprache; **official language** Amtssprache
large [lɑːdʒ] groß
last [lɑːst] letzt(er, e, es); **last night** gestern abend; **last Sunday** letzten Sonntag; **last week** vorige/letzte Woche
late [leɪt] spät; **late afternoon** am späten Nachmittag; **be late (for school)** zu spät (zur Schule) kommen
later [ˈleɪtə] später; **later on** später; **see you later** bis später
latest [ˈleɪtɪst] *in:* **latest attraction** neueste Attraktion
laugh [lɑːf] lachen; **laugh at** auslachen, lachen über
lazy [ˈleɪzɪ] faul
lead (led, led) [liːd] führen
leader [ˈliːdə] Führer
lean [liːn] lehnen; **leaning** schief
learn [lɜːn] lernen; **learn about somebody** lernen über jemanden
least [liːst] *in:* **at least** mindestens
leave (left, left) [liːv, left, left] (weg)gehen, lassen; **leave something at home** etwas zu Hause (liegen) lassen; **leave work** das Büro verlassen, nach Hause gehen
Lebanese [ˌlebəˈniːz] Libanese, libanesisch
left [left] link(er, e, es); **on the left** links, auf der linken Seite; **turn left** links abbiegen
leg [leg] Bein
lemon [ˈlemən] Zitrone
lemonade [ˌleməˈneɪd] Zitronenlimonade
lend (lent, lent) [lend, lent, lent] (ver-, aus-)leihen
less [les] weniger
lesson [ˈlesn] (Schul-, Unterrichts-)Stunde
let [let] lassen; **let's play** laßt uns spielen, spielen wir!
letter [ˈletə] Brief; **post a letter** einen Brief aufgeben, in den (Brief)kasten werfen
library [ˈlaɪbrərɪ] Bibliothek
lie (lay, lain) [laɪ, leɪ, leɪn] liegen
life [ˈlaɪf] Leben
lifetime [ˈlaɪftaɪm] Leben
light [laɪt] hell; Licht; **light years** Lichtjahre
lights [laɪts] Licht, Beleuchtung, (Verkehrs)Ampel
like [laɪk] gern haben, mögen; **I like swimming** ich schwimme gern
like [laɪk] gleich, wie; **like this/these** so, wie folgt, folgendermaßen, (so) wie dies(e); **it's not like him** es sieht ihm nicht ähnlich; **what's it like?** wie ist es?
likes (n.) [laɪks] Neigungen; **likes and dislikes** Neigungen und Abneigungen
line [laɪn] Bahnlinie
list [lɪst] Liste
listen (to) [ˈlɪsn] zuhören; **listening text** Hörtext
literature [ˈlɪtrɪtʃə] Literatur
litter [ˈlɪtə] Abfall
little [ˈlɪtl] klein; **a little** ein bißchen
live [lɪv] leben, wohnen; **live off something** von etwas leben
living-room [ˈlɪvɪŋrʊm] Wohnzimmer
local [ˈləʊkl] örtlich
lock [lɒk] abschließen, zusperren
lonely [ˈləʊnlɪ] einsam, verlassen
long [lɒŋ] lang; **long jump** Weitsprung
look [lʊk] schauen, sehen; **look after** aufpassen auf, sich kümmern um; **look around** sich umschauen; **look at** ansehen; **look for** suchen nach; **look forward to** sich freuen auf; **look forward to...ing** sich freuen darauf, etwas zu tun; **look nice** nett aussehen; **look up** nachschlagen; **look up to somebody** zu jemandem aufschauen; **have a look** sich etwas anschauen
lord [lɔːd] *(britischer Adelstitel)*
lose (lost, lost) [luːz, lɒst, lɒst] verlieren
lot [lɒt] *in:* **a lot (of)** viele *in:* **lots of things** viele Dinge, eine Menge von Dingen
loud [laʊd] laut
loudspeaker [ˈlaʊdˌspiːkə] Lautsprecher
love (n.) [lʌv] Liebe; **love from dad** herzliche Grüße von Papa; **be in love with someone** in jemanden verliebt sein
love (v.) [lʌv] lieben; **I love walking** ich wandere sehr gerne; **I'd love to live there** ich würde sehr gerne dort wohnen
lovely [ˈlʌvlɪ] wunderschön, herrlich
low [ləʊ] niedrig
luck [lʌk] Glück; **no luck** kein Glück
luckily [ˈlʌkɪlɪ] glücklicherweise, zum Glück
lucky [ˈlʌkɪ] glücklich(er, e, es); **lucky you!** du Glücklicher; **I'm very lucky** ich habe großes Glück
lunch [lʌntʃ] (leichtes) Mittagessen; **lunch hour** Mittagspause; **have lunch** zu Mittag essen

M

madam [ˈmædəm] *(höfliche Anrede an eine Dame)*
magazine [ˌmægəˈziːn] Magazin, Zeitschrift
magnificent [mægˈnɪfɪsnt] großartig
main [meɪn] wichtigste(r, s), Haupt-; **main thing** Hauptsache
mainly [ˈmeɪnlɪ] hauptsächlich
majority [məˈdʒɒrətɪ] Mehrheit, Überzahl

make (made, made) [meik, meid, meid] machen; **make it** es schaffen; **make somebody do something** jemanden etwas tun lassen; jemanden zwingen, etwas zu tun; **make somebody laugh** jemanden zum Lachen bringen; **make sure** sich vergewissern, sicherstellen; **make up a dialogue** einen Dialog erfinden; **make friends with** Freundschaft schließen mit; **that makes £ 1** das macht (kostet) 1 Pfund
man/men [mæn, men] Mann
manager ['mænɪdʒə] Manager, Direktor, Leiter
many ['menɪ] viele
map [mæp] Landkarte, Plan
March [mɑ:tʃ] März
mark [mɑ:k] markieren, kennzeichnen
market ['mɑ:kɪt] Markt
marry ['mærɪ] heiraten
marvellous ['mɑ:vələs] herrlich, wunderbar
master ['mɑ:stə] Herr, Meister
match [mætʃ] Wettkampf, Spiel; **football match** Fußballspiel; **he is in the match** er nimmt an dem Wettkampf teil
mate [meit] Kamerad(in), Frau
material [mə'tɪərɪəl] Unterlagen
maths [mæθs] (Kurzform für „Mathematics", Mathe)
matter ['mætə] in: **what's the matter?** was ist los?; **as a matter of fact** tatsächlich, in der Tat; **it doesn't matter** es macht nichts
May (n.) [mei] Mai
may (v.) [mei] dürfen, können; **may I ask?** darf ich fragen?
maybe ['meibɪ] vielleicht
mayor [meə] Bürgermeister
me [mi:] mir, mich, ich; **help me!** hilf mir!; **watch me!** beobachte mich!; **who? me?** wer? ich?
meal [mi:l] Mahlzeit, Essen
mean (meant, meant) [mi:n, ment, ment] bedeuten, heißen, meinen
meaning ['mi:nɪŋ] Bedeutung
meat [mi:t] (Schlacht)fleisch
mechanic [mə'kænɪk] Mechaniker
medieval [,medɪ'i:vl] mittelalterlich
medium ['mi:dɪəm] Medium
meet (met, met) [mi:t, met, met] begegnen, (sich) treffen, kennenlernen
meeting ['mi:tɪŋ] Kundgebung; **meeting place** Treffpunkt
member ['membə] Mitglied
mend [mend] reparieren, flicken, ausbessern
mention ['menʃn] erwähnen
menu ['menju:] Speisekarte
message ['mesɪdʒ] Meldung, Nachricht; **urgent message** dringende Durchsage
metre ['mi:tə] Meter
middle ['mɪdl] Mitte
might [mait] in: **they might** sie könnten; **you might have** du hast vielleicht
mile [mail] Meile
milk [mɪlk] Milch

million ['mɪljən] Million
mind [maind] in: **never mind** mach dir nichts draus; macht nichts; **would you mind...?** würde es dir etwas ausmachen,...?; **I wouldn't mind living there** ich würde ganz gerne dort wohnen
mind (n.) [maind] Sinn, Geist, Bewußtsein; **change one's mind** die Meinung/Ansicht ändern; **the question in everybody's mind is** jeder stellt sich die Frage
mine [main] mein(er, e, es); **a friend of mine** ein Freund von mir
minibus ['mɪnɪbʌs] Kleinbus
mining ['mainɪŋ] in: **coal mining** Bergbau
minute ['mɪnɪt] Minute; **wait a minute** Moment mal
mirror ['mɪrə] Spiegel
miserable ['mɪzərəbl] unglücklich
Miss (Anrede) (n.) [mɪs] Fräulein
miss (v.) [mɪs] vermissen, verpassen; **miss the bus** den Bus verpassen; **I miss you** ich vermisse dich
mistake [mɪ'steɪk] Fehler
mix [mɪks] mischen
model ['mɒdl] Modell
modern ['mɒdən] modern
moment ['məʊmənt] Moment, Augenblick; **at that moment** in diesem Augenblick; **at the moment** im Augenblick, augenblicklich
Monday ['mʌndɪ] Montag
money ['mʌnɪ] Geld
money-back guarantee ['mʌnɪ,bæk 'gærəntɪ] garantierte Geldrückerstattung
month [mʌnθ] Monat
monument ['mɒnjʊmənt] Denkmal
moody ['mu:dɪ] trübsinnig
moped ['məʊped] Moped
more [mɔ:] mehr; **more interesting** interessanter; **not...any more** nicht mehr
morning ['mɔ:nɪŋ] Morgen, Vormittag; **(good) morning** (guten) Morgen; **early in the morning** früh am Morgen; **in the morning** am vormittag, vormittags; **Saturday morning** Samstag morgen; **this morning** heute morgen
most [məʊst] die meisten, am meisten; **most of the people** die meisten der Leute; **most of us** die meisten von uns; **most people** die meisten Leute; **most popular** am beliebtesten; **most visitors** die meisten Besucher
mother ['mʌðə] Mutter
motorbike ['məʊtəbaɪk] Motorrad; **ride a motorbike** Motorrad fahren
mountain ['maʊntɪn] Berg; **mountain walking** Bergwandern
mountaineering [,maʊntɪ'nɪərɪŋ] Bergsteigen
mountainous ['maʊntənəs] bergig, gebirgig
mouse/mice [maʊs, maɪs] Maus
moustache [mə'stɑ:ʃ] Schnurrbart
mouth [maʊθ] Mund
move [mu:v] sich bewegen; **move (to)** ziehen (nach), umziehen
Mr ['mɪstə] (bei Namen) Herr
Mrs ['mɪsɪz] (bei Namen) Frau
much [mʌtʃ] viel; **(not) very much** (nicht) sehr viel; **how much?** wieviel?; **how much is it?** was kostet es?; **thank you very much** danke sehr
mum [mʌm] Mama, Mutti
museum [mju:'zɪəm] Museum
music ['mju:zɪk] Musik; **folk music** Folk (Musik); **pop music** Popmusik
musical ['mju:zɪkl] musikalisch; **musical box** Musikdose; **musical evening** Musikabend
musician [mju:'zɪʃn] Musikant
Muslim ['mʊslɪm, 'mʌzlɪm] Muslim
must [mʌst] müssen; **must not** nicht dürfen
my [mai] mein(e)
myself [mai'self] in: **all by myself** ganz allein; **I can't make...myself** ich kann nicht selbst...bauen; **I enjoyed myself** ich vergnügte mich, ich hatte Spaß

N

nail [neil] (Finger)Nagel
name [neim] Name; **my name is** ich heiße; **what's your name?** wie heißt du? wie heißen Sie?; **name somebody after...** jemanden nennen nach...
Napoleonic [nə,pəʊlɪ'ɒnɪk] napoleonisch
narrator [nə'reitə] Erzähler
narrow ['nærəʊ] schmal, eng; **narrow gauge railway** Schmalspurbahn
nasty ['nɑ:stɪ] gehässig, ungezogen
national ['næʃnəl, 'næʃnl] national
nationality [,næʃə'nælətɪ] Nationalität, Staatsangehörigkeit
naturally ['nætʃrəlɪ] von Natur aus; **happen naturally** von selbst/alleine passieren
near [nɪə] nahe (bei); **near here** hier in der Nähe
nearly ['nɪəlɪ] beinahe, fast
necessary ['nesəsərɪ] notwendig, nötig
need [ni:d] brauchen, benötigen; **need something badly** etwas sehr brauchen; **needn't + verb** nicht müssen, nicht brauchen zu
negative ['negətɪv] negativ
neighbour ['neibə] Nachbar(in)
neighbouring ['neibərɪŋ] Nachbar-, angrenzend, benachbart
neither...nor... ['naɪðə...nɔ:] weder...noch...
nephew ['nevju:] Neffe
nervous ['nɜ:vəs] nervös
net [net] Netz
never ['nevə] nie(mals); **never mind** mach dir nichts draus, nichts macht nichts
new [nju:] neu
news (sing.) [nju:z] Nachrichten; **news has just come in** soeben erhielten wir die Nachricht; **here is the news** wir bringen Nachrichten, Sie hören Nachrichten

newspaper ['nju:s,peɪpə] Zeitung
next [nekst] nächst(er, e, es); **next to** neben; **next time** das nächste Mal; **on the next day** am darauffolgenden Tag
nice [nais] schön, freundlich, liebenswürdig
niece [ni:s] Nichte
night [nait] Nacht; **at night** nachts, abends; **on Friday night** Freitag nacht, abend
no [nəʊ] nein, kein; **no money** kein Geld
no. (Abkürzung für „number") ['nʌmbə] Nr.
nobody ['nəʊbədɪ] niemand
noise [nɔɪz] Lärm, Krach
noisy ['nɔɪzɪ] laut, geräuschvoll
nonsense ['nɒnsəns] Unsinn, Blödsinn
nor [nɔ:] in: **nor do/did I** ich auch nicht; in: **neither...nor...** weder...noch...
normally ['nɔ:məlɪ] normalerweise
north [nɔ:θ] Norden
northwest [,nɔ:θ'west] nordwestliche Richtung
not [nɒt] nicht; **not...at all** überhaupt nicht; **not ever** niemals; **not...any more** nicht mehr
note (n.) [nəʊt] Banknote, Geldschein, Bemerkung, Anmerkung
note (v.) [nəʊt] beachten
notes [nəʊts] Notizen
nothing ['nʌθɪŋ] nichts
notice (v.) ['nəʊtɪs] bemerken
November [nəʊ'vembə] November
now [naʊ] jetzt, nun
nowadays ['naʊədeɪz] heutzutage
number ['nʌmbə] Nummer, Zahl, Anzahl
nurse [nɜ:s] Krankenschwester

O

object ['ɒbdʒɪkt] Gegenstand
ocean ['əʊʃn] Ozean
October [ɒk'təʊbə] Oktober
of course [əf'kɔ:s] natürlich
of [ɒv, əv] von; **a bottle of milk** eine Flasche Milch
off [ɒf] an, abseits von; **off the beaten track** weg vom Eingefahrenen
offer (v.) ['ɒfə] anbieten
office ['ɒfɪs] Büro; **office worker** Büroangestellter; **head office** Hauptgeschäftsstelle
official (n.) [ə'fɪʃl] in: **gate official** Torwächter
official [ə'fɪʃl] offiziell, öffentlich; **official language** Amtssprache; **official statement** öffentliche Erklärung
often ['ɒfn] oft
oil [ɔɪl] Öl
old [əʊld] alt
old-fashioned [,əʊld'fæʃnd] altmodisch
on [ɒn] auf, an; **on holiday** in Ferien, auf Urlaub; **on Sunday** am Sonntag; **on Sundays** sonntags; **on the bus** im Bus; **on the left** links; **on the radio** im

Radio; **on the wall** an der Wand; **on the way home** auf dem Heimweg; **on TV** im Fernsehen; **a western was on** ein Western lief; **an article on sport** ein Artikel über Sport; **on board** an Bord; **on the next day** am darauffolgenden Tag; **what was on?** was war los? was stand auf dem Programm?

once [wʌns] einmal; **once a week** einmal die Woche

one [wʌn] eins, ein, eine; **one day** eines Tages; **the big one(s)** der, die, das große (die großen)

onion ['ʌnjən] Zwiebel

only ['əʊnlɪ] nur; **an only child** ein Einzelkind; **he's only nine** er ist erst neun; **the only** der (die, das) einzige

open ['əʊpən] offen, geöffnet, öffnen, sich öffnen; **open the door!** öffne die Tür!; **the door is open** die Tür ist offen; **the door opens** die Tür öffnet sich

opinion [ə'pɪnjən] Meinung; **in my opinion...** meiner Meinung nach...

opportunity [ˌɒpə'tjuːnətɪ] Möglichkeit, Gelegenheit; **opportunity for...ing** Gelegenheit etwas zu tun

opposite ['ɒpəzɪt] gegenüber

or [ɔː] oder

orange juice ['ɒrɪndʒdʒuːs] Orangensaft

orchestra ['ɔːkɪstrə] Orchester

order ['ɔːdə] befehlen

organization [ˌɔːgənaɪ'zeɪʃn] Organisation, Verband

organize ['ɔːgənaɪz] veranstalten, organisieren

other ['ʌðə] ander(er, e, es); **the other boys** die anderen Jungen; **the others** die anderen

ought to [ɔːt] in: **you ought to** du solltest; **you ought to forget it** du solltest es vergessen; **you ought not to** du solltest nicht

our ['aʊə] unser(e)

ours ['aʊəz] unser(er, e, es)

ourselves [ˌaʊə'selvz] in: **we made-...ourselves** wir bauten...selbst; **we enjoyed ourselves** wir vergnügten uns, wir hatten Spaß

out [aʊt] aus; **out of** aus...heraus; **out there** da draußen; **look out of the window** aus dem Fenster sehen

outdoor [ˌaʊt'dɔː] draußen, im Freien stattfindend

outing ['aʊtɪŋ] Ausflug

outside [ˌaʊt'saɪd] außerhalb, vor, draußen

outstanding [ˌaʊt'stændɪŋ] herausragend, außergewöhnlich

over ['əʊvə] über, mehr als; **over there** dort drüben; **school is over** die Schule ist aus; **the room over the garage** das Zimmer über der Garage; **over an hour** über eine Stunde

overalls ['əʊvərɔːlz] Overall, Arbeitsanzug

overnight [ˌəʊvə'naɪt] über Nacht

own [əʊn] eigen; **a room of my own** ein Zimmer für mich, ein eigenes Zimmer; **my own room** mein eigenes Zimmer; **of its own** eigenständig; **on my own** allein

P

pack [pæk] packen

packet ['pækɪt] Packung, Päckchen; **a packet of tea** eine Packung Tee

page [peɪdʒ] (Buch)Seite

pain [peɪn] Schmerz(en)

paint [peɪnt] malen

painting ['peɪntɪŋ] Malen

pair [peə] Paar; **a pair of scissors** eine Schere; **a pair of shoes** ein Paar Schuhe

pan [pæn] in: **frying pan** Bratpfanne

panic ['pænɪk] in Panik geraten

pants [pænts] Unterhose

paper ['peɪpə] Papier, Zeitung; **a sheet of paper** ein Blatt Papier

pardon? ['pɑːdn] wie bitte?

parents ['peərənts] Eltern

park (n.) [pɑːk] Park; **car park** Parkplatz; **wildlife park** Wildpark

park (v.) [pɑːk] parken;

part [pɑːt] Teil; **in this part of (London)** in diesem Teil (Viertel)...

partner ['pɑːtnə] Partner

party ['pɑːtɪ] Party

pass [pɑːs] vorbeigehen (an), vorbeifahren; **pass by** vorbeifahren, vorbeigehen

passenger ['pæsɪndʒə] Passagier, Fahrgast

past [pɑːst] Vergangenheit; **go past** vorbeigehen, -fahren; **half past one** halb zwei; **walk past something** an etwas vorbeigehen

pause [pɔːz] Denkpause; **after a moment's pause** nach kurzer Überlegung

pay (paid, paid) [peɪ, peɪd, peɪd] (be)zahlen

peaceful ['piːsfʊl] friedlich

peanut ['piːnʌt] Erdnuß

pen [pen] Füllfederhalter, Füller, Kugelschreiber

pen friend ['pen frend] Brieffreund(in)

pencil ['pensl] Bleistift; **pencil case** Federtasche

penny, pence ['penɪ, pens] Abkürzung: p (englische Münzeinheit)

people ['piːpl] Leute, Menschen

pepper ['pepə] Pfeffer; **hot pepper** scharfe Pfefferoni

peppermints ['pepəmɪnts] Pfefferminzbonbons

perfectly ['pɜːfɪktlɪ] völlig, vollkommen

perform [pə'fɔːm] ausführen

perhaps [pə'hæps] vielleicht

period ['pɪərɪəd] Zeitabschnitt, Periode; **a period of time** (Zeit-)Spanne, Periode

permission [pə'mɪʃn] Erlaubnis; **ask permission** um Erlaubnis bitten

person ['pɜːsn] Person

pet [pet] Haustier; **pet shop** Tierhandlung

phone [fəʊn] Telefon; anrufen, telefonieren; **phone box** Telefonzelle; **put the phone down** den Hörer auflegen

photo ['fəʊtəʊ] Foto

photography [fə'tɒgrəfɪ] Fotografie

phrase [freɪz] (Rede)Wendung, Ausdruck

piano [pɪ'ænəʊ] Klavier

pick someone up [pɪk] jemanden abholen, mitnehmen

pick up [pɪk ʌp] auf-, hochheben, in die Hand nehmen

picnic ['pɪknɪk] Picknick

picture ['pɪktʃə] Bild; **go to the pictures** ins Kino gehen

piece [piːs] Stück

pity ['pɪtɪ] in: **what a pity!** wie schade!

pizza ['piːtsə] Pizza

place [pleɪs] Ort, Stelle, Platz

plan (n.) [plæn] Plan

plan (v.) (to do) [plæn] planen, vorhaben (zu tun)

plane [pleɪn] Flugzeug

planet ['plænɪt] Planet

plateau ['plætəʊ] Hochebene, Plateau

play (n.) [pleɪ] (Theater)Stück; **radio play** Hörspiel

play (v.) [pleɪ] spielen; **play area** Spielplatz, Spielgelände; **play football (tennis)** Fußball (Tennis) spielen; **play the guitar (the piano)** Gitarre (Klavier) spielen

player ['pleɪə] Spieler(in)

please [pliːz] bitte

pleased (with) [pliːzd] zufrieden (mit), erfreut (über)

plenty of ['plentɪ] sehr viel(e), jede Menge

p. m. [piː'em] Uhrzeit nach 12 Uhr mittags

pocket ['pɒkɪt] Tasche; **pocket money** Taschengeld

poetry ['pəʊɪtrɪ] Dichtung, Dichtkunst

point (at, to) (v.) [pɔɪnt] zeigen, deuten (auf)

point (n.) [pɔɪnt] Punkt; **a point of time** (Zeit-)Punkt

police [pə'liːs] Polizei; **police station** Polizeirevier

policeman [pə'liːsmən] Polizist

polite [pə'laɪt] höflich

politics (sing.) ['pɒlɪtɪks] Politik

pony trekking ['pəʊnɪ 'trekɪŋ] Ponyreiten

poor [pʊə] arm

pop Pop; **pop group** Popgruppe; **pop music** Popmusik; **pop star** Popstar; **pop concert** Popkonzert

popular ['pɒpjʊlə] beliebt

population [ˌpɒpjʊ'leɪʃn] Bevölkerung

port [pɔːt] Hafen; **inland port** Binnenhafen; **main port** wichtigster Hafen eines Landes

Portuguese [ˌpɔːtjʊ'giːz] portugiesisch, Portugies(e, in)

positive ['pɒzɪtɪv] positiv

possession [pə'zeʃn] Besitz

possible ['pɒsəbl] möglich; **that's just not possible** das ist doch wohl nicht möglich

post [pəʊst] (Brief) aufgeben, zur Post geben

post office ['pəʊst ˌɒfɪs] Postamt

postcard ['pəʊstˌkɑːd] Postkarte

poster ['pəʊstə] Plakat

pot [pɒt] Topf

potato [pə'teɪtəʊ] Kartoffel

pottery ['pɒtərɪ] Töpferei

pound [paʊnd] (engl. Gewicht), (engl. Geld, Abk.: £); **a pound of apples** ein Pfund Äpfel; **that makes £ 1** das kostet 1 Pfund

pour [pɔː] gießen

practise ['præktɪs] üben

pray [preɪ] beten

prefer [prɪ'fɜː] vorziehen

prepare [prɪ'peə] vorbereiten

present (n.) ['preznt] Geschenk

present (v.) [prɪ'zent] (der Öffentlichkeit) vorstellen

preserve [prɪ'zɜːv] erhalten, (auf)bewahren

president ['prezɪdənt] Präsident

press conference ['presˌkɒnfərəns] Pressekonferenz

pretty ['prɪtɪ] hübsch; ziemlich

prevent [prɪ'vent] (ver)hindern

price [praɪs] Preis

prince [prɪns] Prinz

private ['praɪvɪt] privat

prize [praɪz] Preis (beim Wettbewerb)

probably ['prɒbəblɪ] wahrscheinlich

problem ['prɒbləm] Problem, Schwierigkeit

programme ['prəʊgræm] Sendung, Programm

prohibit [prə'hɪbɪt] untersagen, verbieten

project (v.) (on to) [prə'dʒekt] projizieren, (Bilder) an die Wand werfen

promise ['prɒmɪs] versprechen

pronounce [prə'naʊns] aussprechen

pronunciation [prəˌnʌnsɪ'eɪʃn] Aussprache

properly ['prɒpəlɪ] richtig, ganz und gar, gründlich

protect [prə'tekt] schützen, Schutz bieten

proud (of) [praʊd] stolz (auf)

provoking [prə'vəʊkɪŋ] verletzend

pub [pʌb] Wirtshaus

pullover ['pʊlˌəʊvə] Pullover

pupil ['pjuːpl] Schüler(in)

push [pʊʃ] schieben; **push away** wegschieben; **push back** zurückdrängen

put (put, put) [pʊt, pʊt, pʊt] setzen, stellen, legen; **put on** anziehen; **put out** ausmachen; **put out the fire** das Feuer löschen; **put up** aufstellen; **put the phone down** den Hörer auflegen

puzzle ['pʌzl] Puzzlespiel

puzzled ['pʌzld] in: **be puzzled** erstaunt, perplex sein

Q

quarter ['kwɔːtə] Viertel; **a quarter past six** viertel nach sechs; **a quarter to seven** viertel vor sieben
question (n.) ['kwestʃən] Frage; **question word** Fragewort; **ask questions** Fragen stellen
question somebody (v.) ['kwestʃən] jemanden befragen, verhören
questionnaire [ˌkwestʃə'neə] Fragebogen
quick [kwɪk] schnell
quiet ['kwaɪət] ruhig, still
quite [kwaɪt] ganz, ziemlich; **quite a long time** eine ganz schön lange Zeit
quiz [kwɪz] Quiz

R

race (v.) [reɪs] rasen
Radio ['reɪdɪəʊ] Radio; **radio report** Radioreportage, Bericht; **radio play** Hörspiel
railway ['reɪlweɪ] Eisenbahn; **railway track** Bahn(gleis); **narrow gauge railway** Schmalspurbahn
rain (v.) (n.) [reɪn] Regen; regnen; **rain heavily** stark regnen
raincoat ['reɪnkəʊt] Regenmantel
rainy ['reɪnɪ] regnerisch
rather ['rɑːðə] ziemlich, eher, lieber; **he'd rather get ...** es wäre ihm lieber, wenn er ... bekäme, **I'd rather play** ich würde lieber spielen
reach [riːtʃ] erreichen
reaction [rɪ'ækʃn] Reaktion
read (read, read) [riːd, red, red] lesen; **read aloud** vorlesen, laut lesen
real ['rɪəl] echt, wirklich
really ['rɪəlɪ] wirklich, tatsächlich, eigentlich; **I don't really know** ich weiß nicht recht
reason ['riːzn] Grund
reasonable ['riːznəbl] preisgünstig, preiswert
recipe ['resɪpɪ] (Koch)Rezept
recommend [ˌrekə'mend] empfehlen
record ['rekɔːd] Schallplatte
recording [rɪ'kɔːdɪŋ] Tonaufnahme
red [red] rot
refectory [rɪ'fektərɪ] Speisesaal
refer to [rɪ'fɜː] sich beziehen auf
refrigerator [rɪ'frɪdʒəreɪtə] Kühlschrank
refuse [rɪ'fjuːz] ablehnen, sich weigern
regret (v.) (n.) [rɪ'gret] bedauern; Bedauern
relationship [rɪ'leɪʃnʃɪp] Verhältnis, Beziehung
relative ['relətɪv] Verwandter
relax [rɪ'læks] faulenzen, sich entspannen
reliable [rɪ'laɪəbl] verläßlich
religion [rɪ'lɪdʒən] Religion
remain [rɪ'meɪn] bleiben
remark (n.) [rɪ'mɑːk] Bemerkung

remember something [rɪ'membə] sich an etwas erinnern, an etwas denken
remind someone of something [rɪ'maɪnd] jemanden an etwas erinnern
repair [rɪ'peə] reparieren; **get something repaired** etwas reparieren lassen
repeat [rɪ'piːt] wiederholen
report on [rɪ'pɔːt] Bericht (über), berichten (über)
reporter [rɪ'pɔːtə] Reporter
reproach someone for something [rɪ'prəʊtʃ] jemandem Vorwürfe machen
republic [rɪ'pʌblɪk] Republik
request (help) (v.) [rɪ'kwest] (Hilfe) erbitten
rescue (v.) ['reskjuː] retten; **rescue from the smoke** aus dem Rauch retten (holen)
rescue (n.) ['reskjuː] Rettung; **come to someone's rescue** jemandem zu Hilfe kommen
reserve [rɪ'zɜːv] reservieren
responsible [rɪ'spɒnsəbl] verantwortlich
rest (v.) [rest] sich ausruhen; **resting place** Ruheplatz
rest (n.) [rest] Rest; Pause
restaurant ['restərɔ̃ː, 'restərənt] Restaurant
result [rɪ'zʌlt] Ergebnis, Resultat
return [rɪ'tɜːn] zurückkehren
rewrite [ˌriː'raɪt] noch einmal schreiben
rice [raɪs] Reis
rich [rɪtʃ] reich
ride (n.) [raɪd] Fahrt; **go for rides** Fahrten machen
ride (rode, ridden) (v.) [raɪd, rəʊd, 'rɪdn] reiten; **ride a bike (motorbike)** radfahren (Motorrad fahren)
ridiculous [rɪ'dɪkjʊləs] lächerlich
rigging ['rɪgɪŋ] Takelage
right [raɪt] richtig, recht, recht(er, e, es), rechts; **right away** sogleich, sofort; **all right** in Ordnung, jawohl; **he is right** er hat recht; **on the right** rechts, auf der rechten Seite; **right across** geradewegs über; **that's right** richtig, das stimmt; **that's all right** (auf einen Dank) bitte sehr!
ring (rang, rung) [rɪŋ, ræŋ, rʌŋ] läuten, klingeln; **ring someone up** jemanden anrufen
risk [rɪsk] Risiko, Wagnis, Gefahr; **take risks** Risiken eingehen, sich Gefahren aussetzen
river ['rɪvə] Fluß; **underground river** unterirdischer Fluß
road [rəʊd] Straße
rock [rɒk] Fels(en); **rock climbing** Bergsteigen
rocky ['rɒkɪ] felsig
roller skates ['rəʊləskeɪts] Rollschuhe
romantic [rəʊ'mæntɪk] romantisch
roof [ruːf] Dach
room [ruːm] Zimmer
rope [rəʊp] Seil, Tau; **rope-ladder** Strickleiter
rough [rʌf] rauh, schroff, zerklüftet

round [raʊnd] um ... herum; **round the corner** um die Ecke (herum); **turn round** (sich) umdrehen
route [ruːt] Weg, Route
rucksack ['rʌksæk] Rucksack
rugby ['rʌgbɪ] Rugby
ruin ['ruːɪn] Ruine
rule [ruːl] Regel, Vorschrift; **a set of rules** eine Serie/Gruppe von Regeln
run (ran, run) [rʌn, ræn, rʌn] laufen, rennen; **run away** weglaufen; **run into difficulties** in Schwierigkeiten geraten; **run into trouble** in Schwierigkeiten geraten
rural ['rʊərəl] ländlich
rush (v.) [rʌʃ] rasen

S

sad [sæd] traurig
safe [seɪf] sicher, in Sicherheit
sail (n.) [seɪl] Segel
sail (v.) [seɪl] segeln; **sailing** Segeln
sailor ['seɪlə] Matrose, Seemann
salad ['sæləd] (gemischter) Salat
sale [seɪl] Verkauf, Schlußverkauf
salt [sɔːlt] Salz
same [seɪm] gleich; **the same** der-, die-, dasselbe
sand [sænd] Sand
sandwich ['sænwɪdʒ] Sandwich
sandy ['sændɪ] sandig
satisfied (with) ['sætɪsfaɪd] zufrieden (mit)
Saturday ['sætədɪ] Sonnabend, Samstag
sauce [sɔːs] Soße
sausage ['sɒsɪdʒ] Wurst, Würstchen
save [seɪv] retten, sparen
saw (n.) [sɔː] Säge
say (said, said) [seɪ, sed, sed] sagen
saying (n.) ['seɪɪŋ] Sprichwort, Redensart
scare [skeə] erschrecken; **scared** erschrocken
scarf [skɑːf] Tuch, Schal
scene [siːn] Schauplatz, Ort des Geschehens, Szene
scenery ['siːnərɪ] Landschaft
school [skuːl] Schule; **school day** Schultag; **at school** in der Schule; **go to school** zur Schule gehen
schoolgirl ['skuːlgɜːl] Schulmädchen
science ['saɪəns] Naturwissenschaft
science fiction ['saɪəns 'fɪkʃn] Science Fiction
scissors (pl.) ['sɪzəz] Schere; **a pair of scissors** Schere
score (n.) [skɔː] (Spiel)Ergebnis, Spielstand
score a goal [skɔː ə gəʊl] ein Tor schießen
Scottish ['skɒtɪʃ] schottisch
sea [siː] Meer
search [sɜːtʃ] in: **search party** Such-, Rettungstrupp
search something for etwas durchsuchen nach

seaside ['siːsaɪd] See-, Meeresküste; **at the seaside** an der See/Küste
season ['siːzn] Jahreszeit
second ['sekənd] zweit(er, -es, -e)
see (saw, seen) [siː, sɔː, siːn] sehen; **see you on Monday** Tschüs (dann) bis Montag; **see you!** Tschüs!; **(let's) go and see Mike** (laß uns) Mike besuchen
seem [siːm] scheinen
seeping water ['siːpɪŋ] sickerndes Wasser
selfish ['selfɪʃ] selbst-, eigensüchtig
sell (sold, sold) [sel, səʊld, səʊld] verkaufen
send (sent, sent) [send, sent, sent] schicken, senden; **send for someone** jemanden holen lassen
Senegalese [ˌsenɪgə'liːz] Senegalese, senegalesisch
sensible ['sensəbl] vernünftig
sentence ['sentəns] Satz
separate ['seprət] extra, gesondert
September [sep'tembə] September
serious ['sɪərɪəs] schwerwiegend, ernst(haft); **we are serious about each other** wir meinen es ernst mit einander
seriously ['sɪərɪəslɪ] in: **seriously injured** schwer verletzt
serve [sɜːv] servieren
service ['sɜːvɪs] in: **bus service** Busverbindung
set (set, set) [set, set, set] setzen; **set off for ...** aufbrechen, sich aufmachen nach ...; **set out** aufbrechen; **set fire to something** etwas in Brand setzen
several ['sevrəl] einige, eine Reihe von
shaft [ʃɑːft] Schacht
shake hands with somebody [ʃeɪk] jemandem die Hand geben
shall (should) [ʃæl, ʃʊd] [ʃə, ʃəd] sollen; **what shall/should I do?** was soll ich tun?
share [ʃeə] Teil, Anteil; teilen
she [ʃiː] sie
sheep (pl. sheep) [ʃiːp] Schaf, Schafe; **sheep dog** Hirtenhund; **sheep farming** Schafzucht
shelf/shelves [ʃelf, ʃelvz] Regal
shine (shone, shone) [ʃaɪn, ʃɒn, ʃɒn] scheinen, leuchten
ship [ʃɪp] Schiff
shirt [ʃɜːt] Hemd
shock [ʃɒk] schockieren
shoe [ʃuː] Schuh; **a pair of shoes** ein Paar Schuhe
shoot (shot, shot) [ʃuːt, ʃɒt, ʃɒt] schießen
shop [ʃɒp] Laden, Geschäft; **shop window** Schaufenster
shopping ['ʃɒpɪŋ] Einkauf, einkaufen; **go shopping** einkaufen
short [ʃɔːt] kurz
shorts [ʃɔːts] Shorts, kurze Hosen
shout [ʃaʊt] rufen; **shout at someone** jemanden anschreien
show (n.) [ʃəʊ] Schau (künstlerische Darbietung)
show (showed, shown) [ʃəʊ, ʃəʊd, ʃəʊn] zeigen; **show someone round (the**

town) jemandem (die Stadt) zeigen
showcave ['ʃəʊkeɪv] Höhle mit Besichtigungsmöglichkeit
shy [ʃaɪ] schüchtern
side [saɪd] Seite
sightseeing ['saɪtˌsiːɪŋ] Besichtigung von Sehenswürdigkeiten
sightseer ['saɪtˌsiːə] Schaulustige(r)
sign [saɪn] Schild, Wegweiser
signal ['sɪgnl] Signal
signature ['sɪgnətʃə] Unterschrift
silly ['sɪlɪ] dumm
similar to somebody/something ['sɪmɪlə] ähnlich
since [sɪns] seit
sincerely [sɪn'sɪəlɪ] *in:* **yours sincerely** viele/herzliche Grüße; mit freundlichen Grüßen
sing (sang, sung) [sɪŋ, sæŋ, sʌŋ] singen
singer ['sɪŋə] Sänger
sink (sank, sunk) [sɪŋk, sæŋk, sʌŋk] sinken, untergehen
sir [sɜː] *(Anrede)* (mein) Herr
sister ['sɪstə] Schwester
sit (sat, sat) [sɪt, sæt, sæt] sitzen; **sit down** sich (hin)setzen
site (= camp site) [saɪt] Campingplatz
situated ['sɪtjʊeɪtɪd], **be situated** gelegen sein
situation [ˌsɪtjʊ'eɪʃn] Situation
size [saɪz] Größe; **What's your size?** Welche Größe haben Sie?
skate [skeɪt] Schlittschuh, schlittschuhlaufen
skateboard ['skeɪtbɔːd] Skateboard; skateboardfahren
ski [skiː] skifahren; **skiing** Skifahren
skirt [skɜːt] Rock
sky [skaɪ] Himmel
skyscraper ['skaɪˌskreɪpə] Wolkenkratzer
sleep (slept, slept) [sliːp, slept, slept] schlafen; **go to sleep** schlafengehen
sleep (n.) [sliːp] Schlaf; **an hour's sleep** eine Stunde Schlaf
slightly ['slaɪtlɪ] *in:* **slightly injured** leicht verletzt
slow [sləʊ] langsam
small [smɔːl] klein
smell [smel] riechen, stinken
smile (n.) [smaɪl] Lächeln
smile (v.) [smaɪl] lächeln
smoke (n.) [sməʊk] Rauch
smoke (v.) [sməʊk] rauchen
snack bar ['snækbɑː] Imbißstube
snow [snəʊ] schneien, Schnee
snowfall ['snəʊfɔːl] Schneefall
so [səʊ] so, also; **so can/would/am/have I** ich auch; **so do/did I** ich auch
soap [səʊp] Seife
social ['səʊʃl] gesellig
society [sə'saɪətɪ] Gesellschaft
sock [sɒk] Socke
solution [sə'luːʃn, sə'ljuːʃn] Lösung
some [sʌm, səm] einige, ein paar, etwas; **some apples** ein paar Äpfel; **some tea** etwas Tee
somebody ['sʌmbədɪ] jemand

somehow ['sʌmhaʊ] irgendwie
someone ['sʌmwʌn] = **somebody** jemand; **someone else** jemand anders
something ['sʌmθɪŋ] etwas
sometimes ['sʌmtaɪmz] manchmal
somewhere ['sʌmweə] irgendwo(hin)
son [sʌn] Sohn
song [sɒŋ] Lied
soon [suːn] bald; **as soon as** sobald
sorry ['sɒrɪ] *in:* **I'm sorry** es tut mir leid
sound (v.) [saʊnd] klingen
sound (n.) [saʊnd] Geräusch
soup [suːp] Suppe
south [saʊθ] Süden
souvenir [ˌsuːvə'nɪə] Andenken, Souvenir
space [speɪs] Raum, Platz
Spanish ['spænɪʃ] Spanisch, spanisch
spare... [speə] Ersatz-, Reserve-
speak (spoke, spoken) (to) [spiːk, spəʊk, 'spəʊkən] sprechen (mit)
special ['speʃl] besonder(er, e, es)
speciality [ˌspeʃɪ'ælɪtɪ] Spezialität, Besonderheit
speech [spiːtʃ] Sprache
spell (spelt, spelt) [spel, spelt, spelt] buchstabieren
spelling ['spelɪŋ] das Buchstabieren
spend (spent, spent) [spend, spent, spent] ausgeben, verbringen; **spend money on something** Geld für etwas ausgeben
spill (spilt, spilt) [spɪl, spɪlt, spɪlt] verschütten, auskippen
spit (spat, spat) [spɪt, spæt, spæt] spucken
sport [spɔːt] Sport; **sports** Sportarten; **sports centre** Sportzentrum
spread (spread, spread) [spred, spred, spred] sich ausbreiten
spring [sprɪŋ] Frühling
square [skweə] Platz
square (mile) [skweə] Quadrat(meile)
staff [stɑːf] Personal, Belegschaft; **cleaning staff** "Putzkolonne", Gebäudereinigung
stage [steɪdʒ] Stadium, Phase; **critical stage** kritischer Punkt, Phase
stairs [steəz] Treppe
stalactite ['stæləktaɪt] Tropfstein, der von oben nach unten wächst
stalagmite ['stæləgmaɪt] Tropfstein, der von unten nach oben wächst
stamp [stæmp] Briefmarke
stand (stood, stood) [stænd, stʊd, stʊd] stehen; **she can't stand...ing** sie kann es nicht leiden
stand-still ['stændstɪl] Stillstand; **come to a stand-still** zum Stillstand kommen
Standard ['stændəd] **British English** hochsprachliches Englisch;
start [stɑːt] Start, anfangen
statement ['steɪtmənt] Aussage, Feststellung; **official statement** öffentliche Erklärung; **make a statement** eine Erklärung abgeben
station ['steɪʃn] Sender, Bahnhof; **at the station** auf dem Bahnhof, im Bahnhof

statue ['stætʃuː, 'stætjuː] Statue
stay (v.) [steɪ] wohnen, bleiben; **stay (n.)** Aufenthalt; **stay at a hotel** in einem Hotel wohnen; **stay out** ausbleiben; **stay with** wohnen bei
steal (stole, stolen) [stiːl, stəʊl, 'stəʊlən] stehlen
steam train [stiːm] Zug mit Dampflok
steep [stiːp] steil
still [stɪl] jedoch, trotzdem; noch, immer noch
stomach ['stʌmək] Magen; **stomach-ache** Magenschmerzen
stone [stəʊn] Stein
stop [stɒp] aufhören, anhalten; **stop laughing!** hör auf zu lachen!; **oh, stop it!** hör bloß auf!
storey (AE story) ['stɔːrɪ] Etage, Stockwerk
storm [stɔːm] Sturm
stormy ['stɔːmɪ] stürmisch
story ['stɔːrɪ] Geschichte
stove [stəʊv] Herd
stow away [stəʊ] verstauen, wegpacken
straight on [streɪt] geradeaus; **straight down** hinunter; **go straight back** sofort zurückkehren
strange [streɪndʒ] fremd, fremdartig; seltsam
street [striːt] Straße; **in the street** auf der Straße
strip [strɪp] Streifen
stroke (v.) [strəʊk] streicheln
strong [strɒŋ] stark, fest
structure ['strʌktʃə] Struktur, Sprachmuster
studio ['stjuːdɪəʊ] Studio
study (v.) ['stʌdɪ] studieren, lernen; **he's got to study** er muß lernen
stupid ['stjuːpɪd] blöd, dumm
succeed [sək'siːd] Erfolg haben
success [sək'ses] Erfolg
successful [sək'sesfʊl] erfolgreich
such [sʌtʃ] solch, so; **such a** solch ein(e), so ein(e)
suddenly ['sʌdnlɪ] plötzlich
sugar ['ʃʊgə] Zucker
suggest [sə'dʒest] vorschlagen
suggestion [se'dʒestʃən] Vorschlag
suitable ['suːtəbl, 'sjuːtəbl] geeignet, passend, angemessen
suited to each other ['suːtɪd, 'sjuːtɪd] zueinander passend
summary ['sʌmərɪ] Zusammenfassung
summer ['sʌmə] Sommer; **in summer** im Sommer
sun [sʌn] Sonne
Sunday ['sʌndɪ] Sonntag
sunny ['sʌnɪ] sonnig
super! ['suːpə] toll!, prima!, Klasse!
superlative [suː'pɜːlətɪv] superlativ
supermarket ['suːpəˌmɑːkɪt] Supermarkt
supper ['sʌpə] Abendessen
support [sə'pɔːt] unterstützen
suppose [sə'pəʊz] *in:* **I suppose** vermutlich
supposed to [sə'pəʊzd] *in:* **we are supposed to** wir sollen/müssen; **we are not**

supposed to wir dürfen nicht
sure [ʃʊə] sicher, gewiß; **be sure** (sich) sicher, gewiß sein; **make sure** sich vergewissern, sicherstellen
surprise [sə'praɪz] Überraschung; **have a surprise** eine Überraschung erleben
surprised [sə'praɪzd] überrascht
surround [sə'raʊnd] umzingeln
suspense [sə'spens] Spannung, Ungewißheit
sweater ['swetə] Pullover
sweet [swiːt] süß, niedlich
sweets [swiːts] Süßigkeiten, Bonbons
swim (swam, swum) [swɪm, swæm, swʌm] schwimmen
swimmer ['swɪmə] Schwimmer(in)
swimming match ['swɪmɪŋmætʃ] Schwimmwettkampf
swimming pool ['swɪmɪŋpuːl] Schwimmbad
Syrian ['sɪrɪən] Syrer, syrisch
system ['sɪstəm] System

T

table ['teɪbl] Tisch
table tennis ['teɪblˌtenɪs] Tischtennis
tablespoon ['teɪblspuːn] Eßlöffel
take (took, taken) [teɪk, tʊk, 'teɪkən] (mit)nehmen, (hin)bringen; **take a photo** ein Foto machen; **take home** nach Hause bringen; **take part in** teilnehmen in; **take part in something** an etwas teilnehmen; **take place** stattfinden; **take that book!** nimm das Buch!; **take the bus** mit dem Bus fahren, den Bus nehmen; **take the dog out** den Hund ausführen; **take Tom this book!** bring Tom dieses Buch!; **it takes long** es dauert lange; **take risks** Risiken eingehen
talk [tɔːk] sprechen, reden; **talk about** reden über; **talk to** reden mit; **have a talk with someone** eine Besprechung mit jemandem haben
tall [tɔːl] groß
tape [teɪp] Tonband(kassette)
taste (n.) [teɪst] Geschmack, Kostprobe; **taste (v.)** schmecken
taxi ['tæksɪ] Taxi
tea [tiː] Tee
teach (taught, taught) [tiːtʃ, tɔːt, tɔːt] beibringen, lehren; **teach myself something** mir (selbst) etwas beibringen
teacher ['tiːtʃə] Lehrer(in)
team [tiːm] Mannschaft
teeth [tiːθ] Zähne
telegram ['telɪgræm] Telegramm
telephone ['telɪfəʊn] Telefon; anrufen
television ['telɪˌvɪʒn] Fernseh(en)
tell (told, told) [tel, təʊld, təʊld] erzählen, sagen; **tell the way** den Weg beschreiben
tennis ['tenɪs] Tennis
tennis court ['tenɪskɔːt] Tennisplatz
tense [tens] Zeit *(Grammatik)*

163

tent [tent] Zelt
terrible ['terɪbl] schrecklich
test [test] Test, Klassenarbeit; **do a test** eine Klassenarbeit schreiben; **do (badly) in a test** in einer Prüfung (schlecht) abschneiden
Texan ['teksən] Texaner
text [tekst] Text
than [ðæn] als; **smaller than** kleiner als
thank someone for...ing [θæŋk] jemandem danken, daß er...; **thank you very much** vielen Dank; **thanks** danke; **thanks a lot** vielen Dank
that [ðæt] jen(er, e, es); der, die, das (da); **that's 10 p** das macht 10 p; **the boys that you met** die Jungen, die du trafst; **a letter that someone wrote** ein Brief, den jemand schrieb
the [ðə, ði:] der, die, das
theatre ['θɪətə] Theater
their [ðeə] ihr(e)
theirs [ðeəz] ihr(er, e, es), die ihrigen
them [ðem] sie, ihnen
themselves [ðəm'selvz] **in: they made... themselves** sie bauten... selbst; **they enjoyed themselves** sie vergnügten sich, sie hatten Spaß
then [ðen] dann, danach, damals, denn
there [ðeə] dort; **go there!** geh dorthin!; **over there** dort drüben
these [ði:z] diese (hier); **these photos** diese Fotos
they [ðeɪ] sie
thief [θi:f] Dieb
thin [θɪn] dünn
thing [θɪŋ] Ding, Sache, Gegenstand
think (thought, thought) [θɪŋk, θɔ:t, θɔ:t] denken, glauben; **think about something** nachdenken über; **think of...ing** daran denken, etwas zu tun
third [θɜ:d] dritt(er, e, es); **a third of** ein Drittel von
thirsty ['θɜ:stɪ] durstig; **I'm thirsty** ich habe Durst
this [ðɪs] dies(er, e, es); **this evening** heute abend
those [ðəʊz] diese (dort), jene
though (nachgestellt) [ðəʊ] allerdings, in der Tat
thousand ['θaʊznd] tausend
throne [θrəʊn] Thron
through [θru:] durch
throughout the year [θru:'aʊt] das ganze Jahr über, während des ganzen Jahres
throw (threw, thrown) [θrəʊ, θru:, θrəʊn] werfen
Thursday ['θɜ:zdɪ] Donnerstag
ticket ['tɪkɪt] (Fahr-, Eintritts-)karte
tidy (tidied) (v.) ['taɪdɪ] aufräumen, in Ordnung bringen
time [taɪm] Zeit, Uhrzeit; Mal; **for the first time** zum erstenmal; **next time** das nächste Mal; **on time** rechtzeitig; **spare time** Freizeit; **the first time** das erste Mal; **this time** dieses Mal, diesmal; **three times** dreimal; **what time is it?** wie spät ist es?
timetable ['taɪm,teɪbl] Fahrplan

tin [tɪn] (Konserven)Dose, Büchse
tiny ['taɪnɪ] winzig
tip [tɪp] Tip, Hinweis
tired ['taɪəd] müde; **be tired of something** einer Sache überdrüssig sein; **be tired of...ing** satt haben, etwas zu tun
tiring ['taɪərɪŋ] ermüdend
title ['taɪtl] Titel
to [tu:, tʊ, tə] zu, nach, bis; **a quarter to six** viertel vor sechs; **from six to eight o'clock** von 6 bis 8 Uhr
toast [təʊst] Toast
today [tə'deɪ] heute
toenail ['təʊneɪl] Zehennagel
together [tə'geðə] zusammen; **keep together** zusammenbleiben
toilet cabinet ['tɔɪlɪt 'kæbɪnɪt] Waschraum, -ecke
tomato/tomatoes [tə'mɑ:təʊ, -z] Tomate
tomorrow [tə'mɒrəʊ] morgen
tonight [tə'naɪt] heute abend
too [tu:] zu, (nachgestellt) auch
tooth [tu:θ] Zahn, Zähne
toothache ['tu:θeɪk] Zahnschmerzen
toothbrush ['tu:θbrʌʃ] Zahnbürste
toothpaste ['tu:θpeɪst] Zahnpasta
torch [tɔ:tʃ] Taschenlampe
total ['təʊtl] gesamt, Gesamt-
touch [tʌtʃ] anfassen, berühren
tour (n.) [tʊə] Rundfahrt, Tour; **guided tour** Besichtigung mit Führung
tour (v.) [tʊə] umherreisen, umherfahren
tourism ['tʊərɪsm] Tourismus
tourist ['tʊərɪst] Tourist
towards [tə'wɔ:dz] in Richtung auf, nach
towel ['taʊəl] Handtuch
tower ['taʊə] Turm
town [taʊn] Stadt; **town centre** Stadtmitte
toy [tɔɪ] Spielzeug
track [træk] Weg, Spur; **railway track** Bahn(gleis); **off the beaten track** weg vom Eingefahrenen
traditional [trə'dɪʃnl] traditionell
traffic ['træfɪk] Verkehr; **traffic lights** Verkehrsampel
train (v.) [treɪn] ausbilden, trainieren; **fully trained** hervorragend ausgebildet
train (n.) [treɪn] Zug; **steam train** Zug mit Dampflok
training ['treɪnɪŋ] Training
translate [træns'leɪt] übersetzen
transport ['trænspɔ:t] Transportation
trap [træp] (in einer Falle) fangen, einschließen; **trapped** eingeschlossen
travel ['trævl] reisen; **travel agent's** Reisebüro; **travel around** umher reisen
tree [tri:] Baum
tribe [traɪb] (Volks)stamm
trip [trɪp] Ausflug, Fahrt
trouble ['trʌbl] Schwierigkeit; **get into trouble** in Schwierigkeiten geraten; **run into trouble** in Schwierigkeiten geraten; **(be) in trouble** in Schwierigkeiten sein
trousers ['traʊzəz] Hose

true [tru:] wahr, richtig
try [traɪ] probieren, versuchen; **try harder** sich mehr Mühe geben; **have a try** versuchen
Tuesday ['tju:zdɪ] Dienstag
tunnel ['tʌnl] Tunnel
turn [tɜ:n] drehen, ein-, abbiegen; **turn back** umkehren; **turn left (right)** links (rechts) ab-, einbiegen; **turn out (all right)** (ganz gut) abgehen; **turn round** (sich) umdrehen
TV [,ti:'vi:] Fernsehen; **watch TV** fernsehen
twice [twaɪs] zweimal
typical ['tɪpɪkl] typisch
typist ['taɪpɪst] Stenotypist(in)

U

U.S. [,ju:'es] (= The United States) die Vereinigten Staaten
umbrella [ʌm'brelə] (Regen-)schirm
uncle ['ʌŋkl] Onkel
uncomfortable [ʌn'kʌmfətəbl] **in: feel uncomfortable** sich unwohl fühlen
under ['ʌndə] unter
underground ['ʌndəgraʊnd] U-Bahn; **underground river** unterirdischer Fluß
understand [,ʌndə'stænd] verstehen
underworld ['ʌndəwɜ:ld] Unterwelt
unfortunately [ʌn'fɔ:tʃnətlɪ] unglücklicherweise
unhappy [ʌn'hæpɪ] unglücklich
uniform ['ju:nɪfɔ:m] Uniform
unique [ju:'ni:k] einzigartig
until [ən'tɪl] bis
unusual [ʌn'ju:ʒʊəl] ungewöhnlich
up [ʌp] hinauf, oben; **be up** auf(gestanden) sein; **walk up** hinaufgehen
uphill [,ʌp'hɪl] bergauf
upstairs [,ʌp'steəz] die Treppe hinauf
urgent ['ɜ:dʒənt] dringend; **urgent message** dringende Durchsage
us [ʌs] uns
use (v.) [ju:z] gebrauchen, benutzen; **be used as** verwendet werden als
use (n.) [ju:s] Gebrauch, Einsatz; **it's no use...ing** es hat keinen Sinn; **the use of** den Einsatz von
used to [ju:st tʊ] **in: get used to something** sich an etwas gewöhnen; **they used to live** sie lebten früher
useful ['ju:sfʊl] nützlich, praktisch
usual ['ju:ʒʊəl] gewöhnlich, normalerweise
usually ['ju:ʒʊəlɪ] normalerweise, gewöhnlich

V

valley ['vælɪ] Tal
van [væn] Lieferwagen
variety [və'raɪətɪ] Vielfalt; **a variety of** eine Vielfalt von

version ['vɜ:ʃn, 'vɜ:ʒn] Fassung (eines Textes), Version
very ['verɪ] sehr
vest [vest] Unterhemd
victory ['vɪktərɪ] Sieg
village ['vɪlɪdʒ] Dorf
villager ['vɪlɪdʒə] Dorfbewohner
violence ['vaɪələns] Gewalt(tätigkeit)
visit ['vɪzɪt] Besuch; besuchen
visitor ['vɪzɪtə] Besucher
voice [vɔɪs] Stimme

W

wait (for) [weɪt] warten (auf); **wait and see** mal abwarten
wake (woke, woken) up [weɪk, wəʊk, 'wəʊkən] aufwachen
walk (v.) [wɔ:k] (zu Fuß) gehen; **walk (n.)** Spaziergang, Gang, Spazierweg; **walk down (over, up)** hinunter- (hinüber-, hinauf-) gehen; **go for a walk** spazierengehen; **walk past something** an etwas vorbeigehen
wall [wɔ:l] Mauer, Wand; **on the wall** an der Wand; **wallpaper** Tapete
want [wɒnt] wünschen, brauchen, (haben) wollen; **want a...?** (umgangssprachlich): **do you want a...?**; **want somebody to do something** wollen, daß jemand etwas tut; **he wants us to meet...** er möchte, daß wir uns mit... treffen; **I want to come** ich möchte (gern) kommen
war [wɔ:] Krieg; **be at war with** Krieg führen gegen
warden ['wɔ:dn] Aufseher, Leiter
wardrobe ['wɔ:drəʊb] Kleiderschrank
warm [wɔ:m] warm; **I'm warm** mir ist warm
warn [wɔ:n] warnen; **warn someone not to do something** jemanden davor warnen, etwas zu tun
warning ['wɔ:nɪŋ] Warnung
wash [wɒʃ] (sich) waschen; **wash up** abwaschen, Geschirr spülen
waste basket (AE) [,weɪst 'bɑ:skɪt] Papierkorb
wastepaper basket (BE) [,weɪst-'peɪpə,bɑ:skɪt] Papierkorb
watch (n.) [wɒtʃ] Armbanduhr
watch (v.) [wɒtʃ] zusehen, beobachten; **watch TV** fernsehen
water ['wɔ:tə] Wasser
water skiing ['wɔ:tə,ski:ɪŋ] Wasserskifahren
waterproof ['wɔ:təpru:f] wasserdicht
wave [weɪv] winken
way [weɪ] Weise, Art und Weise, Weg; **way out** Weg nach draußen; **ask the way** nach dem Weg fragen; **I'm on my way to** ich bin auf dem Weg nach; **tell the way** den Weg beschreiben; **that way** so wie es ist (war); **the same way** genauso; **this way** so, auf diese Weise; **what's the best way to get there?** wie kommt man am besten dorthin?

we [wi:] wir
weak [wi:k] schwach
wear (wore, worn) [weə, wɔ:, wɔ:n] *(Kleidung)* tragen
weather [ˈweðə] Wetter
weather forecast [ˈweðəˌfɔ:kɑ:st] Wettervorhersage
wedding [ˈwedɪŋ] Heirat
Wednesday [ˈwenzdɪ] Mittwoch
week [wi:k] Woche
weekend [ˌwi:kˈend] Wochenende; **at the weekend** am Wochenende
welcome to [ˈwelkəm] willkommen in...
well [wel] gut, nun, naja; **well done** gut gemacht; bravo!; **do something well** etwas gut machen
well-known [ˌwelˈnəʊn] bekannt
Welsh [welʃ] Waliser(in), walisisch
Welshman [ˈwelʃmən] Waliser
west [west] westlich, Westen; **west of** westlich von
wet [wet] feucht, naß; **get wet** naß werden
what [wɒt] was, welch(er, e, es); **what a pity!** wie schade!; **what about...?** wie steht es mit...?; **what for?** wozu?; **what is it like?** wie ist es?; **what kind of...?** welche Sorte (Art)?; **what time is it?** wie spät ist es?; **what's the matter?** was ist los?; **what's wrong?** was ist los?; **what's your name?** wie heißt du?; **what's your size?** welche Größe hast du?
when [wen] wann?, als, wenn
where [weə] wo, wohin
whether [ˈweðə] ob

which [wɪtʃ] welch(er, e, es)? der, die, das; **the record which I...** die Schallplatte, die ich...
while [waɪl] während
while (n.) [waɪl] Weile, (kurze) Zeit; **after a while** nach einer Weile
white [waɪt] weiß
who [hu:] wer? der, die, das, wen? den, die, das; **the teacher who asks** der Lehrer, der fragt
whole [həʊl] ganz, gesamt
whom [hu:m] wen
whose [hu:z] dessen, deren, wessen
why [waɪ] warum?
wide [waɪd] breit
wife [waɪf] (Ehe)Frau
wildlife park [waɪld laɪf pɑ:k] Wildpark
will [wɪl] letzter Wille, Testament
will [wɪl] *in:* **I will be here** ich werde hier sein; **I won't** ich werde nicht
win (won, won) [wɪn, wʌn, wʌn] gewinnen
wind [wɪnd] Wind
wind surfing [ˈwɪndˌsɜ:fɪŋ] Windsurfen
window [ˈwɪndəʊ] Fenster; **shop window** Schaufenster
windy [ˈwɪndɪ] windig
winter [ˈwɪntə] Winter; **in winter** im Winter
with [wɪð] mit, bei
without [wɪˈðaʊt] ohne
woman [ˈwʊmən] Frau
wonder [ˈwʌndə] *in:* **I wonder** ich frage mich, ich wüßte gern
wood [wʊd] Wald, Holz
word [wɜ:d] Wort

work [wɜ:k] **(n.) (v.)** Arbeit, arbeiten; **work out** herausbekommen; **leave work** das Büro verlassen, nach Hause gehen; **work hard** viel arbeiten
world [wɜ:ld] Welt, Erde; **in the world** auf der Welt
worried [ˈwʌrɪd] *in:* **be worried** sich Sorgen machen, besorgt sein
worry [ˈwʌrɪ] *in:* **don't worry** mach dir keine Gedanken
worse [wɜ:s] schlechter, verschlechtert
worst [wɜ:st] am schlechtesten; **the worst** der, die, das Schlimmste/Schlechteste
worth [wɜ:θ] *in:* **it's worth** es lohnt sich; **it's not worth...ing** es lohnt sich nicht
would [wʊd] *in:* **would you mind...ing...?** möchtest du...?; **I'd rather** ich würde lieber; **I'd love to go there** ich würde sehr gerne dorthin gehen; **would you like to come?** würdest du gerne kommen?; **I wouldn't go if I were you** ich würde an deiner Stelle nicht gehen
write (wrote, written) [raɪt, rəʊt, ˈrɪtn] schreiben; **write down** auf-, hinschreiben; **in writing** in der Schriftsprache
wrong [rɒŋ] falsch; **that's wrong** das stimmt nicht; **there is something wrong with** etwas stimmt nicht mit; **what's wrong?** was ist los? wo fehlt's denn?

Y

yawn [jɔ:n] gähnen

year [jɜ:, jɪə] Jahr; **she is 13 years old** sie ist dreizehn Jahre alt; **light years** Lichtjahre
year-old [ˌjɜ:ˈəʊld]...jährige(r, s)
yes [jes] ja
yesterday [ˈjestədɪ] gestern; **yesterday afternoon** gestern nachmittag; **the day before yesterday** vorgestern
yet [jet] *in:* **not yet** noch nicht
you [ju:] du, ihr, Sie; dir, euch, Ihnen; dich, euch, Sie
young [jʌŋ] jung
your [jɔ:] dein(e), euer, eure, Ihr, Ihre
yours [jɔ:z] eurer, -e, -es; Ihrer, -e, -es; **Yours** [jɔ:z] Dein(e)... *(als Briefschluß);* **Yours faithfully** mit freundlichen Grüßen; **Yours sincerely** viele/herzliche Grüße, mit freundlichen Grüßen
yourself [jɔ:ˈself] *in:* **did you enjoy yourself/-selves** hast du dich / habt ihr euch / haben Sie sich vergnügt?; **did you make...yourself/yourselves?** hast du / habt ihr / haben Sie... selbst gemacht?
youth [ju:θ] Jugend
youth club [ju:θ klʌb] Jugendclub
youth hostel [ju:θ ˈhɒstl] Jugendherberge

Z

zoo [zu:] Zoo, Tierpark

Publisher's note

We wish to record our special thanks to Madalynn Carey for her valuable and perceptive comments on the final manuscript of this book.

Acknowledgements

We are very grateful to the following for their kind permission to reproduce copyright photos, texts and other materials:

BBC, London for "The Skye Boat Song", page 74;
British Tourist Board, Frankfurt/Main for photo on page 74 and brochures on page 102, front cover (castle, house);
Bruckmann Verlag, München for "Queen Victoria" and "Shakespeare" on page 101;
Chicago Fire Department for photos on pages 2, 4 and 5;
Thomas Cook Ltd., Peterborough for brochures on page 67 and one photo (right) on page 78;
Deutscher Fernsehdienst for "Charlie Chaplin", "The Beatles" and "Laurel and Hardy" on page 101;
Interfoto, München for 2 photos (right) on page 54;
Langenscheidt KG, München for dictionary extract, page 99;
Herr Lenz (Neckermann), Frankfurt for pages 54 (bottom left), 59, 66, front cover (Gambians);
Longman Group Ltd., Harlow, Essex for the story in Unit 9;
Kunstsammlungen der Veste Coburg for "Bonnie Prince Charlie", page 73;
Staatliche Kunstsammlungen Dresden for "Nelson", page 96 and "Sir Christopher Wren", page 101;
USICA, Bonn for page 3;
Wales Tourist Board, Cardiff for pages 31, 37, 38, 39.

Our thanks also go to:

Dr. Siegfried Birle, Berlin for one photo on page 48;
Barbara Lehmann, München for 4 photos on page 48;
Michael Stemple, Hamburg for page 32;
Dr. Reiner Schwarz-Kaske, München for one photo on page 48 and girl's photo on page 70.

We would also like to thank the following for their contributions to the book:

Illustrations

Jutta Bauer, Hamburg pages 35, 45, 77, 78, 80, 91, 94, 105;
Jan Gulbransson, München pages 11, 26, 27, 28, 62;
Sabine Kaske, München pages 21, 29, 31, 69, 83;
Dietmar Noworzyn, Leverkusen pages 68, 106, 107;
Colin Shearing, London pages 7, 14, 19, 22, 23, 46, 47, 57, 60, 86, 90, 92.

Photos

Hermann Adler, München pages 39 (top left), 51 (house), 68, 87 (2 photos left);
Hans-Peter Fründt, München pages 70 (bottom), 71;
Peter Jäger, Neufahrn pages 15, 24, 30, 33, 42, 51 (boy), 52 (boy);
Corinna Kaske, Aschaffenburg page 94;
L. Mazzoni, München pages 96 (top), 52–53 (beach), 103;
R. Suthoff-Gross, München page 13;
Dr. E. Winter-Heller, München page 67.

Maps

Christel Langer, München pages 9, 37, 40, 65, 66, 72, 73, 79, 80;
Renate Ludwig, München pages 30, 83, 87, 98 and the rear inside cover.

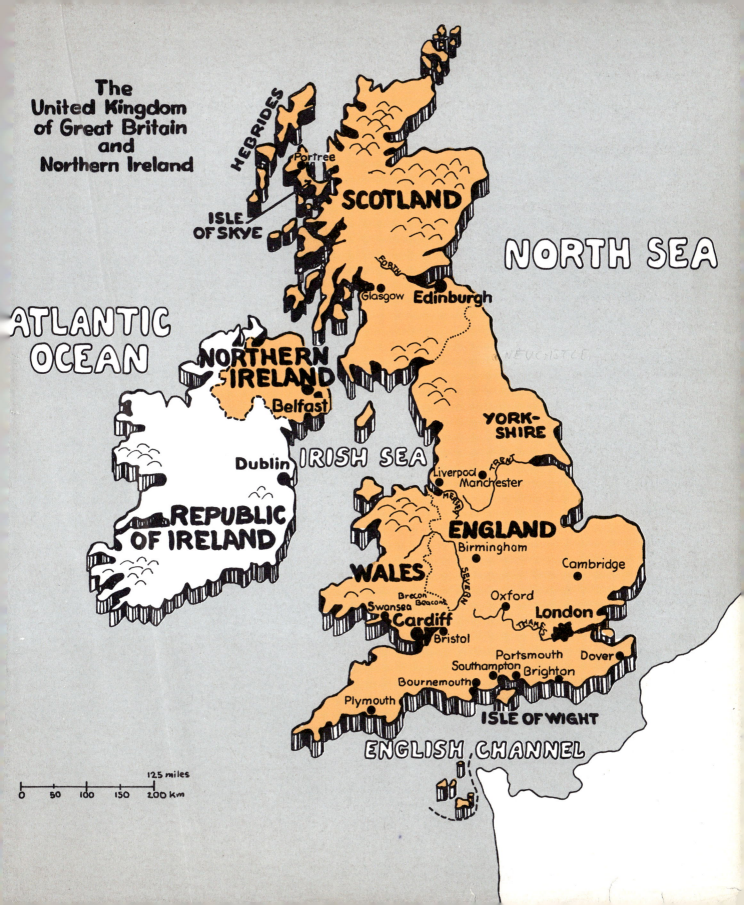